BEYOND BULLSHIT TO BLISS

A Transformative Guide To Self-Love,
Abundance & In-Lightenment

SAMANTHA SPIRO & NOAH DAVID
www.samspiro.com

Publisher's Note

We've changed, or abbreviated, the names and details of the people mentioned in the case studies throughout the book to ensure their privacy. Furthermore, while the exercises in the chapters are powerful tools for self-discovery, they are not a substitute for medical or therapeutic help. If you experience any discomfort or distress, please stop immediately and seek professional assistance. Your well-being is our priority. Ultimately, this book is for entertainment purposes only. Therefore, the views expressed are those of the authors alone, and should not be taken as expert instruction or commands.

Beyond Bullshit To Bliss: A Transformative Guide To Self-Love, Abundance & In-Lightenment

Embark on a transformative journey of self-discovery with Beyond Bullshit To Bliss. Through profound tools like self-enquiry prompts, breathwork, and Tantric energy exercises, you'll uncover your true potential, embrace Self-Love, and cultivate abundance in all aspects of your life.

This book empowers you on your inward journey by providing tools and information for deep exploration. Remember, you are ultimately responsible for your own well-being, and seeking professional support when needed is a sign of strength.

Beyond Bullshit To Bliss: A Transformative Guide To Self-Love, Abundance & In-Lightenment

ISBN Print: 978-1-83556-106-5

TESTIMONIALS

"Sam has been my coach and mentor for the last 4 years. I have worked with many coaches, teachers, and healers, but Sam is definitely the best and only person I will keep going back to whenever I need advice. Sam is one of the wisest people I have ever met, and she is full of love. Her love is not those 'spiritual nonsense' or 'spiritual bypassing' kind of 'love'. Her love is a tough love. Her love is honest and authentic. She truly wants the best for her clients, and she gives her 100% all the time. I recommend Sam to anyone looking for a wise teacher/coach/mentor for guidance!" **H, Singapore**

"I had a wonderful experience with Sam and Noah. They confirmed many things for me and helped me to feel relieved with some amazing guidance. I felt lighter after the session. Thank you Sam and Noah for your time. I can't thank you enough. I am blessed to have been connected with you both," **L, Noosa, Australia**

"Sam, Omgggggg. I am in heavenly mode… I can't thank you enough for a most heady, intoxicating session. I truly enjoyed it. Loved seeing you, and absorbing your mind-blowing ENERGY… Mostttt unforgettable indeed… You are amaaaaaaazingggg," **S, Delhi, India**

"I had a great session with Noah. The most tangible result I've seen is that I'm now a lot less scared of death. I'm also much less sensitive and no longer hold onto things. Internally, I'm more aware of negative thoughts when they arise, and have started to observe them more. I'm learning to step out of victim consciousness and have greater emotional freedom. Noah provides heartfelt support and I would definitely recommend him," **D, Byron Bay, Australia**

"Thanks for the session yesterday, it really helped to be open, especially about the intimacy side. Once it's out there, then I can deal with it rather than pretending everything is OK. I spoke to [X] about us needing to click more and try different things. He's completely on board with that. We had a really nice, close and intimate time yesterday. I'll also look at those times when I get uncomfortable and the easiest actions I can take," **R, London, UK**

"My session with Sam was wonderful, and I'm looking forward to the next one. I will record everything today and will start the practice. I did wake up happy and told myself, 'I am the creator,' which always makes me smile," **A, Toronto, Canada**

"I recently had a profound session with Noah and experienced a real shift. With his insightful guidance and overwhelming love, I finally experienced self-love, which is huge for me. Noah demands commitment – you have to really want to free yourself. And trust me, I really do, especially as I deal with cancer. Thank you so much Noah for this experience," **J, Bali, Indonesia**

"I have worked with Sam multiple times with Reiki, hypnotherapy, and intuitive coaching. She is truly connected on an intuitive level. For example, she helped me to open my heart chakra and used hypnotherapy to help me to clear tension with a close friend. Sam is a wonderful and intuitive person to work with and I look forward to seeing her again," **K, Rishikesh, India**

"Thank you so much for your time, Sam. I'm lost for words! We should do this again. We must have drained your energy. I'm so sorry but your gift really blessed us. Especially his wife! She has been finding it so hard being so young and widowed with two young kids. I just want to thank you from the bottom of my heart. Your gift is amazing," **A, Hong Kong, China**

"Sam has been an amazing mentor. I have experienced some beautiful shifts specially in the area of relationships. My perceptions have been greatly enhanced, which helps me to see people and situations from a broader perspective and understand others' points of view. Her tips have helped me to experience a lot of Aha moments. Looking forward to taking my life to the next level with your guidance again," **T, Hong Kong, China**

"Hey Sam! Thank you for the amazing guidance as always! I've already been looking at jobs this afternoon! Really seems like a smart move and you hit the nail on the head about being valued and dazzling them! I'm on holiday, so going to use the time to take up your suggestions. I'll keep you posted on how I get on!" **B, London, UK**

Sam and Noah's transformational coaching and therapy services have helped me to overcome my personal obstacles, enabling me to achieve happiness and fulfillment. Their mission is to empower you to find your own path to success, Self-Love and return to Bliss. Thank you both!" **D, Mumbai, India**

"Thank you so much Sam for the generous session yesterday. I I felt so much better after talking with you. Still a lot to process but feeling incredibly better. It was a big shift. I wish to maintain the positive attitude. I may have a question pop up in the next couple days and if so, will let you know. Thank you," **E, Hong Kong, China**

"I was sceptical about therapy at first, but working with Noah helped me to realise 'Who am I'. That enquiry has helped me to overcome my fear of cancer. His support and guidance is delivered with compassion and a lot of understanding," **T, Melbourne, Australia**

"A special shout-out to Sam who has been amazing and very on point with tuning into my energy. Her intuitive Reiki session left me with much to think about and a feeling of freedom. After the Reiki, she was able to offer me the tools to help myself. She also confirmed a lot of things that have recently been happening to me. I look forward to growing through connecting more," **T, Rishikesh, India**

"Thank you Sam. Our session made me realise just how much of my power I've been giving up. This realisation is uncomfortable but I think it's an important step towards change. I'll be putting aside some time for my homework this week. Thanks so much again. Onwards and upwards!" **F, New York, USA**

To the True Vast Eternal Nothing that you always ARE. It's always YOU. It's always True!

~❖~

Every human has the capacity to wake up to their own bullshit, train their attention to live within, and revel in Bliss. Now it's your turn.

~❖~

CONTENTS

Acknowledgements 12

Welcome 13

Sam's Story: From Self-Loathing To Self-Love 15
Noah's Story: No More A Sex-Hungry Hedonist... 19

Introduction 26

Who Is This Book For? 28
Our Playful Exploration Of Certain Words 28
How To Use This Book 30

1. You're Feeling Shit, Right? 32

You're Living In Your Own Bullshit Hell 32
Never Mind – It's Not The Boss Of "You" 37
Client Cases: Janet, Tony And Aja Struggled 38
Wake-up Call: Awakening To Your Comparisons 40
Sam's Story: Loosening The Grip Of Self-Dislike 41
Client Case: Carol's Path To Peace 43
Noah's Story: Stepping Back From My Bullshit 44
Wake-up Call: Facing The Force Of Negativity 47
Looking For Evidence – It Fuels What You Think 50
Wake-up Call: Using Coping Phrases To Detach 52
The True Game Of Life – Focus On The Joy 53
The Past Is Where Your Misery Begins 56

2. Being Trigger (Un)Happy 58

Unlocking The Triggers Hidden In Your Life Story 58
The Mechanics Of Being Triggered 59
Accept Your Reactions, Find Your Inner Compass 60
Wake-up Call: Unmask Your Default Responses 61
Client Case: Kristina's Past Became Her Jailer 64
Noah's Story: My Unresolved Anger Has Hurt Others 66
Wake-up Call: Defusing Triggers In The NOW 69
Sam's Story: Confronting My Unhealed Wounds 71
Address Your Patterns Or Face The Fallout 74

3. Release Your Bullshit, Get Healthier.................................77
Ignoring Your Raw Emotions Is A Fool's Game.................................77
Noah's Story: Battling Rage And Cancer – Twice!.................................79
Client Case: Alice's Struggle With Grief.................................81
Are You Blocking Your Body With Bullshit?.................................82
Sickness Reflects Your Perceptions Of The Past.................................83
Wake-up Call: There's "Nothing" In The NOW.................................84
Sam's Story: Accepting Sadness To Heal.................................85
Wake-up Call: How To Deal With Emotional Pain.................................87
Mastering The Art Of Releasing Bullshit.................................89

4. Letting Go – The Life Laxative You Need 91
Stop Clinging, Start Living.................................91
Sam's Story: "Just Drop The Fear..." 94
Wake-up Call: Eight Paths To Physical Release.................................95
Noah's Story: Feel The Hurt And Move On.................................106
Client Case: Lisa Grew When She Turned Within 109
Pivoting Away From The Bullshit Towards Bliss 111

5. Awakening To The True Self...113
Can You Wake Up In Stages? 113
Inner Peace Is Not Complicated.................................114
Wake-up Call: Snap Back to Awareness Fast.................................117
Client Case: Violet Moves Beyond Overwhelm.................................118
Sam's Story: Losing The Story I Was Addicted To.................................119
When You Wake Up, You See Yourself Differently.................................121
When You Wake Up, You See Others Differently Too.................................123
Noah's Story: Seeing My Behaviour Was A Real Gift.................................124
The Mind Will Resist When You Start To Awaken.................................126
Wake-up Call: Quick Process To Return To Love.................................128
Tap Into The Overflowing Love Within.................................130

6. Love And All Its Disguises 132
True Love Vs. Ego-Love. What Sets Them Apart?.................................132
Demystifying The Hype.................................134
Self-Love Is NOT A Quick Fix 135
True Self-Love Is Experienced ONLY In The Body.................................136
Sam's Story: Chasing Fairy Tales... 136
What Does Saying "I Love You" Actually Mean?.................................140
The Dysfunction Of Ego-Love Attachment.................................140
Knowing The "True Self" Leads To Deeper Relating.................................142

The Importance Of Healthy Attachment 143
How Do You Know If You Love Him Or Her? 145
Wake-up Call: Understanding Rejection 146
Client Case: Cassie Began To Process Her Pain 147
Stop Defending Your "Mindfool" Indignation 148
Noah's Story: From Ego Clashes to Inner Peace 149
How Self-Enquiry Leads To True Self-Love 151

7. Meeting "*Who Am I?*" 153
A SLAP Reminds You That Self-Love Is There 153
Being *IshQ* And Basking In The Indescribable 154
Noah's Story: The Guru In Me Is The Guru In You 156
"*Who Am I?*" 158
Wake-up Call: Step 1 – Cracking "*Who Am I?*" 160
Wake-up Call: Step 2 – Focusing On The "Self" 162
Wake-up Call: Step 3 – Deepening The Enquiry 163
Client Case: Henri's Senses Shifted Beyond Sounds 165
Sam's Story: Finally "Filling Up" On Self-Love 166
The True Self Is Unbreakable 168

8. Staying Grounded In Love Amid The Bullshit 170
Radiant Self-Love Is Always Accessible To You 170
Sam & Noah's Story: Love In The Time Of Covid 173
Wake-up Call: The "*Who Am I?*" Journey 176
Wake-up Call: Find Your "Self" After A Fight 180
Client Case: Sarina's Relationship Revolution 184
Wake-up Call: Return to "Self" When Feeling Stuck 186
Wake-up Call: Count On Your "Self" Despite Money Woes 190
I Am "Everything" – And Anything Is Possible 193

9. The Bounty Of Blissful Manifestation 195
Unleashing Your Inner Architect 195
The Key To Successful Manifestation 197
Where Is The "Universe"? 199
Sam's Story: How I Manifested My Big Love 200
Wake-up Call: Shift Your Vibration In Minutes 205
Client Cases: Sadie And Arti Shape Their Reality 207
Three Stages Of Manifestation: Where Are You? 209
Noah's Story: Awakening To The Riches Within 213
Are You Ready To Receive? 215
Wake-up Call: Expanding From Doubt To Delight 217

The True Self Never Complains 219
Wake-up Call: The Steps To Manifest Anything 221
Peaceful Living Is Simpler Than You Think 227

10. Living An In-Lightened Life 230
Embark On A Unique Journey 230
When You Live More As The True Self... 233
Sam & Noah's Story: We Choose Love 234
To Meditate Or Not? 236
Client Case: Chandra Unlocks True Meditation 237
Wake-up Call: More Aware Of Awareness 239
Do You Need A Daily Routine To Wake Up? 243
Your Basic In-Lightenment Blueprint 244
Dealing With Death 249
Wake-up Call: How To Find Peace in Death 250
The In-Lightening Shift Begins 252

11. Opening To *IshQ* – The Final Challenge 255
28 Days To Boost Your Experience Of The "Self" 255
Ready To Go Beyond The Bullshit Towards Your Bliss? 256
How To Get The Most From Your Challenge 257
Day 1: Time To Transmute (Use On Days 1, 8, 15 & 22) 259
Day 2: Tuning Into Sounds (Use On Days 2, 9, 16 & 23) 261
Day 3: Journey Into Silence (Use On Days 3, 10, 17 & 24) 263
Day 4: Unveiling Stillness (Use On Days 4, 11, 18 & 25) 265
Day 5: Cultivating Peace (Use On Days 5, 12, 19 & 26) 268
Day 6: Meta-Awareness (Use On Days 6, 13, 20 & 27) 270
Day 7: Recognising *IshQ* (Use On Days 7, 14, 21 & 28) 273
Moving Forward, Living as *IshQ* 275

ACKNOWLEDGEMENTS

This book wouldn't exist without the tapestry of life experiences woven into its pages. We are deeply grateful for the laughter and love that have filled our hearts, for the lessons learned through moments of profound struggle, and for the individuals who, intentionally or unintentionally, have challenged us to grow. Every twist and turn, even the most gut-wrenching, has become a stepping stone on our journey to self-discovery and the Bliss of knowing the True Self.

A special thank you to those who have played a significant role in our flights of passage: our past relationships, children, families, and yes, even experiences like battling cancer, other illnesses, and surviving a war. Each encounter, each scar, has helped us to uncover the wisdom that lies within.

But most importantly, we thank each other. Without our deep, complex relationship and the willingness to push each other to our edges, this book would not have come to fruition. Our life together has been a catalyst, forging a bond that transcends words, and fuelling the creative fire that birthed this expression of eternal Love.

WELCOME

Let's make this clear from the start, we're not gurus or self-proclaimed saviours. We're just two ordinary people who've suffered, much like you are now. We too have faced that breaking point, that excruciating moment when you sense, deep in your bones, that there must be more to life than the bullshit that you're going through.

Our journeys have been a rollercoaster of emotions. Of course, we tried desperately to heal, but nothing we did was effective enough to shake off the trauma that clung to us like an unwavering shadow. Between us, we carried scars that cut deep:

- Emotional, sexual, and economic abuse that left its mark.
- The relentless grip of feeling bad about ourselves.
- Expecting too much from others and living with a constant sense of disappointment.
- Heart-wrenching echoes of a mass-murder family tragedy.
- The tangled mess of failed relationships and divorce.
- A fierce battle with addictions to sex, drugs, and booze.
- The gut-twisting stress of cancer-related anxiety.
- Confronting death and the paralysing fear it brings.
- The haunting impact of being abandoned as a child in Beirut during the 1976 war.
- Aching loneliness and isolation. And,
- Seeking solace in emotional overeating as a key coping mechanism to get through life's challenges.

Our lives, far from picture-perfect, were a mess – a tangled web of struggles. Yet, amid the chaos, we shared a common longing for Peace, Self-Love, and meaningful connections – goals that seemed perpetually out of our reach.

It was in India, sitting together with a Zen Master, that the truth hit Noah and I. The charade, the self-inflicted bullshit, the endless attempts to decipher its meaning – it all dissolved. We finally saw it for what it was: an unrelenting struggle, dragging us deeper into the quagmire of negativity. Pampering to the mind's wounded inner child, we realised, was not a balm, but a burden, perpetuating the very stories we desperately sought to escape.

Our time with the master was intense, with no escape routes or distractions. We had no choice but to confront our angst, summon up the courage to release it, and embark on a journey of self-discovery to unearth the True Self and awaken to the eternal Love within.

It was a disruptive journey. What catalysed our transformation wasn't someone else guiding us, but the first-hand realisation that no one else could do it for us. The key revelation was simple – only YOU can embark on this journey of self-discovery. Only you can dismantle the deceptive story of "you" and recognise the True Self.

The beauty lies in its simplicity: you don't need to scale mountains or empty your bank account; the truth lives quietly within you. All you need to do is wake up to the bullshit and consciously train the mind to live beyond it. In essence, this involves consistently redirecting your focus to the breath and Joy inside, resisting the temptation to get pulled back into the narratives of the mind. You simply acknowledge its chaos and steadfastly choose not to participate in it.

As Noah and I expanded into the Bliss of the True Self, something extraordinary unfolded between us as well. Gazing into each other's eyes, we posed a profound question, *"Who Am I?"*. In that moment, we saw our own eternal Love mirrored in each other. The Love that surged within us was beyond the mind's comprehension – it radiated out, for ourselves and each other. It was intoxicating, as if we were getting "high" on Love. We call it *IshQ*.

When you commit to waking up, conscious-love stories become a recurring theme. That's not to say that our journey is all sunshine and rainbows; far from it. We've had our share of raw moments. If we don't catch our triggers quickly, we find ourselves spiralling down into the same old rabbit hole of hell, engaging in screaming arguments, shedding tears, and even threatening to walk away.

But we stay, held together by an unspoken bond. What binds us is our determination to transcend the drama and live as the awakened True Self. That's the bedrock of our commitment to each other.

Today, we're on a mission to share our awakening experience. We are spiritual-growth teachers and Conscious-Tantra facilitators who guide people to turn their attention inwards and ask themselves, *"Who is this 'I' who automatically believes the bullshit stories that I repeat to myself about myself and others?"* It's a deep question that lies bare the chasm between the truth of existence and the human race's addiction to incessant suffering.

Sharing this, along with other secrets to knowing the True Self and True Self-Love, is our passion. A passion we call "In-Lightenment", and one that we now humbly offer to you.

On a personal level, our stories are a litany of heart-wrenching experiences, but they are JUST stories. We present them to you as proof that if we can stop being prisoners to our past, release it, and live consistently as the True Self, so can YOU! This is the truth, and it can be your freedom too.

Sam's Story: From Self-Loathing To Self-Love

I'm Samantha, and I used to be plagued by anxiety, self-doubt, and neediness. I was brought into this world by a beautiful, artistic mum, battling mental illness, and a debonair father whom I always saw as a James Bond-like figure. Little did I know, he actually was.

Working as an undercover operative, my father served various government agencies, including the CIA and British intelligence (he is mentioned in a book called *The Octopus* about US government conspiracies). He collaborated with figures like Oliver North, a US Marine veteran connected to the Iran-Contra affair, and Terry Waite, a representative of the UK's Church of England. Together, they negotiated with Shiite Muslims to secure the release of British and US hostages who were being held in war-torn Beirut in the mid-1980s.

My early life with my father was like appearing in the US TV show *Homeland.* At the age of five, he "abducted" me from my mother, whisking me away from the familiar streets of Northwest London, and plunging me into the chaos of Beirut. In his misguided attempt to protect me, he chopped off my hair to make me look like a boy, and essentially abandoned me in a boarding school. Regrettably, he paid little attention to my emotional well-being. Overnight, my perception of my "self" shifted from that of a pretty little girl to an ugly, desolate, and sorrowful creature. It left an enduring imprint on my heart.

Yet, those were not the only constraints imposed upon me. I was given a meagre allowance, forcing me to resort to begging in the school just to buy a drink at break time. I was also cut off from my mother and family in the UK, and told to lie about my family background. It took three years before I was reunited with my mother.

My father's story reached a devastating climax in 1992, when my two half-sisters, half-brother, and stepmother were murdered in their beds in San Diego. Two days later, my father was found dead in his car in California, a victim of cyanide poisoning. The precise details of those events remain shrouded in mystery, but it's evident that my father had incurred the wrath of some powerful, clandestine government agencies. The Internet is full of conspiracy theories as to what happened, yet the full truth may never be known.

Nevertheless, life continued. On the bright side, I didn't end up a crack-whore. Instead, I focused on my education and gained a joint-honours business degree. Along the way, I developed a kind heart, strong sense of humour, and deep spiritual understanding of life and people. Furthermore, I honed my talents as a writer, therapist, healer, and mystic.

On the emotional-regulation front, however, I didn't fare as well. It took me years to come to terms with the loss of my father and siblings, and even longer to navigate my relationship with my mother. I grappled with self-esteem issues and developed a superior knack for attracting emotionally unavailable, critical men.

This came as no surprise, given the circumstances. In my mind, my father had never really loved me (he'd used me as an emotional pawn to manipulate my mother), which only reinforced my belief that I was inadequate. I questioned my worthiness – was I good enough, pretty enough, intelligent enough, or simply enough for anyone to love?

Despite these challenges, I did form romantic relationships, including a decade-long, loving partnership. However, throughout it all, I compromised my inner calling to recognise the True Self. The bottom line was that I suffered.

Then, a voice inside my head screamed, *"Enough."* I'd grown weary of living with my self-loathing attitude, putting myself down, and chasing emotionally unkind men. Determined to break free, I delved into therapy and sought the guidance of a spiritual teacher.

I also retrained as a spiritual, clinical, and cognitive behavioural hypnotherapist. I immersed myself in becoming a Reiki Master Practitioner and Teacher, and later a Conscious Yoga and Meditation Teacher. Additionally, I sought mentoring from proven psychic mediums to deepen my ability to channel the living, the dead, and the Great Unknown.

However, the breakthrough occurred only when I asked myself that one important question, *"Who Am I?"*. Previously, this query had felt confrontational, but this time, I just sat with it. Two days later, I experienced a delicious answer – an opening sensation (or click) in my heart. It felt as if infinity itself was gazing out through my eyes. As the great Indian spiritual teacher Sri Ramana Maharshi (Ramana) put it, asking *"Who Am I?"* is not meant to illicit an answer, it's meant to dissolve the questioner. And that's exactly what it did for me.

The realisation was what I'd been waiting for. It pushed me to resign from my well-paid but lonely life in Hong Kong, where I'd been working as a journalist, corporate financial editor, and PR executive. I cashed in everything and headed to Bali and India, to get to know the True Self. The timing was perfect. I met beautiful people and, most important, I met my "Self".

This recognition transformed me. I started to let go of the negative thoughts and feelings that I'd been subconsciously repeating to myself. With a sense of relief, and Joy, I expanded into the True Self, liberating myself from the bullshit story of "me". It was during this time that Noah and I embarked on our romantic journey together.

Today, I live with a heightened inward focus, unwavering in my commitment to experience the True Self. I've witnessed first-hand the direct correlation between living as this expansive "Self" and manifesting more of my dreams. I've also learned to be present, which has transformed my life into something much more enjoyable.

Nevertheless, it's not always joyful. When I catch myself slipping back into the bullshit, I drop the story (see **Chapter 4** on Letting Go), practise heart breathing, repeat the *"Who Am I?"* self-enquiry process (refer to **Chapter 7**), and guide myself back to Peace.

Consistently training my attention to pivot inwards, beyond the bullshit, has made it easier for me to focus on BEING Stillness, Silence, Peace, Love and Joy most of the time. However, in the beginning, it was a more manual process.

To access Stillness, I would ask myself *"Who Am I?"* while looking at a plant, or wall. Then, I would relax into the corresponding opening sensation in the chest. To unveil Silence, I would use all the external noise around me to cut through the mental chatter and attune myself to the serenity within. To know Peace, I would stretch my Awareness to the ceiling, observing myself and my actions until my Awareness expanded even more. And by being aware of it all simultaneously, I was able to tap into the Love and Joy emanating from the True Self – the *IshQ* of BEING (see **Chapter 7** for the steps on how to experience yourself as the four existential elements of Conscious Awareness).

Recognising myself as an In-Lightened being has been the most fulfilling experience of my life. The intelligence of Conscious Awareness never ceases to amaze me. My life is a continuous interaction with the Universe and, with each passing day, my inherent understanding of the True Self and Conscious Manifestation deepens.

I LOVE this Awareness, and I love sharing it with others so that they can recognise it too. My approach involves teaching them how to breathe through the heart. I then guide them on how to turn within, beyond the bullshit of the mind. Following that, I lead them through "correct" self-enquiry. Lastly, I tune into them energetically to help them pinpoint when they're experiencing themselves as pure Awareness. It begins as a subtle opening sensation (or heat, or tingling) in the body that we can ALL recognise.

Everyone, including YOU, has the capacity to awaken and realise the True Love that you ARE. As soon as you've experienced yourself as this even once, you can direct your attention inwards, repeating the process until it becomes your default state of being.

This practice is profound yet simple. So have faith. You really were born to BE vast and free!

Noah's Story: No More A Sex-Hungry Hedonist...

While writing this book, the timeless words of William Shakespeare resonated within me, *"To be or not to be?"* This contemplation has echoed at the very heart of my being, encapsulating the profound enquiry, *"Who Am I?"* – a singular question of major significance in my quest for In-Lightenment.

My story might not parallel Sam's shocking tale, yet its impact on my psyche has been profound. I am called Noah – a name that has accompanied me throughout the years, albeit shadowed by a multitude of descriptors: labelled an arrogant, narcissistic, drug-abusing, pleasure-seeker – a relentless womaniser, consumed by sex and pleasure. But the truth is, I never really identified with any of those labels. All I wanted was to give and receive love, and bask in the pure radiance of self-acceptance.

I began life as a happy kid in Scotland during the swinging sixties. My mother, an attractive woman and a bit of a socialite, and my father, a well-known BBC presenter, producer, and director, appeared to live the good life. However, at the heart of it, all was not well. My strict, career-driven, philandering father was often absent and, when he was at home, it was a loveless and turbulent environment. I can vividly recall tears streaming down my face as I listened to my parents' heated arguments and the sound of doors slamming.

When I turned eight, my father left us for another woman, abandoning us in a large, expensive rental with no income to pay for it. I felt unwanted, unloved, and uncared for. Deep down, I believed it was my fault. Was it because I'd been naughty? My mother, heavy with resentment towards my father, struggled to provide the emotional support we needed. Whilst I knew she loved us deeply, her attention was consumed with trying to keep a roof over our heads, putting food on the table, and ensuring I continued at my private school.

However, amid the emotional turmoil, I had deep yearning for love and connection. This longing, I now understand, fuelled my early sexual exploration. My first kiss arrived at the age of seven. At eight, I'd rubbed bottoms with a girl who taught me the art of shoplifting chocolate. And just before my 14th birthday, I'd had full-blown sex with a girl I'd played football with, right there in the local park.

My sexual education had really begun and I embraced it. At 15, one of my mum's university-student lodgers decided to "take me under her wing". She guided me in the art of lovemaking, showing me how to give her pleasure. It was a mind-blowing experience and it definitely helped me to suppress memories of being sexually abused by a family friend when I was 11.

By the time I was 16, I'd fallen "in love" with my sexy art teacher. I was doing my exams and used to go to her home for art "classes". I loved the attention and the colour of passion. I only saw her a few times but, by the time that was over, I knew I'd truly graduated.

As a boy, football was another passion and I was pretty good. I played for local teams and even secured a trial with a professional Scottish club. Unfortunately, my dreams of becoming a top footballer were shattered when I suffered a knee injury. While some would have crumbled under such circumstances, I brushed myself off and set new goals. If I couldn't chase a ball, I could still chase women – and that's precisely what I did, gammy knee and all!

Humour, often tinged with sarcasm, became my coping mechanism throughout the tumult of my childhood and teenage years. It also served as a magnet, attracting girlfriends who gladly partook in my adventurous lovemaking. However, I never really committed; love and romance was all just part of an adventurous teenage life.

Saying that, I DID love sex and I did take that seriously. I loved showing woman how experienced I was with my "carnal knowledge". I revelled in being a lady-pleaser. Charming them, kissing them, making love to them, and then moving on when I'd found my next "hit". It was the seventies after all, and I was in my twenties.

I was living the dream. Not only was it easy for me to attract women, but I also created a glamorous lifestyle. I found myself employed by some of the richest and most powerful people on earth. I worked on their mega-yachts, in their luxury homes, and in five-star hotels. I partied with popstars and famous actors, dated models, beauty queens, and Hollywood starlets, and even appeared in several TV shows and commercials as an extra.

Of course, all of this success went straight to my head (along with the pot and booze). I embraced the role of the egotistical protagonist in my clichéd production of life, indulging in every pleasure available. It was inevitable that it would eventually come crashing down. Nonetheless, I managed to save enough of my not-so-hard-earned cash, which I later invested in my own production company, specialising in making documentaries on music and the arts.

Yet, regardless of my professional triumphs and failures, the pursuit of authentic love remained my goal. I got engaged for the first time at 18, but it ended after four years, mainly due to my lack of commitment. By the time I was 28, I thought I'd met the woman of my dreams. We got married in a lavish church ceremony, embarking on a journey around the world, achieving success, and revelling in the pleasures of life.

However, complacency eventually set in. I succumbed to temptation and got entangled with another woman. My wife walked out and our paths never crossed again. It left me feeling lonely and helpless – abusing pot and alcohol even more, and having sex with anyone who would have me.

Fortunately, I refused to allow that sad situation to consume me for too long. Three years later, I'd cleaned up my act and, ever the hopeful romantic, I got married a second time. My new wife was a PhD medical researcher and, early into our marriage, we had our first child. I was 36 years old and the experience of becoming a father proved life-altering. However, even that monumental event failed to stop me from self-destructing again.

When I was 40, I had a mid-life crisis and convinced myself to abandon my wife and daughter for yet another woman. It was a drug-booze-and-sex-fuelled decision that took me a long time to accept. I couldn't admit it, but I'd broken my own heart by leaving my family.

In the midst of this turbulent cycle of despair, I continued my philandering ways. Surprisingly, or not, it was during this period that I met the woman who would become my third wife. She soon became pregnant with my second child, filling me with a sense of hope and happiness. I felt as though I'd been given another chance and was determined to fulfil my role as a loving husband and present father to our son, whilst also strengthening the bond with my daughter.

For 14 years, I embraced my commitment to family life, forming loving relationships with both my son and daughter, who regularly joined us for holidays. Outwardly, we appeared to be a blissful and prosperous family living on the fabulous Sunshine Coast in Australia.

My third wife was a software entrepreneur. She was generous and helped me to get my video-production company up and running again. We certainly enjoyed a great life and all that went with it – a beautiful home, pool, high-end cars, the best equipment, designer clothes, and private schooling. It was five-star all the way.

However, behind closed doors, I felt our relationship was often emotionally challenging. I knew something had to change. Then, as if on cue, the *"Play of Life"* unfolded, bringing Act One, *"The Bullshit"*, to a close and opening the curtain on Act Two, *"The Bliss"*.

It began, though, with a huge kick in the gut. At 57, I received a devastating diagnosis: advanced bowel cancer. The doctor told me that I had just six months to put my affairs in order. However, I chose to reject his negative suggestion and pursued a new direction in life. Determined to heal, I began to let go of my vices and explore my spiritual core instead.

Miraculously, I survived, but almost everything else crumbled away – my marriage, my thriving business, and the majority of my friendships. I even let go of some of the characters I used to be. It seems that when a version of the ego-self "dies", so too do the connections associated with it.

As I focused on releasing the emotional pain that had been weighing me down, I discovered something even more vital. I recognised that chasing success couldn't buy me love, health, or happiness. I'd felt trapped on a treadmill of negative thinking, being, and doing.

I uncovered the truth that pain cannot be healed through self-hatred; it can only be released by turning inwards, letting go, and letting BE. I learned that I am not, and never will be, a victim. Not of abuse, emotional neglect, or even cancer. I refuse to define myself as a cancer survivor. Instead, I proudly proclaim myself a cancer "thriver".

Through introspection, I've enjoyed the Bliss of getting "high" on something much healthier – my own Self-Love. I've allowed every experience to contribute to my healing. Every moment has become a guiding light. I've dared to ask that most challenging of questions, *"Who Am I?"*, and have chosen to live with a deep internal focus.

In my determination to shed the confines of the story that I once believed defined me, I have dropped my greatest addiction of all – to charming women and seeking sexual gratification. While women will always hold a place in my heart, my hunger for flirtation and sex no longer drives me. I've stopped being a man who betrays his partner. What matters to me most now is honouring myself and those closest to me, embodying the True Self that I AM.

In recognising this, I've finally manifested what I've always desired. Authentic love with just one other – my beloved wife and partner Sam, my co-author in life. I've realised that the "Zensual" way of living, as we call it, is the most joyful and fulfilling.

After being diagnosed with cancer, not once, but twice, I didn't know if there would be a tomorrow. Now, I spend my days focusing on the present and helping others to do the same. I use my training in Breathwork, EFT, NLP, Reiki, Tantra and Transcendental Meditation to support people to let go of their drama.

I don't sugar coat it or indulge them, especially not when it comes to "relatingshits" (as Sam and I call them). That's never going to bring people Peace, Self-Love, or help them to heal. The only way to do that is to drop the bullshit and live from within, radiating as the Stillness, Silence, Peace, Love and Joy that you ARE.

I've come to understand that the only way to move forward is to stare into the darkest corners of your psyche. You must be prepared to unravel all illusions of grandeur, turning inwards to embrace every emotion – all forms of sadness, anger, fear, and happiness (which psychology views as the four primary emotions).

Whilst it might all seem real, it is in fact just a narrative crafted by the ego-self, a story it boldly defines as being "you". However, it's not a genuine reflection of who "You" really ARE at all.

As you join us on this intimate journey of awakening, we humbly bow to the True Love that we know you always ARE – this is *IshQ,* this is YOU!

With Love, only Love,

Sam & Noah

INTRODUCTION

Welcome to the anti-bullshit revolution. This book is not for casual browsers seeking fleeting self-improvement; it's for the desperate, disillusioned, battle-scarred veterans of suffering who have tried everything and still ache under the soul-crushing weight of existence. We know you're ready to ditch the angst and reclaim the Bliss of being.

We're talking about radical self-realisation, a direct route to the In-Lightenment you crave. No vague promises, just potent tools to cut through the bullshit. You will:

- **Shatter the illusion.** Recognise the false "self" that is burdened by anxiety and regret.
- **Liberate your past.** Learn powerful methods to release the grip of your life story and step into present freedom.
- **Establish instant distance.** Separate the observer from the observed, quickly finding sanctuary from the mind's bullshit.
- **FEEL Self-Love on demand.** Tap into the profound Love of the "Self", in minutes, not months. It's your birth right, not a bonus prize.
- **Embrace unwavering Peace.** Realise your inherent serenity, a refuge that's accessible forever.
- **Pose the big question.** Ask *"Who Am I?"* and silence the ego-self's narrative, revealing the In-Lightened Self that's always waiting to embrace you.
- **Know the True Self.** Experience the profound Stillness, Silence, Peace, Love and Joy that you already ARE, and recognise first-hand that you can NEVER lose them.

- **Manifest with ease.** When you understand the limitless "Nothing" at the heart of being, you simultaneously grasp the potential of "Everything". It's then easier to recognise yourself as the True Vast Eternal Nothing from which all of life flows, drawing your desires to you naturally. And,
- **Expand your vibration.** Fuel your personal growth with the radiant power of True Self-Love. Release fear, inviting in abundance and positive change. (Note: it's important to realise, however, that the power of Conscious Manifestation is rooted in the vibration a person emits. It doesn't depend on their morals).

This journey is no magic pill. We're not selling sugar-coated epiphanies or "*Satori*" shortcuts. It's a raw excavation, a conscious choice to rewrite your story. But you don't need guru status; this journey is for every seeker, for the you who longs for more. The potential for Bliss already resides within you. So, are you ready to unlock it?

If so, you can forget passive reading. This book is your detonator, a literary Molotov cocktail designed to blast apart the bullshit holding you back from the Joy that's rightfully yours. Having spent over three decades cracking open our own hearts, we now help ordinary people blossom into the same embodiment of Peace that we ourselves have achieved. This isn't some theoretical promise; it's a truth forged in the fires of human experience, extending to every warrior searching for Joy amid the embers.

We're offering you a toolkit packed with empowering exercises and liberating sparks – deep psychotherapeutic self-enquiry prompts and Conscious Tantra nudges designed to ignite your inner rebellion. We'll guide you through recognising True Self-Love, navigating the minefield of relationships, emerging from the ashes of heartbreak, and mastering the Zen of your own mind.

Imagine shedding the shackles of self-doubt and stepping into the sun-drenched freedom within. No dancing naked under the stars waiting for "signs" – we're inviting you to experience In-Lightenment, right here, right now, in the ordinary magic of your own breath.

This book is your torch, and your inner revolution starts with a single match. Light it up and let the alchemy begin.

Who Is This Book For?

It's for you if you can answer *"Yes"* to at least two of the following questions:

1. Are you yearning to experience yourself as the In-Lightened True Self and FEEL lasting Self-Love?
2. Do you frequently experience loneliness?
3. Do you find it challenging to let go of friendships and relationships?
4. Do you engage in active self-enquiry, yet find it doesn't lead you to lasting Peace?
5. Do you meditate regularly on the mat but notice that it makes little difference to your emotional regulation or well-being?
6. Have you had therapy, or are you currently undergoing it, yet still feel stuck in life?
7. Are you a Reiki user or practitioner, and curious to learn how it can deepen your recognition of pure Conscious Awareness?
8. Do you consistently apply the principles of manifestation to draw to you a new job, romantic partner, and other desires, yet feel frustrated by your limited progress? And,
9. Have you had your first recognition of the True Self but can't figure out how to experience it again?

If these questions resonate with you, then this book is precisely what you need. Prepare to have your mind blown as we take you on a journey from "in-slavement" to In-Lightenment.

Our Playful Exploration Of Certain Words

This book is your opportunity to dive deep within, shedding illusions, and unearthing the True Self and its four elements of Stillness, Silence, Peace, and the combined essence of Love and Joy (referring to the Love of the "Self", not the impermanent love of the ego).

Think of these terms as signposts, each illuminating a facet of your authentic being, leading you deeper into the True Vast Eternal Nothing (aka Consciousness). We intentionally capitalise them to highlight their significance, hence you'll find: the True Self, True Self "You", the True "You", the "Self", Conscious Awareness, and more.

But wait, there's another "you": the ego-self is the story-driven part that often takes the wheel. We use lowercase for this, and terms like the mind-self, or small "self", to distinguish it from the True Self.

Some associate self-discovery with "mindfulness", but we invite you to explore "mindlessness". It's not about being "full of mind", but rather about letting go of the constant chatter and simply resting in the present moment. So, be mindful of the mindfool within (we all have one), but don't get caught up in the chase for perfect "mindfulness".

As you recognise yourself as the True Self, Peace permeates your being, impacting every area of your life. It's like your Specific Energetic Love Frequency (SELF), your vibrant essence, expands as you embrace your own Love. Knowing yourself as True Self-Love correlates directly with a more expansive vibration. This draws to you more positive, high-vibing situations and people. So, when we talk about "manifesting" your life, we're referring to this alignment, not manipulating the world from your egoic desires.

To help cut the ego-self's attachment even more, we generally refer to "the body" and "the mind" (not "your body" and "your mind").

Now, let's address the elephant in the room (or rather, the bullshit in the mind). We use this term playfully, not disrespectfully, to challenge the limiting narratives your ego spins. These stories of fear and lack are simply your own bullshit. It's vital to see them for what they are, while simultaneously acknowledging that they don't define "You". This is where our revolutionary Self-Love Awakening Process (SLAP) comes in.

Think of SLAP as a gentle push, urging you to break free from the bullshit and turn inwards. Here, in the Love and Joy that you are, you'll rediscover the radiant warmth of *IshQ* (a Sufi term for divine Love). Our aim is to guide you to live from this Awareness, permanently.

Although this inner revolution requires consistent effort, the profound Bliss that awaits you makes it infinitely worthwhile. So, take a deep breath, embrace the playfulness of self-discovery, and SLAP yourself awake to the magnificence of who you truly ARE!

How To Use This Book

You can use the chapters in any way you feel to, but here are a few suggestions:

- Read the book sequentially. This will give you a solid foundation in the process of experiencing yourself as the True Self and True Self-Love.
- Select a page based on how you're experiencing life today. If you're feeling tense and unhappy, read a chapter on how to let go of the bullshit. If you're feeling expansive and want to deepen your experience of the True Self, read the last few chapters and jump into the 28-day *Deepening IshQ Challenge*. And,
- Trust your intuition. If a particular chapter or self-enquiry exercise speaks to you, focus on that. There's no right or wrong way to use this book.

"Wake-Up Calls" And Processes

Many of the chapters include at least one self-enquiry "Wake-Up Call" – exercises that are designed to shake you from your own self-deception. Approach them with curiosity, not fear; they're intended to wake you up to the layers of your limiting beliefs and bullshit, not give you a reason to wallow in it. So, take a deep breath, find a quiet corner, and dive in.

Client Cases, Noah Stories And Sam Stories

Throughout the book, you'll also come across Client Cases (all names and ages have been changed to protect identities), Noah Stories, and Sam Stories. These real-life narratives serve as powerful examples of how ordinary people have transcended their bullshit and discovered True Love and Peace. By sharing them, the intention is to ignite a spark within you, inspiring you to shift inwards, beyond the drama, and embrace the path of transformation instead.

Read Beyond The Mind

Finally, imagine these words as stepping stones leading you beyond the mind's bullshit maze. With each step, feel the ground beneath you solidify, revealing more of the True "You" – radiant and whole. So, take your time, savour the journey, and let the Bliss of your own inner rebellion welcome you home.

Above all, remember, transformation isn't linear. Trust the process and enjoy the journey!

CHAPTER 1

YOU'RE FEELING SHIT, RIGHT?

"The truth is that comparison is a treacherous game. It's a crime against your very being. It shackles you with dissatisfaction, an insatiable longing for something or someone you don't have. And, so, you compare and complain, drowning in an abyss of your own making."

You're Living In Your Own Bullshit Hell

Have you ever noticed that you're often trapped in a never-ending cycle of torment – a self-imposed sentence within the prison of your own mind? It usually sounds something like this, but it could be any words that incite the feeling of despair to flood your being:

- "I hate myself."
- "I'm such an asshole."
- "I'm stuck with him or her."
- "What's wrong with me?"
- "Why doesn't anyone ever pick me?"
- "I'm broken and wounded; I'll never recover."
- "Will life ever work out for me?"
- "I'm a disappointment."
- "What if he or she leaves me?"

- "She doesn't trust me."
- "He's always criticising me."
- "Why am I always screwing up my life?"
- "I don't know why but I just don't feel good."
- "How could this happen to me?"
- "Everyone else is better than me."
- "I'm so lonely." And,
- "Surely, there must be more to life than this bullshit?"

Does any of this sound familiar? Welcome, dear reader, to the cesspool of suffering that fills YOUR mind.

These thoughts (and thousands of others like them) bombard you, both in moments of perceived disappointment and triumph. They may also manifest as a knot of tension, a constant reminder of your failings in life. It comes as no surprise then that you struggle to find peace and generally don't feel good about yourself.

Understanding why you suffer is the start of your journey to waking up to the bullshit. This realisation will ignite the flame of self-discovery, guiding you from self-loathing towards True Self-Love. The key lies in unravelling the enigma of the mind, that formidable tool you believe successfully guides you through life.

Right now, you believe "you" are the ego-self that's walking around the planet posing as "you". You BELIEVE everything you feel, don't you?

- Every picture that flickers through the mind, you accept as being the truth.
- Every emotion that surges within you, you take as being real.
- Every thought and memory that emerges, you deem as fact.
- Every time the body goes into its fight-or-flight response, you're convinced that something bad is going to happen to you.

- Every belief you justify to your weary heart, you accept as truth. And,
- Every event that has unfolded in your life, you interpret as being an accurate reflection of your worth.

From your perspective, it's all undeniably true. Positive or negative, it would never occur to you to question its validity. After all, it's YOUR mind, the compass that has steered you and protected you for your whole life. Surely, then, it must be correct. Alas, it's not so – it's all mostly indoctrinated bullshit!

What you might not realise is that you filter every situation using the lens of your unique life story – and feelings about that story. You then compare it to what you think the situation should look like, triggering either positive or negative emotions. You believe your interpretation is the truth, oblivious to the objective reality that exists beyond your own narratives. Essentially, you judge situations not based on their intrinsic nature, but on the bullshit perceptions of the ego-self known as "you".

For those living with the ongoing effects of trauma, the impact is often debilitating. Trauma, with its gnarled roots, finds its way into the very core of your being, distorting the balance of your nervous system. It ignites the primal response of fight, flight, or freeze, leaving you feeling trapped in a blur of emotional turmoil. When trauma lingers, it results in a hypersensitive state, where even the gentlest breeze can stir up a bullshit storm within.

In the realms of emotional regulation, unresolved emotional pain (and trauma) casts a shadow that obscures the essence of the True Self. Powerful emotions bring you down, making it challenging to find the Peace that lies beneath the surface. Sadness, anger, and fear (and all forms thereof) become turbulent currents that complicate your very existence.

Remember, you're not alone in this struggle. Many find themselves drowning in their self-constructed stories, inadvertently leading lives fuelled by emotional angst and drama. Consider the following examples of what this could look like for you:

- If a long-awaited text fails to arrive, and you believe the whispers in the mind, concluding that the person in question no longer cares about you.
- If you argue with your partner, and keep fuelling the fear in the mind, convincing yourself that the relationship is over (when it's really just hot air).
- If a work promotion eludes you, and you listen to the bullshit in the mind, allowing it to confirm your failings when it comes to your career.
- If you constantly draw to you the same types of relationship, and you believe it when the mind tells you that it's because "there must be something wrong with me".
- If your partner walks away, and you succumb to the habitual negativity of the mind, labelling yourself as not good enough or successful enough, etc.
- If the property you want to buy slips through your fingers, and the echoes in the mind insist that fortune favours others but not you.
- If your wallet vanishes, and the bullshit mind declares you were born "unlucky" or states, "Typical, it always happens to me." And,
- If a stranger on social media criticises you, and you fall apart emotionally as a result.

It could be any scenario, but one thing's for sure – most people are deeply invested in their life-long narratives, mistaking them for the Gospel Truth. This IS the very root of suffering. However, there IS a simple alternative:

1. Learn to step back from your bullshit thoughts, and consciously shift your attention to something more uplifting (e.g., watching a heart-centred video, or going for a walk).
2. Practise soothing your nervous system by using grounding exercises, such as EFT (tapping), breathwork, and body scanning, to bring your focus back to the NOW.
3. Recognise that the True "You" is way vaster than the story of "you" that you tell yourself about yourself all the time. And,
4. Turn your attention within consistently, living more often as the eternal Stillness, Silence, Peace, Love and Joy that you ARE. This is what you're striving for. This is how you get to know your Buddha Nature, or the In-Lightened True Self.

When you live with your attention mostly inside, the burdens that weigh upon you dissipate. No longer do you perceive yourself as old, fat, ugly, poor, stupid, or inadequate. Emotional discomfort no longer clings to your every move. The need to compare yourself to others, or criticise them, evaporates. You choose not to engage in arguments or defend your fragile ego-self. In fact, you decide not to listen to the siren call of your bullshit at all.

Noah and I envision the mind as a vast library, brimming with stories from the past and files containing hopes and fears for the future. It's cluttered with a mix of joyous and agonising bullshit. It was only when we realised that we could live beyond the library, in the Silence of the present moment, that we began to let go of suffering – and oh, what a revelation that was!

Now, it's your turn to start your own transformative journey. Learn to move beyond the raw reality of your bullshit and bask in the light of self-discovery that awaits you within.

Never Mind – It's Not The Boss Of "You"

There's a reason why newborns exude an air of Bliss. It's because they're still connected to the eternal Love and peace that precedes their physical incarnation. They don't judge the life they've been born into as being good or bad; in fact, they don't think at all.

Through our own self-enquiry, we recognise that newborns possess an innate recognition of the True Self. However, this blissful state doesn't last for long. By the age of eight, the nightmarish onslaught of bullshit descends. You too, like all of us, started to judge everything by then – your appearance, your body, your home, and more. Everything became a mirror and you compared yourself to your parents, siblings, peers, etc. You questioned:

- *"Am I as pretty as them?"*
- *"Am I as popular as them?"* And,
- *"Am I as rich as them?"*

It's no wonder that you started to feel self-conscious about certain aspects of yourself at such a young age. If left unchecked, the ego-mind acts like a mischievous puppy, causing you to suffer. All the puppy wants to do is roam, bark, and run off freely. It seeks to fulfil its own desires without restraint.

When it barks, it wants attention. When it's hungry, it demands food. But above all, it craves attention – any attention, all the time. It's demanding and expects immediate gratification. And if it doesn't get what it wants, the barking intensifies, leading to even greater suffering.

The ego-mind (i.e., the puppy) falsely believes that it's the boss of "You". It guides and protects you based on its observations during your formative years. You constantly heard people dictate how you should behave. You were told to stay busy, strive for more, and respect your elders. You were indoctrinated with notions of right and wrong as determined by those who claimed to know better.

If you take a step back, you can see that most of your life has been consumed by distractions and "mindfool" pursuits. Rarely were you encouraged to let go of external input and stimulation. No one ever instructed you to just BE, to experience the blissful present moment. And nobody guided you to recognise the True Self, the Vastness that exists beyond the ego-personality known as "you".

However, if you wish to escape the burden of bullshit lies that you tell yourself every day, you must acknowledge that it is, in fact, all bullshit. You must pivot inwards and experience yourself as Conscious Awareness – the Stillness, Silence, Peace, Love and Joy that you ARE. This is the authentic boss of "you".

Just as you learned to walk as a child by getting up after every fall, you can train the mind to transcend the bullshit automatically by moving your attention within every time you notice that you've become distracted by it. The more you consciously practise this, the easier it will become to experience yourself as Conscious Awareness.

Here are a few more examples of what real-life psychological suffering can appear as.

Client Cases: Janet, Tony And Aja Struggled

Let's start with Janet, 43, who was married with children. On the surface, she appeared to be happy, but inside, she was suffering. Despite her love for her four children, she resented the lack of time she had for herself. Her husband was constantly preoccupied with financial worries. Janet blamed herself for his stress and internalised it as a reflection of her worth. She believed she wasn't a good-enough mother or an interesting-enough wife. Nothing changed until she became aware of her distorted perception and learned how to let it go.

Then there was Tony, 62, who went through a divorce after 26 years of marriage. To his friends, he seemed successful and confident, but in reality, he was really struggling. Fear consumed him as he approached the end of his career. He worried about money and being alone, drawing parallels with his father's experience. Tony took the time to shift his attention from what he didn't want to what he desired instead, drawing to him interesting people and opportunities. He realised that the issue was not his age but, rather, his fixation on the lack of what he sought.

Meanwhile, Aja, 45, was divorced and appeared to have it all – beauty, success, and material possessions. However, she lacked romantic love and craved it. Like many individuals with emotionally absent fathers, she attracted unavailable partners and resented it. She was afraid to let go of toxic sexual relationships because she didn't trust that something better would come along. We assisted her in recognising her own True Self-Love, and taught her how to expand internally to manifest healthier, more loving connections.

The common thread is that all these clients made their circumstances mean there was something wrong with them. They continuously sabotaged themselves by focusing on "the not having of what they desired" until it became a truth in their reality. In other words, they bought into their own bullshit, or suffering, and held onto it.

As part of their treatment plans, we helped them to understand that by stubbornly focusing on certain beliefs, they were actually hypnotising themselves to create the opposite of what they desired. This is what happens when you consistently identify with a story of lack and keep reliving it.

Another way to understand this is by recognising that you hypnotise yourself by focusing on your expectation of a particular outcome happening. If you live as if a positive result has already occurred, success is more likely to follow. Conversely, if you live as if a negative outcome has taken place, failure is more probable. (Note: Hypnosis, as we define it, refers to focusing on specific suggestions and feelings whilst excluding all else.)

Ultimately, if you continually internalise and embrace the negative story that you have constructed about yourself, it's not unsurprising that positive opportunities don't materialise often. It's time to liberate yourself from this cycle. How, you might wonder? You must become more aware of how your story holds you back. Let's delve deeper into that now.

Wake-up Call: Awakening To Your Comparisons

The aim of these exercises is to help you to see your limiting story of "you" so that you can stop engaging with it. You start to wake up when you become more aware that the True "You" is way vaster than the bullshit narratives that you keep telling yourself about "you".

Take a moment now, close your eyes, and bring to mind someone close to you. Notice your immediate thoughts. Don't censor or filter them. Whatever the thoughts were, recognise that they were a judgment. Whether you compared yourself to them, positively or not, felt sympathy for them, or argued with them, it's all just judgment of yourself and others.

Now, take a deep breath and, again, let those familiar thoughts about that person flood the mind. Notice how many there are. Recognise how often you think about and judge others, even those you hold dear. It's quite a distraction, isn't it? To gain more insight into this pattern, ask yourself:

1. *"What thoughts do I tend to have about them (and others)?"* And,
2. *"What do I experience in my body as I think about them?"*

Make a note of your answers and reflect on them. Are you able to observe that judging others, even if the judgment appears positive, doesn't feel nurturing inside? It actually feels quite hollow. This realisation serves as your wake-up call. If thinking about others feels uncomfortable, it's time to redirect your focus inwards and explore self-loving thoughts instead. This exercise is guiding you towards that realisation.

Acknowledging your own thinking patterns can be daunting, yet it's definitely the first step towards waking up. So, if this exercise feels challenging, take a few moments to breathe and remind yourself that this is where the transformation begins.

The truth is that comparison is a treacherous game. It's a crime against your very being. It shackles you with dissatisfaction, an insatiable longing for something or someone you don't have. And, so, you compare and complain, drowning in an abyss of your own making.

There's nothing more disempowering than comparing yourself to others. The following story shows how I started to liberate myself from the harsh judgments that I used to have about the way I looked.

Sam's Story: Loosening The Grip Of Self-Dislike

For most of my life, I carried a deep sense of feeling unloved and unwanted. Self-esteem eluded me, and I saw myself as ugly, despite the compliments of friends and lovers. I was convinced that they were simply being kind, unable to see the truth as I did.

Through self-enquiry, I traced the dislike of my appearance back to a pivotal moment when I was five and subjected to a dreadful haircut. That experience etched a negative self-image into my psyche, leaving me feeling insecure for years.

"Perhaps my dad left because I wasn't good enough?" The question wasn't a conscious thought, but a whisper that echoed deep within. For over four decades, I held onto this self-sabotaging narrative, blaming my appearance for everything that was wrong in my life. It was a heavy cloak to bear.

Then, like a sunbeam piercing through storm clouds, a journey to India offered a path of liberation. True freedom arrived when I realised that the True Self was not defined by the superficial "me". My internal suffering had never been about my appearance; it had stemmed from my obsessive lack of self-worth and not having had a clear recognition of the True Self.

As I delved deeper into Conscious Awareness, a metamorphosis happened. With each introspective breath, the tyranny of self-blame faded. It wasn't about the reflection in the mirror, but the gentle hum of Peace radiating from my being. There were no rules, no rigid definitions of beauty dictated by the ego-self. Consciousness didn't care if I altered my appearance or learned to love it. This newfound freedom felt exhilarating, like shedding a self-imposed cage, and stepping into the vibrant flow of life, unfettered and alive.

My transformation rippled outwards. In the quiet sanctuary of the True Self, I discovered a magnetic connection with Noah. Our relationship blossomed, nurtured by my steady glow of presence and unreserved flow of Self-Love. Witnessing myself as this Love allowed me to experience it profoundly with another – a romantic love that was, and still is, unequivocally beautiful in all its facets.

The life I once chased, defined by goals and aspirations, faded into the periphery. In its place bloomed a deep acceptance of the present moment, an understanding that the only purpose of life is to experience it fully, in all its messy, breath-taking glory. There is no ultimate "soul calling" or elusive "my truth", just the undeniable reality of being, a symphony of Stillness, Silence, Peace, Love and Joy orchestrated as Consciousness itself.

These realisations were vital. Nurturing the Love within shifted my focus, and my external world began to reflect that Love back at me. Self-enquiry revealed the painful extent to which I'd hypnotised myself with negativity. As I said, I fixated on those who seemingly confirmed my flaws, ignoring any words of kindness. It was a vicious cycle, fuelled by self-doubt.

But I broke free. Through consistent effort, I trained myself to pivot my attention away from the bullshit, towards the True Love inside. I didn't try to suppress the thoughts or rewrite the story; I simply acknowledged them and refused to engage. It felt awkward at first, but with practice, focusing on Peace became effortless. This shift has transformed my life, and if I can do it, trust me, so can you.

Now, let's delve into Carol's journey and learn how she stopped interpreting her painful past as evidence of her own shortcomings.

Client Case: Carol's Path To Peace

Carol, 41, grew up in an environment dominated by her perpetually angry father. This upbringing left her feeling unsafe and lacking in confidence. Despite her ease in meeting men, she struggled to maintain relationships, believing herself to be unworthy of lasting love.

Like most people, Carol internalised every breakup as a reflection of her perceived inadequacy. She interpreted any separation as confirmation that she wasn't good enough or that someone prettier, thinner, or younger had replaced her.

Regardless of what we said, Carol looked for evidence to reinforce her belief that she was undeserving of long-term love and romance. It was an endless debate and she was sure she was right. Her treatment plan involved several steps:

1. She started to challenge the notion that her painful life story determined her worth.
2. Next, she recognised that by repeating her negative self-talk, she'd been setting herself up for constant failure. To counter this, she started to train her attention to switch to more positive thoughts as soon as a negative one popped in. And,
3. Finally, Carol began to turn her gaze inwards, focusing on the Love and Joy that always resided deep within her. She also embraced her passions and pursued activities that expanded who she was BEING a lot more often.

By following this plan as best she could, Carol experienced a breakthrough. She was eager to continue changing her inner dialogue, and reassured when she was able to recognise herself as True Self-Love – for the first time in her life.

Within a few months of experiencing herself as this Love every day, Carol found an inner Peace that had eluded her previously. She felt a softness inside and started to embrace being alive. Consequently, she found herself enjoying life a lot more.

This is the transformative power of shifting the focus of your attention away from the external towards a Love that's internal – and always available to you. But it doesn't happen in a vacuum; often we need inspiration to take the first step in aligning with our own Love.

Look no further than Noah's story. It took him a while to break free from the lies that he used to tell himself about himself and step into the power of the True Self. But he did it. He reached the point where the pain of staying the same outweighed the pain of change.

Noah's Story: Stepping Back From My Bullshit

For years, I bore the heavy burden of disappointment, imprisoning myself within its suffocating clutches. When my father left us for another woman, I swallowed my heartache and stepped into the role of the man of the house, doing my best to support my mother. By the time I was 11, I was already out there, delivering milk and newspapers at the crack of dawn, and hustling for odd jobs in the neighbourhood to keep us afloat.

I should say here that I love and respect my mother deeply. I fully acknowledge that she had to grapple with her own demons after her divorce, navigating the demands of single parenthood on a shoestring budget. It wasn't easy for any of us!

I can remember the day when, at the age of 12, I mustered up the courage to tell her that a trusted male family friend had been sexually abusing me for nearly two years. It was 1967, and Scotland had been hit by a big storm. Our home was devastated and we lost everything.

It was during this time, as we waited for our home to be rebuilt, that the abuse happened. My mother had arranged for my sister and I to stay with friends. However, instead of safeguarding us, I became the victim of the father of the family that we were staying with.

Overwhelmed by confusion and fear, I lived with the daunting prospect that speaking out might lead to us to being kicked out and homeless. After enduring this abuse for more than a year, I felt a profound sense of relief when we returned to our home, and I to the sanctuary of my own bed. But, a few months later, my mother suggested that we stay with the same family again when she was away. Terror gripped me and I knew I couldn't revisit that nightmare.

When I finally confided in my mother about what had happened, she didn't believe me and even defended the man. As I stood before her, trembling, it became clear that the shock was sinking in, yet she remained unable to speak or act. Now, as a parent myself, I can empathise with the emotions she must have experienced. However, in that moment, I felt isolated and betrayed. No action was taken against the man, but alternative arrangements were made.

Meanwhile, the sordid story was never mentioned again. We all carried on as if nothing had happened. From my perspective, I didn't dwell on it. I was simply relieved that it was behind me, thrilled to be a teenager playing football and chasing girls. I didn't consciously see myself as being scarred. But as I moved into adulthood, I understood that I was on my own, and perhaps that's where some of my self-esteem and trust issues sprouted from.

My mother's influence permeated every aspect of my life. Even after leaving home at the age of 17, and getting engaged at 18, the ties to her remained profound – I still felt like "her boy", with scarcely any boundaries between us. When I was 22, my then-fiancée found herself pregnant, and I was looking forward to our future together.

However, my world shattered when I discovered that my mother had persuaded her to have an abortion. This caused my engagement to unravel. I was devastated and angry. But, as was our usual pattern, my mother and I chose to sweep that painful incident under the carpet, never to discuss it again!

It wasn't until many years later that I realised how much my childhood had affected me, turning me into what I can only describe as a "Master of Suppression". I had become convinced that nothing I did would ever satisfy anyone, least of all my mother! This self-doubt pushed me to change jobs, locations, and relationships constantly, all to avoid exposing my vulnerabilities and disappointing those around me, including myself.

As part of my healing process, I came to understand that I'd unwittingly internalised my family's perceptions of me – even into my fifties. It was no coincidence that I heard the word "disappointment" in my mind every day, or that I used it frequently in conversation. This belief had become so ingrained that I'd essentially hypnotised myself with it, constantly feeling like a disappointment, and looking for it within myself and others. Consequently, I resorted to a harsh and joyless way of living.

However, I came to understand that I didn't have to carry this burden forever. Through self-enquiry, I realised that I had the power to release myself from my psychological baggage. Although I couldn't change my traumatic childhood, I could break free from the narratives I'd constructed about myself. No one had forced me to accept these stories as truth. In fact, no one had ever mandated that I should let my childhood define my identity in any way.

Today, I can reflect back and laugh at the stories I once regarded as being indisputably real. I now KNOW, beyond a shadow of a doubt, that the True Self "Me" transcends all the bullshit. It might have taken a while, but I'm grateful that I finally turned inwards and recognised the charade for what it truly was – utter bullshit.

The only lens through which I choose to see myself now is as the embodiment of the Stillness, Silence, Peace, Love and Joy that

I KNOW I am. To just BE in this magnificent moment unfolding before me. Nothing else matters!

Wake-up Call: Facing The Force Of Negativity

Start this exercise by closing your eyes and taking a deep breath. Let go of all thoughts and turn your attention inwards. It's time to confront the core beliefs that govern your life.

We all have our own version of "not good enough" and now is the moment to pinpoint the exact wording of yours. If you're not sure what that is, think about the beliefs that we outlined earlier in the chapter. For example:

- "I'm not worthy."
- "I can't do it."
- "I'm meant to be alone."
- "I'm a failure."
- "No one wants me."
- "No one loves me."
- "No one appreciates me."
- "I'm not attractive enough."
- "I'm too fat, old, ugly, etc."
- "Good things never happen to me." Or,
- "There must be something wrong with me."

If, however, these don't trigger your words, think about the last time you had an argument with someone, or defended yourself in the mind. Notice the words that pop up and whether they are part of your automatic internal dialogue.

Take a moment to make a note of these thoughts and reflect on them. As you begin to notice how often your words automatically fill the mind, see if you can recognise once again how frequently you feel the physical impact of thinking them (i.e., headaches, backaches, etc). It's probably more often than you realised, right?

Now, take a few deep breaths and prepare to confront the addictive pull of your thinking. To do this, go back to your list of negative self-beliefs. Repeat them to yourself a few times and really start to FEEL them in the body.

As you sense that you're about to descend into the spiral of feeling not good enough, clap your hands, and say, *"STOP!"* This command will bring your thinking to an abrupt halt. Stay in this space of no-thinking and do NOT let your attention get sucked into any other thoughts.

Notice that as you do this, it creates a tightness in the body. This is because the mind automatically tries to latch onto the next idea. As soon as you stop engaging with it, it creates tension. However, you MUST. It's in resisting the tug to engage with the next thought that you're able to train the mind to pivot inwards, away from it.

As you become more aware of this pull, slow your thinking right down. Zoom in on your next belief and see how the mind really wants to grab onto it. Notice that reaching for that thought and not engaging with it feels the same as reaching for another drink, biscuit, or cigarette, etc, when you really want it but are trying to abstain. It's as uncomfortable to deny yourself what the mind thinks it wants materially, as it is to deny yourself the perverse pleasure of engaging with that next (usually negative) thought or belief.

Recognising this is empowering – it's allowing you to see the nature of the mind. So, give yourself permission to be OK with it. You want to become very attuned to what it feels like physically to get pulled into your familiar thought patterns. This is how you'll start to train the mind to move beyond them.

Take another deep breath and let's expand the practice. This time, reread your list of beliefs and, without saying *"STOP"*, just quit the negative self-talk. Notice the strong urge to keep going, but DO

NOT engage with whatever is hovering there. Stubbornly hold your space and focus on your breathing. Gradually, the energetic craving to buy into your incessant story will ease.

Next, get up and go to the fridge. To help yourself get in touch with the somatic pull even more, stand in front of it and reach inside for something you'd like to eat or drink. Then stop yourself from taking it and observe the uncomfortable physical sensation that comes from not giving it to yourself.

As you stand there, start to recite your list of beliefs and stop suddenly in the middle, refusing to engage with the next one. Yes, it will feel uncomfortable, but you must be willing to face this discomfort, and not give into it, if you're going to break free from its toxic pull.

Finally, go through the whole process again. Read your list and stop in the middle of it. Then, tune into the body and ask yourself the following:

- *"Can I stop myself from engaging with my thoughts, even for a moment?"*
- *"How do I feel physically if I am able to just observe what I'm thinking?"*
- *"If I do get pulled back in, what happens next?"*
- *"Do these thoughts frequently occupy my mind? Are they familiar?"* And,
- *"If I can stop, what do I experience then?"*

These questions are going to help you to wake up to your default thinking, so be really honest with yourself. Make a note of your answers and reread them once you've finished. Can you observe any incessant thinking (and feeling) patterns starting to emerge? Does anything surprise you about what you've written?

Take a moment to acknowledge and reflect on what you've discovered about the ego-self known as "you". You're beginning to unveil the stories that circulate through the mind 24/7.

If you observe, you'll be able to see how the mind-self combs any situation and pulls out "evidence" to confirm what "you" think and feel. For example, if you only hear criticism from people and can't receive compliments, understand that the ego-self does this to back up the story of "you" that you play out on a continual basis.

Consider this for yourself and think about what you do. Can you see the type of twisted evidence that you look for repeatedly? Is it a sense of stuckness, a belief that your partner (or family) doesn't appreciate you, an assumption of inevitable failure, or a feeling of being stuck and unlucky?

Be thorough, but also treat yourself with compassion. Remember, your objective is not to control your thoughts. Instead, you're choosing to live beyond them, focusing your attention on the Love within.

Looking For Evidence – It Fuels What You Think

Let's dive back into Carol's story; it offers a useful insight when it comes to perception.

Convinced that her father's departure was her fault, Carol developed a belief that all men would leave her. This led her to scrutinise all her relationships, searching for signs that her partner was losing interest. She lived in a constant state of unease, second-guessing her every move. It took time for Carol to accept that men genuinely desired her company.

Had Carol grown up in a more emotionally intelligent and awakened environment, her primary caregiver might have nurtured her differently. They might have taught her how to observe her thoughts and recognise that she didn't have to be defined by them.

Imagine if Carol had received a gentle nudge like this during her formative years: *"Dearest Carol, you shine more brightly than your mind lets you believe. The story you hold about your father leaving, the one where he shouts and the blame falls on you, might not be the whole picture. It's natural to try to understand why things happen, and sometimes we make up stories to make sense of it. Perhaps your father did raise his voice or say harsh things, and it's normal to feel hurt and wonder if it was your fault. But remember, Carol, his words and actions were about him, and his own struggles, not a reflection of your worth. People can be loud and say hurtful things, even when they love you. So, I ask you to consider whether it's possible that he didn't leave because of you at all?"*

Had Carol encountered this kind of understanding and guidance when she was a child, her self-belief might have blossomed like a flower. It's likely that her inner landscape as an adult would have been an oasis of self-nurturing and faith in her own value and ability.

Remember this: your automatic way of looking at the world stems firmly from what you experienced when you were growing up, and how you felt about those experiences. Based on this, the mind constructs a story around the ego-self known as "you" and will tirelessly look for evidence to validate it. Knowing our story and identifying with it is what makes us human. It makes us feel safe.

However, as you begin to wake up, you'll realise that the True Self is way more expansive than the limitations of the ego-self and its (mostly) bullshit voice. As a result, you'll no longer need your old story to feel safe in the world. This is where your freedom begins.

As you expand and recognise that you're a boundless expression of "Nothing", you'll grasp inherently that nothing about your ego-self's perception of "you" is set in stone. The only truth is that "You" are the True Self and its four existential elements of Stillness, Silence, Peace, Love and Joy (remember Love and Joy is classed as one).

Let that sink in – within the realms of the True Vast Eternal Nothing, there is no thinking. Your thoughts are invented by the mind, shaped by your perceptions of the world. This insight is liberating because it means you really can choose to see yourself in any way you desire. The next time you think about yourself, bear this in mind.

Your internal dialogue might feel 100% real, but actually you could tell yourself a different version and very soon that would feel real too! In fact, take a few minutes now to reframe your life story, then repeat it to yourself for a week and notice how you feel about the personality known as "you".

The power of knowing yourself inherently as the True Vast Eternal Nothing is that you believe it when you say to yourself: *"No. I'm not going there. This is ALL bullshit made up by my mind to protect the story of 'me'. I KNOW that everything's working out for me, always has and always will. I therefore release the need to control and embrace the expansiveness of the True Self instead."*

Take a while to reflect on that, then ask yourself the following profound questions:

1. *"Why would I choose to look for evidence to back up my bullshit perception of 'me' when I could choose to focus on a more empowering story instead?"* And,
2. *"Why would I choose to think about 'me' at all when I could revel in the exquisite Stillness, Silence, Peace, Love and Joy that I KNOW I AM?"*

Repeat the questions, allowing the answers to flow through you. Your body inherently knows the truth of who you ARE, so trust its wisdom. When you recognise that you no longer have to believe in the bullshit, the Game of Life begins to shift in your favour.

Wake-up Call: Using Coping Phrases To Detach

Even though your goal is to stop engaging with the mind's bullshit completely, it sometimes helps to repeat "coping" statements like the following as you begin to wake up. The more you repeat them, the faster the mind will learn that it's not the boss of "You".

Start by reading the following statement. Make the commitment to recite it as often as possible so that the mind repeats it automatically the next time the bullshit arises: *"I'm starting to recognise the thoughts and beliefs I use to define the ego-self known as 'me'. I can see that my mind has been consumed by them, leaving no space for Silence. It's no wonder that I've been feeling so tense. I don't have to believe anything that I hear or feel. In fact, I can say to myself, 'Just because I think and feel this way, it doesn't mean it's true.' I remind myself that fear is merely a sensation in the body, not reality. If I feel bad, I now know it's because I believe what's in my head. Although these thoughts and feelings may look like 'me' and feel like 'me', I KNOW that they're NOT the True 'Me'."*

Take a deep breath and continue with: *"I KNOW that the True Self transcends the limitations of the personality known as 'me'. Regardless of my thoughts, I'm not confined to this small sense of 'self'. In reality, I am the True Vast Eternal Nothing from which the essence of life flows. The only elements that define the True Self are Stillness, Silence, Peace, Love and Joy. Everything else is just noise created by the mind."*

Notice that reading this has a calming effect. Repeat it a few times and observe what happens inside of you. If you feel any irritation or tension, spend a minute or two focusing on the breath, following the air flowing in and out of the nose. Remind yourself that you're asking these probing questions to highlight your bullshit, not to torment yourself with it. If you want to break free of suffering, you must start to recognise who your ego-self thinks "you" are.

We know the journey of self-discovery is intense, but it's also liberating. Once you start to understand the nature of the mind, it's much easier to KNOW the True Self "You" that exists beyond it. So be brave. Give yourself the time and space to observe your automatic thinking patterns. This is the start to you feeling lighter and brighter. And that, dear reader, is where the true Game of Life begins.

The True Game Of Life – Focus On The Joy

While society measures a successful life in terms of material accumulation – cars, partners, careers, watches, and homes – true success lies not in our possessions, but in the depth of Joy that we experience.

The more Noah and I tap into Consciousness, the clearer it becomes: chasing the trappings of romance, riches, and social status is like running after the end of a ball of string.

Even if we manage to grab the "perfect" partner, pile up the wealth, buy the car, or retire young, these achievements eventually unravel, leaving us yearning for something deeper. Why? Because these external things are mere extensions of ourselves, temporary and ultimately unfulfilling. They can never quench the thirst for profound inner Joy, which comes not from collecting the trinkets of the world, but from the radiant core of your own being.

The secret to cracking the true Game of Life is buried within. You don't need to hoard more stuff, climb social ladders, or accumulate experiences to know yourself as Love and Joy. It's not about proving anything to anyone, least of all yourself.

Imagine letting go of that ball of string, the one you cling to so tightly in your pursuit of validation. Release your grip and, instead, step fully into the Vastness of your own being, the eternal Universe that is "You". This, dear reader, is the real win, one that transcends the impermanence of material reality.

Life's only true "goal" isn't a goal at all, but an inherent calling: to experience yourself as the True Self. It's a dance of attention, a gentle training of your inner gaze to rest more often on the Love that lives deep within. Through this introspection, you'll discover the fundamental truth – that the True Self IS Stillness, Silence, Peace, Love and Joy (**Chapter 7** delves deeper into recognising each element). This is who you are, untainted by the ebb and flow of your material world. No pile of belongings or intimate social circle can ever match the fulfilment of knowing your eternal Joy.

Standing tall in the light of Conscious Awareness, therefore, we redefine success. It's no longer about the size of your house or the notches on your belt. Instead, it's about:

- *"How much of my life am I able to stop seeking, judging, comparing, and suffering in general?* And,
- *"How quickly can I let the bullshit go and know myself as Love and Joy?"*

The more you can experience yourself as True Love, the more successful your life becomes. It's a simple equation:

- 51% of your time spent in this blissful state translates into a 51% successful life. Or,
- 70% of your days filled with Joy? That's a resounding 70% success rate.

The more you live and FEEL like someone who's filled with Joy, the more you'll manifest circumstances that reflect that Joy. The irony, though, is that the more you live as Joy, the less you'll desire anything other than what you already have. This is not to say that you won't still enjoy the good things in life. You will. You'll just be MORE interested in experiencing True Joy than in revelling in anything material and external to "You".

Once you understand this inherently, it will become a lot easier to receive "more". More abundance, more connections, more fun, more laughter, more magic – more of everything.

This is one of the most basic principles at the heart of feeling lighter about life. And yet, despite its simplicity, so many people still feel stuck, weighed down by dissatisfaction and doubt. Why? There are three main culprits lurking in the shadows:

1. **The Stubborn Believer.** This fella clings to the belief that happiness is some elusive butterfly, forever flitting just out of reach, tied to the strings of "having more". He chases promotions, pursues people, clings to treasures, and frantically ticks boxes on his mental "successful-life" checklist, all the while missing the vibrant Joy that is buried right within.
2. **The Storyteller.** This one whispers a familiar tale in your ear – the narrative of "you" that's woven from past hurts, limiting beliefs, and self-doubt. He tells you who "you" are, what you're capable of, and, more importantly, what you deserve. The problem? This story might be holding you hostage, keeping you chained to a reality far dimmer than your true potential. And,

3. **The Bullshit Clinger.** Ah, the most cunning of the trio. This one convinces you that your sadness, anger, and fear are not just baggage, but badges of honour, essential threads in the story of "you". He whispers that to shed them is to lose a part of yourself, leaving you bare and vulnerable. But the truth? These emotions are clouds obscuring your radiant Joy – clouds you have the power to gently nudge aside.

Now that the three tormentors have been unmasked, the question is: How do you break free from their grip? The answer is buried deep within you, a radiant space untouched by the bullshit. Let's journey there together, and bathe in the healing light of self-awareness.

The Past Is Where Your Misery Begins

With this newfound understanding, turn your attention inwards. Do you ever feel like a puppet, your strings being manipulated by unseen hands reaching from the past? If so, it's possible that your attention dwells primarily in the trenches of your life story.

This can leave you feeling vulnerable and insecure, and most probably a captive to unresolved emotional pain or trauma. It might manifest as sudden outbursts that seem disproportionate to the situation, such as exploding over a spilled coffee or sinking into sadness as you stalk your ex on social media. Alternatively, you may find yourself trapped in a mental echo chamber, replaying past hurts with your unforgiving inner critic.

If any of this resonates, you're not alone. You might well be carrying the weight of unprocessed psychological pain, making you easier to trigger. But the good news is that freedom awaits! Embrace the uncomfortable journey of exploring your triggers. It's not about focusing on the past, but about clearing out the toxic root that empowers you to reclaim your present and future.

To kickstart your inner revolution, here are some thought-provoking questions:

1. *"Who is this 'I' who feels X, Y, Z?"*
2. *"Who is this 'I' who believes everything that 'I' think?"* And,
3. *"Who is this 'I' who gets so easily triggered?"*

As you embark on this self-enquiry, see if you can find a separate "I" who owns these thoughts, feelings, and "self" narratives that you spin. The secret is that there's no such "I". Recognising this is a crucial step – you simply can't hold onto the limiting stories of "you" while simultaneously questioning them. Can you grasp this inherently?

Take your time with these questions. They're invitations to transcend the labels you've pinned on the ego-self – your name, title, relationship status, and so on. Keep asking and keep digging, until the grip of those triggering narratives begins to loosen. Trust your intuition; you'll know when another layer of self-made bullshit has fallen away.

Remember, observing the nature of the mind illuminates the path towards untangling yourself from your emotional shackles. In the next chapter, we'll delve deeper into recognising and mastering those triggers, paving the way for a lighter, freer you.

CHAPTER 2

BEING TRIGGER (UN)HAPPY

"If you recognise that a particular person's behaviour triggers you often, it's time to turn the spotlight on yourself and ask: 'In what way am I similar to them?'"

Unlocking The Triggers Hidden In Your Life Story

Waking up is NOT a soft landing. Life demands a choice: turn inwards, confront your self-sabotaging narratives, and choose to live as an embodiment of eternal Love. Or continue to fixate on the dramas of everyday life, clinging to the limiting story of "you" that the ego-self whispers is the truth.

If you find yourself leaning towards the path of True Love, blessings will overflow. By making this choice, you're starting to shed the illusions of "you", directing your focus inwards towards the Stillness, Silence, Peace, Love and Joy that you ARE. This implies a profound understanding of the need to detach from the dramas and your emotional reactions to it. As a consequence, you're on course to creating an easier, more blissful life.

However, if the ego-self's saga still ensnares you, a wake-up call is in order. This path holds no genuine self-improvement. It only fans the flames of emotional fragility, leaving you vulnerable to your automatic trigger responses.

The burning question now is this: What choice will you make? The initial step towards liberation involves acknowledging those triggers, and embarking on an exploration to unravel their hold on you.

The Mechanics Of Being Triggered

A single word, familiar smell, or fleeting memory can spark an unexpected emotional eruption, positive or negative, regardless of your current mood. These intense reactions are more than just fleeting feelings; they're flashlights into your psyche, revealing unresolved conflicts and limiting patterns waiting to be addressed.

Don't run away. Instead, embrace the power of your triggers. They're an opportunity to confront buried issues, break free from self-sabotaging behaviour, and ultimately cultivate a calmer, more centred response to life's inevitable challenges.

Imagine a scenario where the mind-self, the external persona that you present to the world, leans towards anger, neediness, or emotional numbness. This constant state of high anxiety can feel like you're constantly teetering on the edge of an outburst. Such a state is usually a consequence of your life experience (especially what happened to you during your formative years). Neglect, abuse, or other painful events can leave a lasting psychological imprint, significantly influencing your behaviour.

From a spiritual perspective, when someone triggers you, they're reflecting back something about YOU. Your relationship with the worlds acts as a mirror, showcasing aspects of your ego-self that you both embrace and resist. These reflections serve as guides, illuminating where you've fully embraced your identity and where resistance lingers. They also spotlight judgments that need to be released if you're serious about your own growth.

For example, perhaps you find yourself easily irritated when your partner cries, seeing it as weakness. However, upon deeper reflection (through therapy or self-enquiry), you realise that your discomfort with their vulnerability stems from your own feelings of helplessness. Does that resonate with you?

Alternatively, maybe you're drawn to strong individuals, men and women who subconsciously remind you of a parent. However, in reality, these relationships often feel draining or challenging, leaving you feeling unheard and unseen. If you step back and observe, you'll notice that you feel the same way with them as you do (or did) with your mother, father, or primary caregiver!

We could cite countless examples, but they all have one thing in common – you get negatively triggered because you're still attached to your painful life story and what you believe it means about "you".

However, whilst unsettling, emotional triggers offer the potential to catalyse your personal evolution. By recognising their origins and engaging in self-enquiry, you can deepen your Awareness, enhancing emotional regulation and spiritual fulfilment.

Accept Your Reactions, Find Your Inner Compass

With this in mind, one of the most empowering approaches to alleviate the intensity of your triggers is to stop trying to avoid them and welcome them instead.

The next time someone annoys you, rather than lashing out at them, take a deep breath and remember that their actions are NOT the trigger. Your unresolved emotions ARE!

Remind yourself of this often – ALL your emotions are yours. That snap? It's not about the other person; it's about the pain you haven't learned to process internally. Dumping it, often on people who can't fight back, is tempting, but embracing it inwardly is the route to personal growth and freedom.

The more you welcome your raw emotions – fears, tears, and perceived weaknesses – without resistance, the faster they'll dissipate, granting you a deeper recognition of the True Self.

Let's consider another example. A client used to get upset at any mention of her "gappy" teeth. For years, these comments triggered a deep insecurity about her attractiveness. One day, she decided to start accepting them.

It wasn't an overnight miracle but anytime the trigger arose, she would ask herself, *"Who is this 'I' who hates my teeth?"*

She would then relax into her inner Silence (the answer), while staying present to her emotional discomfort until it shifted. Eventually, the comments stopped bothering her and disappeared altogether.

This is the work and it's empowering. Facing your triggers and letting them go IS the gateway to feeling lighter about yourself and life. It IS the pathway to true Peace. Now, let's explore how to do this together.

Wake-up Call: Unmask Your Default Responses

As you do this exercise, remember that you're not trying to torture yourself by thinking about what might have been. It's essential to remind yourself often that you can't change the past. All you can do is drop the bullshit self-deception that it could have happened any differently.

Start this process by closing your eyes and thinking about the last time your trigger response was activated. Ask yourself:

- *"What triggered me?"*
- *"Who or what was involved in the situation?"*
- *"How did I react?"*
- *"What emotions did I experience?"* And,
- *"What was I thinking about as I reacted? Was it part of my usual inner dialogue?"*

Take a moment to note down and consider your answers. Now, read them again and see if you gain any clarity into why you react in certain ways. Keep in mind that anything can trigger you, whether it's your own inner critic, or unresolved emotions from the past, etc.

If you're finding it hard to recall a specific triggering event, focus on a familiar emotional response instead (for example, the feeling of being wrongly accused, ignored, or unheard), and see if you can trace the associated feeling back throughout your life.

Take, for example, one client who recognised that she'd been emotionally numbing herself for years. Growing up in an abusive home, she'd adopted numbness as a form of self-protection, unaware of how to regulate her own emotions. Her only emotional language was to lash out in anger when her carefully constructed wall cracked.

Uncovering the root of your triggers is a cathartic process but it can also be emotionally challenging. So, be gentle with yourself and allow the process to unfold at its own pace.

Now, let's take a deeper look. If you recognise that a particular person's behaviour triggers you often, it's time to turn the spotlight on yourself and ask:

- *"In what way am I similar to them?"* For example, if you often get irritated with your partner because they're always stressed about money, examine your own relationship with money. Are you also worried about your finances? Could it be that their behaviour is reflecting back your own feelings of financial insecurity that you're reluctant to face? Or is it showing you how secure you feel in yourself, allowing you to offer compassion instead of frustration?
- Similarly, if you find that your partner, family, or friends are critical of you, ask yourself: *"How, when, and why am I critical of myself and others?"* Alternatively, consider whether your personal growth has made you more resilient to negativity?
- Next, if there are aggressive people in your life, go within, and ask: *"How, when, and why do I give out aggressive energy?"* And *"Where in my life have I learned that it's 'normal' to be around angry,*

violent communicators, and is that OK for me?" If it's not, ask yourself, *"If I don't like being in this hostile environment, what's stopping me from just walking away?* And,

- Lastly, if you find that gossip and betrayal surround you, enquire: *"How, when, and why do I gossip about others?"* And *"How, when, and why do I betray myself?"*

Take your time, note down your answers, and observe the ego-self's behaviour without judgment. As you trace back your feelings and triggers, you may discover patterns of overcompensating for people's poor behaviour (when you know you shouldn't), or that you push people away to protect yourself. Keep asking and TRUST that as your Awareness expands, insights and opportunities for positive change will start popping into the mind.

Next, consider the following scenario: today, you shouted at someone, seemingly for no reason. By retracing your emotions, you realise that your outburst wasn't because you're rude. The real trigger is your partner's inconsistent behaviour (or your boss's), which is making you feel insecure. With introspection, you recognise that you're still holding onto feelings of inadequacy from your past. It's this simmering emotional energy that keeps you on edge and easily triggered.

However, it doesn't have to be that way. Owning your emotions and learning to regulate them internally can break the cycle. It's time to turn inwards and be present to yourself, rather than succumbing to your endless, bullshit reactivity.

Here are some additional examples illustrating what emotional triggers look like in action:

- If you can't sleep at night because you're winding yourself up, thinking your partner is going to leave you (when they're actually happy with you).
- If you find yourself shutting down during arguments with people because their emotional meltdowns overwhelm you.

- If your friend doesn't reply to your email and you panic, convinced that you must have upset them.
- If you explode in anger at a taxi driver for taking a wrong turn when you're actually upset because your boss gave you a bad work review, or your mother criticised you.
- If your partner innocently asks about the person you're texting and you feel interrogated, leading to a shouting match. Or,
- If you've been hurt and let down by lovers in the past, you might find yourself constantly on alert, searching for red flags and reasons to justify ending your relationships. This heightened vigilance often originates from the fear of finding yourself back in a painful situation, similar to what you've experienced before. Essentially, the (usually subconscious) reluctance to get close to others emotionally is a result of past trauma, driving you to protect yourself from further distress.

If you EVER find yourself reacting like this, take it as a sign that you have unresolved emotional pain that needs to be released. Living as a prisoner to your emotions is not what you want – the aim of this work is to start observing them, processing them, moving your attention beyond them, and focusing internally on the True Love that resides deep within "You". Let's explore this further through the lens of Kristina's story.

Client Case: Kristina's Past Became Her Jailer

Kristina, 41, sought help in releasing the heavy emotional pain that she had been carrying. Despite years of therapy, she told us that she often felt triggered and generally "heavy" in herself. Anything could trigger her sadness. Whether it was watching a children's cartoon like *Bambi,* or a comedy like *Home Alone*, any depiction of a child being separated from their parents would lead to crying.

During her sessions, Kristina started to see that her tears were not solely due to good storytelling. They tapped into a deeper wound –

her parents' separation and the emotional abandonment she'd experienced as a child. Any film exploring the theme of "lost love" would resonate with her unhealed pain, triggering a flood of emotions.

Similarly, emails or messages from men who'd rejected her in the past would act as potent triggers. A year after sending a closure email to a former lover, she received an unexpected response. Just the sight of it in her in-box shocked her, transporting her back to the moment of rejection, and reopening old wounds.

Kristina's treatment plan involved acknowledging the origins of her triggers. She recognised that her emotional neediness stemmed from unaddressed childhood sadness, hindering her ability to handle rejection later in life. Had she been able to face it sooner, she might have been better equipped to deal with the end of that relationship and subsequent email.

To heal, she dedicated 5 minutes each day to sit with her pain. She would ask herself, *"How am I feeling?"* followed by, *"What do I need?"* Each time, she would repeat her responses back to herself, acknowledging her emotions – she would say, *"I hear that you're feeling X,"* followed by, *"I hear that you need Y."* She would do this for at least three rounds, giving herself the focused presence that she craved.

As Kristina grew more comfortable with the process, she noticed a shift. She became less reactive and more observant of her inner space. She embraced self-enquiry and made it a habit to turn inwards to experience her own True Self-Love. This enabled her to come to the realisation that True Love can NEVER be lost, no matter what the external circumstances are.

Embracing these changes, Kristina made a conscious decision to stop labelling herself as "broken". She also resolved to no longer chase unavailable "bad boys". She was done seeking validation from inappropriate men. Consequently, her relationship with herself and others improved, and she stood stronger and more authentic than she'd been before.

We all have emotional triggers – it's how we deal with them that matters. If we use them to see our bullshit in action, and take appropriate steps to let the triggers go, they can be an effective tool for spiritual evolution.

Kristina's journey highlights the transformative force of understanding and addressing our habitual triggers. They aren't obstacles; they're signposts guiding us towards profound healing and self-discovery. In the following story, we'll explore how Noah confronted and transformed his triggers, offering an important insight into claiming empowerment.

Noah's Story: My Unresolved Anger Has Hurt Others

I've always been a puzzle, a tapestry of complexity that the women in my life have found hard to understand. I didn't intentionally set out to be "complicated" or "difficult", I just know that I was. For years, I found myself entangled in playing out my ego-driven struggles.

Through self-reflection, I have uncovered the root of my issues – low self-esteem. This might raise eyebrows given my outward appearance – tall, attractive, and with an aura of success that I spent years cultivating. But beneath the facade, I felt like a Walter Mitty character, a perpetual pretender. I played the role, dressed the part, and managed to convince myself that I was indeed that character. Yet, none of it truly reflected the real "Me", not even the ego-self that paraded around as "me".

My thirst to elevate my self-worth led me to embellish my story continually. This pattern resulted in an aura of secrecy, a curtain I drew to hide my "self" and my difficult beginnings. However, while this quest for secrecy was my way of seeking emotional safety, it's a trait that's infuriated most of the women I've known. For a long time though, I couldn't accept it.

I never considered myself a conniving person, but I did relish the idea of staying under the radar. Maybe I enjoyed the illusion of being an enigmatic international man of mystery. Whatever it was, it certainly didn't help my relationships. I could always charm women, but most of them regarded me with caution, dubbing me a bit of a "bad boy" – fun to be around but not good to settle down with. That troubled me deeply. After all, in my mind, I was just a hopeful romantic, looking for the "right" girl to do the family thing with.

Logically, I understood how my actions led to mistrust. However, their suspicion also triggered me. My ego-self despised being mistrusted and accused of things that I hadn't done (which is what used to happen to me a lot when I was a child).

I'll give you an example. One Christmas, Sam saw a naked picture of me whilst I was uploading photos to my computer. She questioned why I'd taken it, visibly triggered. I understood her perspective when she said that men only took "dick pics" to send to other women. However, I hadn't sent it to anyone. I'd taken it because I'd been aroused and had a semi-erection, a rarity since my prostate-cancer surgery. I took the photo with a sense of pride, knowing that I could still get a semi!

We managed to diffuse the tension. However, the next day, Sam confessed that she still felt triggered. What I heard felt like an accusation and, in my frustration, I impulsively (and irrationally) declared our relationship over. I was livid that she seemed to repeat the same patterns of mistrust that I'd encountered in previous relationships – failing to trust me or acknowledge the love that I had for her.

Clutching onto my self-righteous anger, I chose to remain irritated for hours. Sam had simply said that she was processing her emotions. However, due to my feeling confronted and accused, I'd erupted in anger. Of course, I soon realised how ludicrous I was being and calmed down, but I knew my exaggerated reaction had hurt us. I had to confront and manage my own patterns of behaviour that caused the mistrust in the first place, as well as my unresolved anger and sadness when it came to my "relatingshits" – Freudian issues, indeed!

Unveiling The Bullshit: Taking Ownership Of My Life

As part of my healing journey, I've learned that when I get triggered, it's important to step away and process my reactions. I've etched into my psyche that my triggers are not the fault of the person who pushed them. I constantly remind myself that no one "makes" me feel anything. Yes, someone can provoke my frustration but the emotions are entirely mine. The moment I began taking responsibility for my reactions, my relationships started to improve.

I've come to recognise that I am the author of my own story, the producer and director of the grand theatrical production that is "Noah". If I was determined to wake up, I knew I could no longer blame anyone else for what happened in my life.

Today, I rarely play out the dramas scripted by "Noah's" mind. However, if I do find myself triggered, I remind myself that these triggers serve a purpose – they're indicating that I'm still holding onto a part of my story that requires my attention in the present moment.

Ultimately, every trigger is an invitation to let go and expand. I've also grasped that I don't have to wait for these triggers to manifest in my external reality to confront them now. I have the ability to face them today, using the vast movie-edit suite of my mind.

Through the power of visualisation, I can revisit my painful narratives, unravel their emotional charge, and defuse them. I am my own editor, capable of cutting and letting go of any character or scene, liberating myself from having to relive these experiences in my 3D reality.

The reason this is possible is because the root of our triggers stems from past pain that we relive and experience in the NOW. When we're triggered, the pain is alive for us in the moment, which is the perfect time to face it and start to let it go. Let's dive into this further right now.

Wake-up Call: Defusing Triggers In The NOW

If you're feeling emotionally fragile, begin this exercise with an event that's not too distressing to recall.

Start by thinking about a situation that still triggers painful memories and feelings that you're willing to release. Close your eyes and let yourself drift back to that event. Immerse yourself in the experience and truly feel what it was like to be there.

If you're struggling to focus on a specific situation, go back to your own not-good-enough beliefs (e.g. "There must be something wrong with me", "No one wants me", or "She's never satisfied with me").

Whatever your words are, start chanting them to yourself, allowing any disturbing scenarios to resurface. As you consistently bring them to mind, you should start to feel those painful emotions welling up more intensely. Aim to reach a discomfort level of at least 5 out of 10 (you can assign a number by asking yourself how uncomfortable it feels to think about the situation. If it rates as a 3/10, continue saying the words until the discomfort rating increases. The higher it is, the more effective this exercise becomes, as it helps you to release emotional energy in the NOW).

As you become more aware of the emotional discomfort surrounding the situation, pay attention to any pain or tension you're experiencing physically. Is it in the chest or stomach? Or is it in other areas such as the kidneys, liver, neck, or lower back? Make a note of it. You're starting to recognise where you store any form of sadness, anger, or fear in the body.

Next, ask yourself how you feel about what happened, and note any thoughts or feelings that arise. Observe whether the discomfort intensifies as you recall the situation. Then, pay close attention to what do you do next:

- Do you feel yourself closing down emotionally?
- Do you have a severe physical reaction like nervous diarrhoea or clammy skin?
- Do you instinctively turn inwards and allow yourself to feel the pain you're experiencing?
- Do you allow yourself to cry or shout in anger?
- Does your automatic response involve distracting yourself to avoid discomfort? Or,
- Do you choose to think the discomfort away by justifying yourself to yourself with thoughts such as, "it's his or her loss" and "I don't need this bullshit"?

Take the time to recognise your typical patterns. If you still feel very triggered, focus on your breathing and observe what you're experiencing. Remind yourself that you're only thinking about the situation so that you can SEE it and move beyond it. Tell yourself that this is NOT the trauma of the past repeating itself. You're not doing this to shame yourself or feel bad!

The longer you've been holding onto any unresolved emotions, the more intense the pain and stress reaction is likely to be. Keep observing and tell yourself that experiencing your raw emotions in this way won't kill you, no matter how uncomfortable they are.

Continue watching and, at the same time, try your best to stand back from the bullshit story of what happened. It's important to recognise that you don't need to relive the narratives of who or what prompted the emotional pain – it's not about that. It's about feeling and releasing the physical discomfort, which is NOT the same thing as rehashing it. And yes, we know it's painful, so be kind to yourself!

The next step is to challenge yourself to stop thinking about the situation altogether (just like you did with the fridge exercise in **Chapter 1**). See what happens if you can just sit with the pain of what happened without going into the "why of it". No matter how uncomfortable it is, allow yourself to FEEL the pain fully. This one step alone will help you to cut through the discomfort in a much more empowered way (we'll discuss it more in **Chapter 4**).

Take another deep breath and keep in mind that you're going through this process to get free. Ask yourself, *"Who is this 'I' who's still so upset about this situation?"* Continue asking while paying attention to any sensations in the body. As soon as you recognise inherently that no such "I" exists, you'll begin to feel more spacious inside.

Remember, although your life story may look like "you" and feel like "you", it's not the True "You". As you distance yourself from the bullshit and allow yourself to experience the waves of sadness, anger, and fear somatically, you'll start to recognise that the True Self "You" is very distinct from the small "self".

This is your rebellion. The start of your everlasting freedom. So, push yourself to step back from the drama and celebrate every moment of your recognition.

Personally, it took me a long time to break free from parts of my own negative narrative, particularly concerning my relationships with men. However, I've always had a deep yearning to liberate myself. The following story illustrates an important step in my personal journey of awakening. See if it resonates with you.

Sam's Story: Confronting My Unhealed Wounds

A few years ago, I had a one-night "fling" with a man introduced to me by a friend (let's call him Will). At the time, I was living in Hong Kong and he was in the UK. Despite not feeling an emotional connection with him, I agreed to meet him for a drink when I was in London. My inner voice, however, was screaming, *"NOOO!"*

To my surprise, the meeting went well. Although he'd been critical on the phone, that evening he was charming. We drank wine and discussed life, including our past relationships. It was fun and I didn't want the night to end. So, when we left the bar, I took his hand and we made our way back to his flat.

We kissed. We touched. We shed clothing, but we didn't have full-blown sex. I left a few hours later, feeling empowered that I'd had a brief sexual connection with him without getting attached. I was glad we were "friends" but genuinely wanted nothing more than that.

Naively, I assumed he felt the same way. But he didn't. He sent me a text the next morning, wishing me a good flight back and telling me he didn't want to continue the conversation. He didn't want friendship. He didn't want anything. I was upset and very triggered.

"Why didn't he want to be friends with me?" I tormented my fragile ego-self, plunging into self-loathing. It felt like an overwhelming rejection and within minutes, my trauma response had kicked in. I was, once again, in the painful grip of my trigger wound – that familiar, excruciating sensation of feeling unwanted by yet another man.

However, even though I could sense my self-doubt starting to engulf me, something stopped me from spiralling too far into despair. This time, I tried to dive into the raw pain instead. Every time I thought about his text, waves of uncomfortable emotional energy moved through me. It was agonising but I stayed with it as best I could, really feeling the pain.

The flight back to Hong Kong was challenging. The tears fell and sadness enveloped me. Of course, I traced it back to when I was aged five and my father left. I was desperate to feel better, but the desire to indulge in the story hit hard. So, I wrestled with: "How could this happen to me? There must be something wrong with me."

For days, I zig-zagged between focusing on the raw discomfort in the body and falling into the pull of my old bullshit story. It was exhausting, but interestingly, I did feel stronger. This was the first time I'd been able to allow emotional pain to move through me, even finding moments to laugh at the absurdity of it all.

Intense insights followed. My reaction to Will's dismissal was not rational – it was fuelled by the unhealed trauma relating to my father's rejection. It had little to do with Will, a man I'd barely known.

I realised that I'd never truly allowed myself to feel the sadness of my father's abandonment. It had been too painful to accept that he hadn't wanted to live with me. If only I'd learned then how to process the grief, how to soothe myself with my own True Love, I might have felt strong enough to avoid Will completely.

Self-enquiry revealed my motivation for meeting him: a desperate craving for male attention – any attention from any man to avoid my loneliness. I was desperate to feel better about myself; I simply had no idea how.

Another realisation also struck: my pattern of accepting "any old shit" to avoid losing love was like repeatedly scratching an emotional scab. By putting myself in situations with unavailable men who mirrored my father's rejection, I kept the wound inflamed, never allowing it to heal. Every flirtation with a "red-flag" man was another scratch. I was starting to understand that this habit didn't reflect the True Self – it was just a reflection of my bullshit mind.

This applies to you too. Your harshest judgments about "you" are entirely constructed in YOUR mind and then projected onto others. They are NEVER fabricated in anyone else's mind. This is the truth. So, FEEL it because it might just start to set you free!

Even though my self-enquiry was awkward then, I received an insight that has stayed with me: "*No matter how traumatic my life circumstances, I don't need to define myself by them. I am NOT wounded or broken unless I believe I am. Only the mind would label me 'broken'. Consciousness would never do that. It NEVER speaks. It just vibes as the Peace and Love of the True Self. I now choose to hold myself with compassion, recognising that I always do the best that I can.*"

Address Your Patterns Or Face The Fallout

If you're committed to waking up but still struggle with the impact of trauma, we suggest incorporating the following steps into your daily routine. The more you apply them, the better equipped you'll be to support yourself when the next emotional reaction surfaces.

1. **Embrace your vulnerability.** We often hear people say, *"I thought I'd worked through that and let it go."* You may have indeed let layers go, but sometimes, there are threads lurking in the shadows. This is OK. The journey towards experiencing true In-Lightenment isn't always smooth, and facing wobbles along the way is part of the process. Trust it, knowing that whatever arises, you have the ability to embrace it and let it go. With growing Awareness, you'll recognise inherently that the True "You" is way vaster than the small "you", building your confidence in the "Self".
2. **Adore your flaws.** Waking up isn't about perfection; it's about embracing imperfections with heightened Awareness. Acknowledge and accept your so-called flaws by repeating: *"I love my anger, I love my frustration, I love my feelings, I love my xxx (add your own words). I acknowledge and accept them, and STILL, I choose not to engage with my bullshit narratives about them. I am Peace and I am free."*
3. **Self-enquiry, breathwork and Reiki.** Use tools such as transmutation, EFT (tapping), breathwork, Reiki, and asking *"Who Am I?",* to regulate your nervous system and recognise yourself as Peace. When you're triggered, remove yourself, splash your face with cold water, tap for a couple of minutes following a YouTube video, give yourself Reiki if you can, and/or breathe through the heart. You WILL start to feel calmer.
4. **Self-compassion.**You can't awaken without fostering compassion for the small "self". Therefore, be gentle with yourself when you get rattled and remember that every trigger offers an

opportunity to "die" another layer of mind. So, don't live in fear, turn towards it and say, "BRING IT ON!"

5. **Integration and growth.** When the shit hits the fan, and you're shaking after a heated argument, breakup, or other difficult situation, push yourself to go within. Despite the mind's resistance, recognise that your triggers and reactions ARE opportunities for growth. It might feel excruciating, but each time you're able to contain yourself when feeling overwhelmed, you deepen your connection to the True Self. Ask yourself, *"Who is this 'I' who's feeling like life is crumbling around me?"*. This can help you to recognise that your temporary reactions are not your core identity, which can bring a sense of calm and perspective. And,
6. **Seek support.** Finally, if you need it, find a therapist, counsellor, or spiritual mentor to help you to deal with trauma and triggers. Seeking help is a sign of strength and will offer additional tools and perspectives for more expansive living.

Ultimately, if we refer back to the Game of Life, the truth becomes obvious – you're NOT here to wallow in a perpetually triggered state of bullshit. Life is meant to be Bliss and that's a natural fact. If you want the suffering to end, you must take a leap and work towards transcending the bullshit you hear in the mind about "you". Otherwise, you'll keep defending your right to remain angry or sad, and remain a prisoner to your reactions.

This is the time to be brave, to stare down the triggers and let them go. But don't just blink past them. You have to face your suffering head on, unflinching, until it sighs in surrender, melting under the intensity of your gaze. There's no other way. The alternative is a life locked into reactivity, and a body tense and taut due to lingering psychological pain.

To empower yourself further, ask yourself this question once again, *"Who is this 'I' who gets so easily triggered?"* Keep asking, pushing past the doubt and mental noise, until you experience a tangible inner shift.

It's at this point that you'll FEEL the True Self, the "You" behind the triggers, waiting to embrace you.

So, keep asking the question and if the mind wavers, remind yourself of this crucial equation: "*Believing the story of 'you' = eventual tension in the body = eventual stress and sickness.*"

This equation unlocks the next chapter, where we'll delve deeper into the physical impact of clinging to the limiting story of "you". We'll unveil the connection between the body and mind, and illuminate the path to freedom through self-awareness and release.

CHAPTER 3

RELEASE YOUR BULLSHIT, GET HEALTHIER

"The important thing to remember is that clinging onto emotional pain really doesn't help you. If you're struggling, the most empowering action you can take is to face it and recognise that the True 'You' is distinct from the suffering 'you'. This will keep you emotionally, physically, and spiritually strong."

Ignoring Your Raw Emotions Is A Fool's Game

"*Smile and the whole world smiles with you, cry and you cry alone.*" How many times did you hear that, or something like it, when you were growing up? Happiness and joy were celebrated, but sadness, anger, and fear definitely weren't.

Noah and I heard the words "stop crying" a lot when we were children. Not once were we told that it was OK to cry, be angry, or feel afraid. And we were certainly never encouraged to just sit with our emotional discomfort. We're sure we're not alone in this experience. Many people don't know how to handle painful emotions because they were never taught how. As a result, society applauds pleasure but deems suffering appalling.

Consequently, most of you do everything you can to avoid feeling your uncomfortable emotions. You try to rationalise and think your way out of them. Alternatively, you resort to self-medication with food, drugs, alcohol, shopping, work, or sexual pleasure. Anything to distract the mind and escape from the story causing you pain, right?

However, you do so at your own peril. True healing begins when you can gently allow yourself to FEEL your raw emotions, rather than running away from them. Cultivating a compassionate curiosity towards your inner landscape, without judgment or resistance, is key to this approach. This doesn't mean wallowing in despair but encourages a deeper acknowledgement of your emotions. (Note: The widely recognised link between the mind and body has been studied extensively by both conventional medicine and holistic approaches. We recommend reading Caroline Myss' *Anatomy of the Spirit.*)

As you explore the infinite realms of Conscious Awareness, you'll notice that there's absolutely NOTHING there. Remember, Consciousness is also referred to as the True Vast Eternal Nothing, the source from which everything in life flows. If you enquire into this state of Nothing, you won't find a pocket labelled "sickness" lurking in a corner. Instead, all you'll observe is your Awareness of the existential elements: Stillness, Silence, Peace, Love and Joy. This means that anything else (including sickness), by virtue of being NOT that, must be a function of the mind.

The crux of the matter is this: if you hold onto your bullshit story of "you", you're not only likely to be easily triggered, but also burdened with tension in the body. Consequently, the SELF you present to the world will radiate denser energy, and you're likely to have emotional, mental, physical, and relationship issues to deal with.

If this resonates with you, take a deep breath and ask yourself, *"Can I afford to spend another moment feeling tense and dwelling on the painful events of my life story, or can I start to drop it all right now?"*

Take a moment to reflect and recognise the truth: life is short and it's insanity to continue living in the pain of the past! Embracing your raw emotions is not a passive surrender, but a courageous act of self-liberation. It's a journey of unravelling the layers of conditioning that have kept you disconnected from the True "Self".

Therefore, even considering the above question just once will plant the seeds of change. Initially, it might feel impossible for the ego-self to let go, especially if you've been through any kind of trauma, but remind yourself often that you definitely CAN if you have the will to face the pain and work through it!

Untangling the link between his emotions and the effect they had on his well-being and body was a gradual process for Noah. We're going to discuss his health story in more detail now.

Noah's Story: Battling Rage And Cancer – Twice!

Prostate cancer – when that diagnosis hit me, it was another glaring wake-up call. A neon sign from the Universe, screaming at me to let go of the lingering anger that had been festering within me, gnawing away at my insides.

Five years after battling life-threatening bowel cancer, I thought I'd dealt with most of my emotional turmoil. Yet, I found myself still buying into the same familiar web of bullshit. It was perhaps no coincidence that I developed prostate cancer as well.

I'd become a "festerer", steeped in bitterness over the wreckage of my third marriage. I'd mutter to myself, "I know I need to move on," followed by, "How could this happen to ME?" This internal dialogue was akin to striking a match to dynamite, igniting a tirade of grievances that I believed had been dealt to me. Clearly, I was still addicted to my self-destructive thoughts and emotions, even though they were corroding me from within.

Through self-reflection, it dawned on me that I was still furious at the way my life had turned out. Finding any sort of internal softness and extending kindness to my ego-self, the one I call "Noah", seemed like an impossible climb. However, I knew that if I was to heal myself of cancer once more, this was the path I had to tread. It was my responsibility to KNOW that I was actually enough – no one else could know it for me.

Digging deeper within, I realised that clutching onto resentment was like sipping poison, all the while waiting for the perceived wrongdoer to keel over. In truth, the only person being poisoned was ME. It had to stop. There was simply no way I could justify my right to nurse my grudges any longer.

I'd read enough about the metaphysics of disease to understand that cancer thrives on harboured resentment. I knew the principles of chakras (the body's energy centres) and that bowel cancer and prostate cancer mirrored the helplessness and insecurity I'd felt as a man navigating life's ups and downs. (Note: Louise Hay, in her book *You Can Heal Your Life*, says that cancer results from resentment "eating away" at the body.)

There was no way around it – if I wanted to triumph over prostate cancer, I had to summon up the courage to exorcise more of my toxic emotional bullshit. I'd already let go of many vices like drugs, alcohol, and meaningless sex. Now, it was time to let go of my addiction to negative thinking and harsh ways of being.

Initially, it wasn't easy. I'd spent a lifetime cultivating a sarcastic and cynical worldview – perhaps fuelled while growing up on the harsh streets of Glasgow! Nevertheless, I was determined to transform myself into a gentler soul. To facilitate my metamorphosis, I dedicated hours to self-reflection and immersed myself in dynamic meditation. Whenever the urge to snap or fret about money hit me, I'd take a deep breath and let it all flow away. I'd whisper to myself, "*Everything's working out for me, always has and always will.*"

This became my mantra. As I released resistance and allowed my emotions to move through me, the present moment rose up to greet me like a flower after the rain. With each conscious breath, I sank deeper into simply being. I sensed a release of tension in my hips and buttocks. It was as if I'd set myself free and was finally in harmony with life's rhythm. My resentment had weighed me down for so long that it's no wonder I'd suffered from physical constipation as well – I was quite literally holding onto a lot of (bull)shit!

True freedom blossoms when you find the courage to face your painful emotional responses as they emerge, while choosing to ignore the stories the mind-self weaves around them.

Sadly, many people shy away from exploring their emotional pain, fearing it will intensify. This is bullshit! It's a limiting belief fuelled by the ego-self's desire for comfort and safety.

Here's the naked truth: avoiding your raw emotions is a fool's game. By acknowledging your pain for even a moment, no matter how excruciating, the floodgates of self-realisation will start to open. This isn't a tepid dip in the shallows of self-improvement; it's a full-body baptism in the fire of your own being. You'll emerge scorched, yes, but immeasurably stronger, clearer, and closer to the unvarnished truth of who "You" really are.

Let's look at Alice's story now – it's an example of how NOT to live your life.

Client Case: Alice's Struggle With Grief

No matter what others told her, Alice, 70, held onto the belief that her first husband left because of her. The conviction that she had "ruined things" haunted her until the day she died. The pain and guilt stemming from his departure simmered inside her, and she couldn't accept, or let go of, the distress his leaving had caused her. Consequently, she grappled with profound physical, emotional, and mental anguish throughout her life.

In addition, Alice developed chronic obstructive pulmonary disease (COPD) later on, a lung condition often attributed to smoking. However, some interpretations, such as those in Traditional Chinese Medicine and Louise Hay's work, connect lung conditions to unresolved grief. For Alice, it may have mirrored the unprocessed grief over losing her first husband and the life she'd once known. (Note: It's important to recognise that medical science doesn't definitively link COPD to unresolved grief, and proper medical care remains crucial.)

The truth is that you can't release yourself from a situation while still clutching onto the emotional pain associated with it. Liberation can only be achieved by accepting it and dropping self-blame. Here's how you can do that:

1. Have compassion for yourself.
2. Accept your actions, regardless of the reasons behind them.
3. If appropriate, reach out to the affected person and make amends. However, be prepared for the possibility that they may not want to engage with you and be willing to accept their choice. And,
4. Make a conscious decision to let go of the attachment to the pain associated with the situation and move forward, knowing that you've done your best to resolve it. This is the path to True Peace and growth.

Alice's story is a stark reminder of the consequences of lifelong self-neglect. It's a wake-up call to turn inwards and recognise that the only Love "you" really need is your own!

Are You Blocking Your Body With Bullshit?

So, based on Alice's story, take a moment to reflect on whether you're like her, or are you more focussed on letting go and getting free? Here are some questions to ask yourself:

- *"Does Alice's story resonate with me?"*
- *"Do I have any medical conditions?"*
- *"Am I holding onto unresolved emotional pain from my past?"*
- *"Does my emotional pain or condition flare up in certain situations, and what are they (e.g., anxiety, or a headache, after an argument?*
- *"Do I punish myself relentlessly by dwelling on my actions or inactions?"* And,
- *"Do I recognise that each time I revisit the past, I'm reliving it in the NOW?"*

Make a note of your answers and observe any recurring thoughts and behavioural patterns. Write it all down and journal on it to get more clarity. Exploring these questions may feel psychologically challenging, especially if you're grappling with a medical condition, but persevere. Remind yourself that the reason you're considering them is to gain insight into the nature of your unique mind and to deepen your Awareness of the mind-body connection. It's NOT to provide ammunition for more self-criticism.

Sickness Reflects Your Perceptions Of The Past

Remember, your physical condition is a reflection of your mental landscape. It constantly reveals your thoughts, emotions, and vibration.

As mentioned earlier, if you've spent most of your life being a generally positive-minded person, your body is likely to feel "lighter" and more spacious within. In such cases, you would probably describe yourself as mostly free from physical pain.

On the other hand, if you tend to worry, or are more pessimistic in nature, your body will feel denser, and you may experience some form of frequent tension or ailment.

If you have a medical condition (or even just aches and pains), place your hand on your heart and take a deep breath. As you exhale, ask the body why you've created it. Give yourself time to delve into this enquiry. If you're not getting much clarity, imagine personifying the condition by drawing a mouth on it. Then ask it to tell you directly why it's there.

Prepare to be surprised by the answers, and keep going until you gain a deeper understanding of the root cause. It will reveal itself to you if you stick with it. (Note: We also recommend reading Lise Bourbeau's *Your Body's Telling You: Love Yourself: The Most Complete Book on the Metaphysical Causes of Illnesses*).

To heal, it's important to acknowledge that any physical issues you experience stem from how you perceived and responded to past events, even if they occurred recently. Why the past? Because when your attention is fixed firmly on the present, you cannot engage in emotionally distressing thinking or relive disturbing situations. Thus, any headache you experience in the NOW, for example, originated from how you felt about yourself or a situation in the past (even if that past was just a few minutes ago). Let's unpack this together.

Wake-up Call: There's "Nothing" In The NOW

Start this exercise by fixing your focus straight ahead. Keep your eyes still, resisting the temptation to let them wander. Understand that when your eyes move, you're thinking.

Next, regardless of what's happening in your life, ask yourself a simple question, "*Are there any problems in my life right now?*" Maintain your steady gaze and repeat the question until you recognise in the body that the true answer is *"NO."*

Don't let your attention move back in time to the (painful) past, or forward to the (fearful) future. Keep your attention in the middle of your eyebrows (third eye), which represents the NOW. Notice that when your attention is there, there's no automatic thinking. There's no running commentary about what you're doing or not doing. There's Nothing there at all.

Take a few moments to embody and appreciate the sensation of being the True Nothing. Then enquire within, asking yourself, *"If there's no thinking in the NOW, how can I have any problems?"* As you keep your eyes focussed on the centre of your forehead, the only answer is, *"I can't. There are no problems in the NOW. Everything is as it should be!"*

Breathe deeply and feel the truth of this answer. Practise this exercise every day. It will invigorate you, help you to release reactive patterns, and keep daily challenges in perspective.

Looking back, I can see that Noah was not the only one clinging to the pain of past hurts. I too was "guilty of that. It was a heavy cloak, weighing me down, and it manifested in ways that I barely recognised. Glandular fever was just the surface – the deeper truth was a compromised immune system, a dimmed sparkle in the eyes, and a constant hum of unease. If I'd been able to let go sooner, I might have been able to avoid getting sick!

Sam's Story: Accepting Sadness To Heal

From the moment I met Henry in the digital universe, his charm and spirituality captivated me. Every message painted a galaxy of hope in my mind, every phone call felt like a seductive moment frozen in time. We talked for hours, diving into depths I never knew existed.

It was intoxicating, a romantic chick-flick dream come alive. I knew I had to meet him. So, I boarded a plane and flew into the unknown. The initial week was a whirlwind of passion, but reality soon set in. Two weeks later, I landed back in Hong Kong, clutching not only heartbreak but also a souvenir: glandular fever, a bittersweet memento of a "love" that burned bright and died fast.

Back home, the weight of loneliness hit me. There was no escaping the raw pain. Too sick to bury myself in work, I was forced to face it fully. However, this wasn't a pain I wanted to get to know. I didn't want to "stare into its bloody eyes" or sit with it spiritually. I felt so sick, and so miserable, that all I wanted was for it to go away. But it didn't, and my resistance to it only made it worse.

It was in this state of misery that I discovered a lump in the breast, absent just six months before. I wasn't surprised. I'd spent those weeks drowning in negative emotions, fuelling that dense energy with my self-blaming thoughts and tears. Suddenly, the phrase "what you focus on grows" resonated painfully. I'd been feeding my own suffering, clinging to the bullshit story that I was unwanted and unworthy.

If only I'd recognised it sooner, I could have reminded myself that the pain stemmed from believing the narrative I was tormenting myself with, not from any inherent flaw in me. I would have also made the effort to shift the emotional energy by moving my body to clear it, expediting my emotional recovery, and possibly avoiding the progression of the lump.

Discovering the lump was a huge wake-up call. I knew from my work and training as a clinical hypnotherapist that breast issues are linked to a lack of nurturing. According to Louise Hay, they are the result of not nourishing ourselves. I had definitely not been nurturing myself. In fact, when I'd needed my connection to the "Self" the most, I'd turned away from it. All I'd wanted was for someone to "save" me from having to face myself!

To heal emotionally, I had hypnotherapy, and spent hours sitting with my spiritual teacher to shift the pain. I also resigned from my well-paid corporate job in Hong Kong.

Thankfully, I discovered the lump in time to address it. I also started to self-enquire more. Looking back, I recognise that, just as with Will, there had been several red flags with Henry that I'd ignored. Yet I don't regret meeting him, as the experience taught me invaluable lessons. First, I promised myself that I would finally stop entrusting my soft heart to "red-flag" men. And second, I vowed to never again allow my thoughts to spiral out of control to the point that they could compromise my health and well-being.

If you, like me, find yourself tangled in emotional turmoil, remember: true nurturing arises when you face your inner battles and let them go. You have to shift your attention away from the limiting narratives and bask in the vibration of the True Self. This is the path to true healing, a route that each of us must tread in our own way.

So, what could I have done differently had I been more self-aware? Understanding energy as a flowing force helped me to shift my perspective. Instead of blaming "bad" energy for the lump, I realised that there's no "good" or "bad" energy. I'd just been blocking my own internal flow with self-loathing and criticism. Emotions are simply energy in motion. Learning to live within as the True Self and observe everything without judgment became my new focus.

In doing so, I soon realised that there are no emotions, feelings, experiences, and stories within the True Vast Eternal Nothing. Moreover, everything that seems solid, including those emotions, feelings, relationships, and experiences, is fundamentally energy. This extends to encompass anything and everything within the vast multiverse.

Since then, I've learned that we can harness the energy of ANY situation to manifest – even a painful one. We can either plough the spark of energy back into manifesting emotionally disturbing outcomes, or redirect it towards pulling in what we truly desire. This is the Tantra of life – the dance of alchemy, where hardship becomes the fuel for Joy, and every wound a chance for rebirth.

Wake-up Call: How To Deal With Emotional Pain

If a client were to come to me today with a similar story to my experience with Henry, I would recommend the following treatment plan (we'll explore this further in **Chapter 9**):

1. **Be kind to yourself.** Begin by acknowledging any unresolved emotional pain that needs to be addressed. Approach yourself with the same compassion and kindness that you would offer a loved one facing a similar situation.

2. **Turn inwards and embrace Awareness.** Make a decision to face your emotional pain full on. Give yourself the transformative power of becoming aware of Awareness, allowing yourself to observe the nature of the triggers that affect you.

3. **Follow the breath.** This will anchor you in the present moment and provide stability during emotional turbulence. Focus your attention on the breath, feeling each inhale and exhale. At the same time, take in all the sensations in the body. This will quieten the mind, making it easier to navigate intense emotions.

4. **Stop thinking.** Do NOT allow yourself to engage in painful thoughts surrounding the situation, especially in moments when another wave of excruciating emotion arises. Don't avoid the physical pain but remind yourself that reliving the story of what happened makes you feel worse! Then gently redirect your focus to the present moment and the grounding techniques we mentioned earlier.

5. **Recognise the power of your thoughts and feelings**. If you cry or shout, and keep rehashing your bullshit thoughts (e.g., "What's wrong with me? or "No one loves me"), all you're doing is sending (neutral) energy to feeling bad and unloved. This keeps you feeling even more unwanted and stuck.

6. **Redirect energy towards healing.** The aim is to cry (shout or shake, etc) and channel the energy towards a more positive intention. In other words, see yourself "sending" a neutral stream of energy towards *"Feeling more peaceful"* or something like that.

7. **Challenge beliefs and patterns.** If the emotional pain resurfaces, remind yourself that you feel troubled because you're holding onto your bullshit thoughts and feelings about the situation. Talk directly to the knot of tension in the body and say, *"I feel bad because I believe what I think and feel about this situation."* Keep saying it until you sense that you've created inner distance and the unease starts to fade. And,

8. **Reflect and integrate.** Once the intense emotions have subsided, take some time for post-trigger reflection, which can provide valuable insights for continued healing.

Mastering The Art Of Releasing Bullshit

The important thing to remember is that clinging onto emotional pain really doesn't help you. If you're struggling, the most empowering action you can take is to face it and recognise that the True "You" is distinct from the suffering "you" (also reread the coping statements in **Chapter 1**). This will keep you emotionally, physically, and spiritually healthier.

Ask yourself: *"Can I recognise that the 'I' who's experiencing this suffering is not the 'I" who's observing the suffering?"*

Take a deep breath and acknowledge that the "I" who's witnessing the struggle is NOT the same "I" who's going through it. Keep asking the question until you experience more spaciousness in the body. Consider what this is telling you. As you become more curious about the nature of the mind, you'll start to see clearly that when you hold onto painful emotions, you keep yourself locked into them!

So, why do you continue to do it? Remember, it takes time for the mind to learn that it's NOT the True Self and step down. In the meantime, it keeps throwing up its habitual dialogue to keep you safe (whatever you interpret that to be). The good news is that you can speed up the recognition process by reminding the ego-self often that it's not the boss of "You". It also helps to ask yourself repeatedly, *"Who is this 'I' who feels so attached to my pain?"*

Continuously questioning the nature of this "I" is crucial as you delve into your spiritual core. With each enquiry, the insight deepens, revealing that there's no separate "I" entity. You'll inherently grasp that you can step back from the "you" that's suffering and recognise that the True Self isn't struggling; it's the silent observer. This realisation will empower you, fostering a sense of comfort as you bravely take the rebellious leap to live beyond the confines of the limited small "self".

Learning to let go is one of the most challenging yet rewarding aspects of spiritual awakening. In the next chapter, we'll dive into practical methods to release the self-limiting beliefs and emotional baggage holding you back from experiencing the True Self "You".

CHAPTER 4

LETTING GO – THE LIFE LAXATIVE YOU NEED

"Letting go is not a mental exercise – it's a somatic experience that transcends thought. While the decision to let go requires an act of will, it's the wisdom of the body that actually feels the emotions and lets them go."

Stop Clinging, Start Living

The phrase "letting go" gets thrown around so often, but when was the last time you actually felt something shift inside of you? If you're tired of settling for a life filled with bullshit, and ready to awaken to your own Love, this is your invitation to experience it.

Think of letting go as the ultimate life hack, the emotional laxative you never knew you needed. It clears out the muck of unresolved feelings, freeing up space for growth, Joy, and the kind of authentic living that sends shivers down your spine in the best way possible.

But before we dive into the nitty-gritty of actually releasing your baggage, let's first identify the sneaky ways that you cling on. Like an overstuffed cupboard, you minds and heart can become cluttered with unwanted memories and emotions.

Noah and I define "holding on" as this: *"You know you're holding on when you're constantly reliving and enduring emotions relating to a person or situation. It's a physical sensation, a tightness in the chest, a pulling and pushing that feels like an internal tug of war. Holding on keeps you anchored in the past. In fact, you're often so attached to the bullshit of what happened that creating a richer, more uplifting, story in the present feels impossible."*

Ultimately, holding on boils down to one thing: FEAR. Fear of accepting reality, of feeling the pain you think will overwhelm you if you let go, of facing what the situation might say about you. "Am I inadequate? Doomed to sad loneliness? Consumed by anger or perpetual lack?" These are the doubts that whisper at you, keeping you clinging on, even if it hurts.

We understand. Letting go is difficult. It's messy, it's raw, and it can feel like ripping open a scab only to discover a festering wound beneath. But trust us, holding on can be even harder, a slow poison that rots your heart from the inside out. If your intention is to wake up and lead a more inward-focused life, there's no way round it. You have to embrace the transformative power of letting go, even if it's just one shaky step at a time.

But how do you know when you're holding on? The following examples will give you a clue:

- **The past haunts you.** Does every thought of your ex-partner, ex-boss, or that one frenemy from school send waves of sadness, anger, or fear crashing over you? If so, you're probably holding onto unresolved emotions from your past.
- **Stuck in replay.** Can't let go of that argument with your friend from five years ago? Does each memory feel like a fresh wound? If so, you're still holding on!
- **People pushers.** If those who've upset you in the past continue to trigger emotional earthquakes in your present, even if they haven't done anything lately, there's a good chance you're carrying unresolved baggage.

- **Past abuse.** For those who've experienced any form of abuse, using that experience as a protection against the present might be a sign of clinging onto past pain. Whilst acknowledging what happened is crucial, holding onto the emotions around it can hold you back. Please consider getting support.
- **Pining for phantoms.** Do you spend your days reminiscing about someone from your past, wishing they were still around? You're likely to be holding onto that person and the fantasy they represented. And,
- **The nostalgia trap.** If past memories leave you feeling sad, angry, or fearful about your present situation, you're holding onto emotions tied to what was, instead of embracing the possibility of what IS.

To be clear, letting go doesn't mean erasing the past or pretending it didn't happen. It's about releasing the emotional charge that keeps you bound to it. It's OK to think about past events or people, but when those thoughts consistently trigger intense negative emotions in the present, it's a sign that you're trapped in their web.

If you find yourself in this situation, it's time to break free. Start by asking yourself the following: "*How would I feel if I got to the end of my life and realised that I'd failed to wake up and embrace my Bliss because I was too engrossed in justifying the bullshit story of what happened to 'me'?*"

This sobering question has a way of jolting you into realising that hanging onto the past is akin to forfeiting your present happiness.

So what is "letting go"? Noah and I define it as this: "*You know you've let go when you STOP trying to force something to happen and turn your attention inwards, accepting what is with openheartedness. It's not about suppressing emotions, but allowing them to flow through you without clinging onto them. Say you've had a fight with your partner, and they're silent and unwilling to communicate. Letting go isn't about trying to change that or justifying your position. It's about accepting their choice and releasing your own need to control the situation. As you do, a sense of spaciousness unfolds within you. The acute pain of holding on softens, replaced by Peace, and a deeper understanding of your own emotional landscape."*

Letting go is not a complicated process and you don't need to be a saint to do it. You just have to want Bliss more than you want to defend your bullshit. You can start by asking yourself the question above and one other: *"Am I willing to let go right now?"* As soon as you can say *"Yes"* to this, you'll notice that you feel a bit lighter.

If, however, a full-on release is too overwhelming, try asking yourself: *"Can I let go for just a second?"* If you can answer *"Yes"* to even that, your inner dialogue is going to start to shift, just like mine did.

Sam's Story: "Just Drop The Fear..."

The concept of "letting go" really hit me when a healer said the following to me in a session many years ago: *"Everything you want is on the other side of your fear. Just let it go and you'll meet the love of your life, and receive everything you've ever wanted."*

In that moment, both excitement and helplessness coursed through me. I sensed the truth in her words but had no idea how to release fear. Seeking advice, I asked her how to do it. Her response was simple, *"You just let it go."* And, with that, the session ended. I left the room feeling frustrated. It was as if she'd told me that I'd been given a large treasure chest of gold coins, but the box was locked and there was no key. I would have to hunt it down for myself if I wanted to get my hands on the loot.

At that point, I had no real understanding of how to let go of anything, but I was determined to unravel the mystery. My first realisation was that in order to let go, I needed to become more aware of when I was holding on. However, I really didn't know what that meant either. How was I "holding on" to my fear?

As I self-enquired, I recognised that I'd been living with a constant tightness in the body. I wasn't actively fixating on my father's murder, my traumatic childhood, my loneliness, or even the uncertainty of finding romantic love again. I wasn't reliving any specific event at all. Yet, I did often feel contracted and I didn't know how to release it.

It was through this exploration that I came to realise that letting go is not a mental exercise – it's a somatic experience that transcends thought. While the decision to let go requires an act of will, it's the wisdom of the body that actually feels the emotions and lets them go. We're going to discuss this in more detail now.

Wake-up Call: Eight Paths To Physical Release

What I learned in my attempt to open my "treasure chest" was that there's an obvious sensation when it comes to letting go. It feels like the insides of the body become wider, or more expansive, and that more inner spaciousness is created.

Over time, Noah and I have tried many techniques to release painful emotions. Here are some of the most effective. We encourage you to use them, as they'll undoubtedly support you in your mission to wake up and keep your attention inside, beyond the bullshit.

1. Squeeze A Pen To Unlock The Spaciousness Within

This is an effective way to start your process of letting go. Begin by picking up a pen and squeezing it for about 10 seconds. Grip it tightly, then on the count of three, let it fall out of your hand. Imagine you're dropping it just like US President Barack Obama did with his famous "mic-drop" at the end of his final term. Notice how, as you drop it, you begin to feel a sense of spaciousness unfolding within.

Repeat the process, squeezing the pen for another 10 seconds. Notice that as you squeeze, there's a tension or contraction within you. This physical sensation mirrors the act of "holding on" in life. Now, once again, drop the pen and notice the immediate inner release – the tension/contraction disappears as soon as you let the pen fall.

This metaphorical exercise provides a profound insight into the nature of letting go. When you're able to release and let go, the inner tension dissipates almost instantly. To train the mind to recognise that feeling, practise this exercise several times a day. As you drop the pen, say to the mind, *"This is what letting go FEELS like."* The more you repeat it, the quicker the mind will start to associate and understand how to let go automatically in life.

2. Drop Illusions By Leaving The Library Of Lies

Another technique to use to let go of painful memories, beliefs, and feelings is to imagine that each of them is represented by a book in a library. This library symbolises the mind (as mentioned in **Chapter 1**).

As soon as you notice that the ego-self has started to pick up another book in your library, drop it. Then visualise yourself stepping out of the library door and walking into space. This space IS the portal to the True Vast Eternal Nothing that you ARE. By dropping the book, you're training the ego-self to disengage from the pictures and words that appear in the mind.

Let's practise this technique now. Start by closing your eyes and recalling a situation that still feels emotionally challenging, but not one that's too disturbing to think about (aim for a discomfort rating of around 3/10).

Try to remember it in as much detail as possible. Keep reliving it until you start to experience the same emotional reaction in the present as you did when it originally happened (try to elevate the discomfort rating to around 4-5/10).

As soon as you feel that unease welling up inside, imagine yourself dropping the book (i.e., the whole situation, including all the thoughts and feelings that are prompting that reaction). Then, turn around and walk out of the room, envisioning yourself entering space, or the True Vast Eternal Nothing (we perceive it as the endless sky at night).

Repeat the process until you start to feel lighter; you'll instinctively know when you've let go of a specific storybook. Practise this on any emotional response (both painful and happy) few times a day. If you can familiarise yourself with this method and get into the habit of using it often, it will help you when the next emotional storm hits!

3. Clap To Break Free From Negative Thinking

Clapping, or startling yourself, is one of the easiest ways to stop negative thinking. When you become aware that you're being pulled into your automatic bullshit story, it's time to act.

Let's try this together. Start by revisiting a stressful situation (or the same one as above if it's still bothering you). Allow the mind to wander back to that moment and immerse yourself in the words associated with it. Perhaps you heard thoughts like, "How could she move on so fast?", "I'm not good enough", "What's wrong with me?", "How could she have left me?", "My money's running out", "I should never have married him or her", and so on.

Replay the situation and keep going until you start to experience an emotional reaction (i.e., you feel tension in the body, or a discomfort rating of about 5/10). When you feel it's there, clap your hands, and say out loud, *"STOP!"* Take a moment to observe what happens inside when you do this. The thinking pauses, right?

Now, recall the situation again, clap your hands, and add a "support" phrase. We've found the following works well: *"STOP! I'm not going there. I KNOW that everything's working out for me, always has and always will. I therefore release the need to control and embrace the expansiveness of the True Self instead."*

By repeating this phrase, you achieves two things. First, it interrupts the mind's tendency to spiral down into the drama. Second, it reminds the small "self" that it's distinct from the True Self, which is constant and much vaster.

If you choose to step beyond the bullshit stories that you believe about your life, and shift your attention inwards to focus on the True Vast Eternal Nothing that you ARE, you'll soon recognise that everything IS indeed always working out for you. This is the truth, even if it's challenging to accept at the material level.

Remember, you are way vaster than the bullshit perception that you have about "you". You are the captain of your own ship. Life naturally supports you because Conscious Awareness IS the essence of life itself. The only obstacle is when you become so identified with your bullshit stories that you can't see beyond them.

This attachment to what the mind perceives, hears, and feels is detrimental. In staying faithful to your habitually limiting story, you contract your vibration, and often miss out on the magic flow of life. This blocks your progress and stops you drawing to you that which the Universe knows is meant for you!

However, we understand why you do this. Noah and I used to do it too. It's hard to trust that life has your back, especially when nothing in your 3D world seems to be working out. Sometimes though this is just the way it has be – it's the Universe doing its thing. Remember, from the perspective of Consciousness, there's no good or bad – it is ALL just energy.

Certain pieces of the puzzle will always have to fall first so that other pieces can fall later. Annoyingly, there's no way of knowing what those pieces are; it's all part of the Universe's greater plan for your life (see **Chapter 9** for more on what this Universe is). All you can do, therefore, is remind yourself that you ARE the Universe (i.e., the True Self) and that all is well. Because it really is. On a bigger-picture level, train yourself to remember that everything IS ALWAYS working out as it's meant to – even if the mind-self says otherwise.

To cultivate a deeper connection with the Vastness of life, we encourage you to write a full (A4) page of the following power statement every day: "*I KNOW that everything's working out for me, always has and always will. What's meant for me will not pass me by. Therefore, if it passes me by, it's NOT MEANT FOR ME! I therefore release the need to control and embrace the expansiveness of the True Self instead."*

By writing and reciting this statement consistently, you'll start to repeat the words automatically when the drama of life occurs. This WILL keep you on track, leading to greater acceptance and openness in facing and dealing with challenges.

4. Talk Gibberish And Embrace White Noise

A fascinating way to confront and let go of the bullshit is to engage in gibberish, or imagine it's white noise, as soon as you catch the mind spiralling into negative thinking. This stops the mind fixating on the bullshit story that you were about to torture yourself with.

Let's put this into practice now. Recall that difficult emotional situation once again (or choose a different one if you feel you've released the previous one). Allow yourself to really get into it, and as soon as you sense your attention being pulled back into the cycle of bullshit (discomfort rating of up to 3/10), start speaking nonsensical words aloud.

Simply open your mouth and let the words flow without attaching any meaning or thought to them. As you utter these sounds for a minute or two, notice the growing lightness inside. You may even find that you've forgotten what you were originally thinking about.

Alternatively, envision yourself pressing an imaginary "white-noise" button as soon as you become aware that your attention is veering towards the negative. This action transforms those angsty thoughts and feelings into a distant hum.

Both versions of this exercise aim to cultivate neutrality towards your thoughts, both positive and disturbing. As you practise it, you'll notice that you're starting to feel more expansive. This is because the mind can't cling to drama and engage in gibberish, or focus on white noise, at the same time.

Allow a few minutes each day to try both versions of this exercise. Observe how quickly they enable you to distance your attention from unsupportive thoughts and feelings.

5. Conscious Breathwork Helps You To Expand

This was one of Noah's favourite release techniques as he began to wake up. Breathwork is a potent tool to help you to cut through the drama; you can't consciously focus on the breath and get sucked into your automatic, negative thinking simultaneously.

Let's do the *Conscious Circular Breathing Technique* now. We suggest you start with 5-10 minutes. However, if you're feeling really stuck, continue for as long as it takes to experience more inner calm.

Begin by seeing yourself being born and taking your first breath – a long, sharp intake of breath through the mouth. As you breathe in, FEEL your birth (renewal) in every cell of the body, while pushing your stomach out and to the side.

Next, connect the in-breath to what you imagine your last breath is going to be like – a long, slow release of air through the mouth. Pull your stomach in whilst exhaling the air, as if letting go of everything that you've ever held onto.

This is what the complete circle looks like (imagine you're blowing on a didgeridoo):

1. Inhale and suck the air down into your abdomen. Push your stomach and sides out.
2. Hold the breath in your lungs for a brief moment. And,
3. Release the breath from deep within, pulling in your stomach as you exhale. The out-breath will always be longer and slower than the in-breath.

The breath can teach you many things. Pay attention to the subtle pause between breaths; this IS the gateway to the True Nothing. As you focus on the pause, allow yourself to expand into the truth of what awaits you there – "Everything and Nothing".

Continue this conscious breathing practice for as long as you can, feeling the nourishing effects of oxygen flooding the body and energising your being. Oxygen is the ultimate superfood, revitalising the body and mind (but if you feel any discomfort, stop, drink some water, and wait until you're ready to carry on).

Conscious breathwork will enable you to live a more expansive existence. As you become more aware of your unique flow of breath, you'll begin to realise that it's safe to let go of the brittle protections that you've put in place to keep the mind-self happy. You'll recognise that you're strong enough to be exactly where you are right now – and that it's OK to relax and be more vulnerable and loving.

Breathing IS the meditation of life. You don't need to sit on a mat to do it. You're already doing it. You don't need to know anything about meditation to practise and benefit from breathwork. The truth is the breath has been meditating you since you were born. All you have to do is be willing to receive the rewards of doing it.

For many people, the experience is a natural "high", offering profound insights – where there was once confusion, now there's more clarity. This is because they're often going beyond the bullshit of the mind for the first time and experiencing that initial delicious Awareness of the True Self.

You may notice as you start to breathe consciously that your hands tingle, your throat is dry, and you lose recognition of the body. These are all temporary effects and tell you that you're "stretching" your inner spaciousness. This is a good thing. You may also experience waves of emotional release and palpable recognition of emotional freedom. Keep breathing and allow your experience to unfold.

So many people overlook breathwork. However, it can have a profound impact on your spiritual evolution. This is why we suggest you incorporate it into your daily life. It's a powerful way to release toxicity from the body, and it WILL speed up your spiritual growth.

6. Move The Body To Enable Emotional Discharge

One direct way to let go of whatever bullshit story is playing out in the mind is to address it via the body. Targeted physical movement can help you to release energetic blocks fast.

For example, if anger arises, remove yourself from the situation and vent your emotions by shouting or screaming into a pillow. Engage in vigorous actions, such as punching the air or stomping your feet, to get the energy flowing. Some yoga poses, such as the Roaring Lion Pose, can also help in moving stuck energy out of the body (in this case, via the throat).

Similarly, if sadness weighs heavy, give yourself permission to express the emotion by crying or shouting. Fear, meanwhile, can be released by focusing on movements that engage the stomach area, such as jumping or shaking.

No matter what uncomfortable emotions you're experiencing, moving the body to shift them directly is going to leave you feeling immediately lighter. So, let the body become the vessel for release, bypassing the mental loop, and allowing the raw emotions to flow through you and out.

To support yourself in this process, imagine a zip running through your eyebrows and mentally close it whenever you feel your attention drifting back to the story. Do NOT allow your focus to move beyond that zip (i.e., into what we call the crazy rave party that's going on day and night in the mind). Just move the body, and keep releasing while focusing on what you want to create next, not on what's holding you back.

This is a very tantric way of using emotional energy to manifest your s (we touched on this in **Chapter 3** and will discuss it further in **Chapter 8**). It's at the very core of living as your most expansive SELF.

7. Unlock The Power Of Reiki Energy Healing

Reiki, an ancient Japanese healing technique, harnesses universal life-force energy to release emotional blocks from the body ("*Rei*" signifies spirituality, mystery, or the divine, while "*ki*" represents life-force energy, vital essence, or cosmic energy).

It took Noah and I a while to realise that Reiki is an effective way to let go of psychological distress and get the energy flowing again, but we're so glad that we persevered. Since then, the Reiki energy has never failed to amaze us.

We've found that this energy is a particularly useful tool to recognise the True Self and True Self-Love. We see it as the equivalent of receiving an injection of eternal Love directly from the Universe straight into the body, bypassing the mind and its limiting narratives.

Rarely, in our experience, are people not touched or moved by it in some way. We've seen clients release tears of pain and cry tears of joy as the Reiki unlocks energy blocks and unveils the True Love within. We've also witnessed them improve their intuitive ability and consciously start to manifest more of what they desire. Overall, nearly everyone seems to improve their well-being by experiencing it.

Reiki is an accessible energy-healing practice open to anyone regardless of prior experience. Once you're attuned to it, and the more you place your hands on the body with the intention that the Reiki will flow, the more it will expand you. Alternatively, you can get a Reiki practitioner to do it for you.

Investing in Reiki, whether through training or receiving treatments, is invaluable for those committed to waking up. It complements the practice of self-enquiry beautifully, as it takes you well beyond the limitations of the bullshit mind.

8. Become More Present, Accept The Moment

One of the most effective ways of letting go is to train the ego-self to become more present to what's happening in the moment. Again, this is because you can't be simultaneously absorbed in drama and be present to what IS. They're mutually exclusive.

Let's practise cultivating presence together right now. Start by directing your attention towards the sensations in the body. Begin by identifying five sensations and then another five that are more subtle. After that, search for an additional five that are the subtlest yet. These could be as delicate as the brush of air on the face, a faint tickle in the throat, or a slight itch in the liver!

Once you've found at least 15 sensations, recall a disturbing event in your life. As you relive it and start to feel your trigger reactions kicking in (discomfort rating of 4-5/10), make yourself switch from focusing on how you're feeling emotionally to find another five sensations in the body instead.

Take your time and recognise how you feel internally as you do this. Initially, the mind might resist, but if you commit to finding sensations in the body, you'll notice that the negative inner dialogue starts to diminish. Therefore, the next time the mind is noisy and focused externally, make yourself turn inwards and find five sensations, and then another.

Check in with yourself again. Notice whether the inner dialogue is quieter, and the discomfort has lessened. As you continue observing sensations, recognise that reliving your automatic bullshit story becomes impossible at the same time. When you focus on the body, the mind calms – it must.

Next, keep part of your Awareness on the body and its sensations while shifting your attention to the environment around you. Move your head slowly, and notice the colours and shapes surrounding you without pausing on any particular object or allowing the mind to pass any judgment. Focus on the factual aspects (for example, "blue curtains or brown table") rather than adding any subjective opinion (i.e., "ugly" blue curtains).

Take a few moments to breathe naturally, then expand your Awareness to encompass everything around you. Keep your movements slow, taking it all in without fixating on anything specific. During this process, ask yourself, *"Who is observing?"* Recognise that Awareness is observing – and that it's expanding as you acknowledge it.

Now, tune into the sounds around you. Can you hear birds chirping, the rustling of leaves, a TV playing, rain falling, distant cars or trains, or the sound of drilling? Listen to all the sounds in your environment without judging any of them. See if you can recognise that as you focus on all the sounds at the same time, your Awareness expands, and the bullshit chatter continues to fade.

The more aware you become of the Awareness that you ARE, the deeper you'll recognise that "You" are everywhere. The True-Self "You" cannot be contained by a physical body; "You" are the Awareness in which the body is experienced.

Take another deep breath and recognise the truth of this. Then, just to prove it to yourself even more, try to widen your Awareness. Visualise it as an elastic band and see if you can stretch it to "touch" the walls, the sky, the earth, and beyond. Really tune in into it and "pull" your Awareness "bigger".

As you sense your internal spaciousness widening, observe who's reading these words. Ask yourself: *"Who is this 'I' who's aware that I'm reading and thinking?"*

The answer may not be immediately obvious, so keep asking the question until you recognise inherently that the correct response is *"Awareness"*. Then say to yourself: *"I'm aware that I'm the silent Awareness that observes the ego-mind reading these words. But the True Self 'Me' is not the ego-mind, it's way vaster!"*

Repeat the question and answer to yourself as many times as necessary, observing the profound and humbling effect it has on the mind and your Awareness.

Remember, letting go doesn't mean avoiding or controlling your thoughts, feelings, and emotions. It's about relinquishing attachment to them and not identifying yourself with them. It's a conscious choice to turn inwards and pay attention to the True "You", not the lies that "you" tell yourself about yourself.

Both Noah and I have used all these methods and recommend them all as you start to let go of the old bullshit story of "you". As you become more present, though, we suggest that you practise and embody the transmutation methods that follow. They are the most effective tools when it comes to releasing your limiting narratives.

Let's shift focus now to the processes Noah adopted to confront his ego-driven need to defend his position.

Noah's Story: Feel The Hurt And Move On

Throughout my exploration of self-discovery, I've experimented with many techniques to release and transform my raw emotional pain. Whilst I rarely slip into the bullshit these days, if I do, I turn inwards and practise what we refer to as the *Direct Transmutation Method* to let go (see below). However, during the initial stages of my spiritual practice, I used the following, more elaborate, transmutation technique.

The Beginners Transmutation Method

Let's take a situation where someone annoyed me. As my intention was to become less reactive, and release irritation as soon as I became aware of it, I would start by:

1. Reminding myself frequently that the responsibility to shift how I felt was MINE.

2. Telling myself that it wasn't my job to judge the person who'd annoyed me. And,
3. Recognising repeatedly that I had a choice. I could continue to relate as the fiery "me", or I could drop the story and relate as the loving "Self" that I know I AM.

If it was my partner who'd irritated me, I would remember that this was the woman I wanted to be with. This gentle prod would help me to soften my heart, particularly when I was feeling guarded and aloof. If I clung to the anger, life inside my body would be uncomfortable and not a fun place to be. It felt much lighter to shift the focus of my attention towards my own Love rather than justifying my right to remain uptight and annoyed.

I noticed that when I was angry, my body would contract, with my chest, sides, shoulders, and arms tensing up and forming a protective cocoon around my heart. To counter this, I would take a breath, exhale, and consciously open up my chest by rolling my shoulders back.

Next, I would recite the following: *"I choose to focus on my breath. With each inhale and exhale, I return to the present moment. I acknowledge the sadness, anger, and fear within, and consciously choose to release them. I'm not better than anyone else. I KNOW that I'm way vaster than my emotions! I choose to take responsibility for them and release them. Through this act of letting go, I expand into the silent True Self that I know I AM."*

By opening up my chest and reciting this mantra for about 10 minutes, I would be able to create a gap between the annoyed ego-self, masquerading as "me", and the silent Awareness that is the True "Me". Eventually, the mind's incessant chatter would stop, the tension would disperse, and I would find myself feeling more emotionally open to my partner.

In my view, this is the most effective way to begin your journey of transmutation. It helps you to understand inherently that ALL the work goes on in YOU. It has absolutely f@ck all to do with the person who triggered you, and certainly doesn't entail trying to change them. Your point of power revolves around releasing your emotional responses and not projecting them onto someone else. This is the essence of true spiritual growth.

However, as I became more adept at shifting emotional energy, I started using what Sam and I refer to as the *Direct Transmutation Method*. It's faster and doesn't involve bodily movements or reciting coping statements. Let's unravel this method together now.

The Direct Transmutation Method

This has become my go-to practice. Now, if I have an emotional reaction to someone or something, I focus immediately on the discomfort in the body.

I become very present to it, imagining myself sitting on a chair in the middle of it, or on a plane gliding through clouds of it. I remain upright and just observe. I don't allow the body to move. I remind myself that if I'm twitching or fidgeting, and not aware of it, then I'm not being present. If I notice that my leg or foot is tapping, I make myself focus on my breathing as I return to Stillness. Sometimes, just repeating the word *"Stillness"* under my breath a few times is enough to bring my attention back to the NOW.

The purpose of this observation is to embrace whatever arises in the moment without passing judgment. It's akin to the True Self impartially observing the ego-self. There must be no wanting to change the emotional unease – that would be resistance. I simply sit in complete surrender of what's unfolding, finally experiencing the psychological pain that's been too uncomfortable to feel in the past.

Throughout this process, I do NOT allow the mind to engage in the story, pictures, or beliefs that triggered the reaction. If necessary, I remind myself that I am the writer, producer, and director of my life. I hold the power to rewrite the script at any time. I also refuse to make my painful emotions mean anything – be it about the situation or the ego-self known as "me".

What I've learned is that it's important to experience my raw emotions, and NOT try to rationalise them away. Furthermore, accepting them does NOT imply any of the following:

- That you're unworthy.
- That you're unloved.
- That the situation is entirely your fault.
- That your partner or friend is about to abandon you.
- That something is fundamentally wrong with you. Or,
- That you're being dismissed or undervalued.

If any of these words resonate with you, we reiterate: acknowledging your pain and permitting it to touch your heart does NOT mean any of these things, or anything else that the mind-self tells you about "you". What it does suggest is that you're brave enough to face your suffering and, beneath it all, the colossal fear of being alone.

Embracing the pain allows its grip to weaken. With consistent practice, you'll eventually reach a point where it no longer consumes you; you'll even reject the urge to hold onto it. Additionally, you'll come to realise that the reality of any situation is often the opposite of what you initially thought or feared it would be.

As you commit to making transmutation your main mental-health exercise, you'll notice that it's your attachment to the stories that you tell yourself about your ego-self that gets you into challenging situations. And it's the act of letting go that gets you out of them.

In the following case study, we'll explore Lisa's approach to transmutation, shedding light on her journey and insights.

Client Case: Lisa Grew When She Turned Within

Lisa, 48, had felt insecure for a long time and constantly sought reassurance from people. However, she was sick of relying on others for emotional security and validation. She wanted to learn how to experience True Self-Love so that she could stop feeling so needy.

As part of her treatment plan, we showed Lisa how to turn inwards and recognise her own Love when she felt insecure. She didn't have to wait long to put the theory into practice.

Shortly after one of our sessions, Lisa experienced a breakthrough. She observed herself on the verge of plunging into the familiar spiral of feeling not good enough when her partner said he didn't like her trousers. But rather than seeking his reassurance, she made a conscious decision to pivot within and transmute her need for approval. This shift empowered her.

By not asking him, Lisa not only saw how fragile her ego-self was, but her recognition of the True Self deepened. However, to reach this point, she had to be willing to face the discomfort of not voicing her insecurity. Doing it once was extremely uncomfortable but, as Lisa discovered, the unease was soon replaced by something much softer – Peace!

Since then, Lisa has been on a mission to experience herself more as the "Self". She's aware, though, that the mind can be cunning and will do anything it can to obtain the validation it thinks she craves. This keeps her vigilant and ready to clap her hands, step back from the bullshit, and redirect her attention deep inside.

Remember, the more you focus on living as Conscious Awareness, the more you'll start to recognise that the mind is NOT the boss of "You". You'll realise that its only "true" job is to stay in the background until it's needed for something practical (rather than stirring the bullshit pot and creating emotional turmoil).

Allowing the mind to run wild will just keep you trapped in cycles of bullshit. Therefore, if you're serious about letting go of the angst, you must be determined to actually let it go. You must be willing to deny the mind the comfort of fixating on its automatic, usually negative, dialogue. This is where the real growth begins.

Pivoting Away From The Bullshit Towards Bliss

By shifting your self-perception, you can rewire your neural pathways, which are the foundation of your thoughts, emotions, and actions. As you embrace new and supportive beliefs and behaviour, you'll gradually replace negative thought patterns and destructive habits with healthier ones. This profound shift is how you transform who you're BEING.

Liberation comes when you commit to waking up and seeing your particular behavioural tendencies. As you do, you'll find yourself spending less time defending your dramas, and more time turning inwards and experiencing yourself as the Stillness, Silence, Peace, Love and Joy that you ARE (we'll discuss how to embody this further in **Chapter 7**).

You'll also find that you're no longer afraid of your pain. In fact, you'll begin to respect it; you'll know that it offers the opportunity to transmute and taste the Joy that's waiting just beneath it. And my, what Bliss that is.

However, letting go isn't always easy and you might find yourself in situations where you're feeling very emotionally disturbed. If this happens, support yourself by asking yourself once more:

- *"Who is this 'I' who's experiencing this bullshit?* And,
- *"Who is this 'I' who believes the bullshit story of 'me' is true?"*

Asking these questions might feel like prodding a sleeping giant, but with each enquiry, you pave the way towards a profound truth: this "I" dissolves into the vibrant expanse of the True Self.

This realisation isn't a sudden flash, but a gradual unveiling as your Awareness illuminates the interconnectedness of all that is. Like morning dew touched by first light, your limitations dissolve, revealing the radiant wholeness that twinkles just beneath.

There's no denying that the awakening journey is an emotional one. It demands the destruction of everything you thought you were. While this can feel really challenging, especially if you're attached to the personality known as "you", it ultimately leads to a profound expansion of Consciousness and deeper connection to the True Self.

Don't worry though, we're going to explore this awakening process in more detail in the next chapter, offering tips and guidance to navigate your revolutionary journey of self-discovery.

CHAPTER 5

AWAKENING TO THE TRUE SELF

"The desire to wake up and 'die' the ego-self is the ONE true desire that every human has, whether they realise it or not. This is not a fickle want created by the mind. It's not a desire to avoid suffering. It's the longing to face the suffering full on and let it go, knowing that it doesn't define the True Self 'You'."

Can You Wake Up In Stages?

Absolutely, *"YES"*. You can wake up gradually. You CAN experience the ego-personality "dying" bit by bit.

While some, like the spiritual teacher Eckhart Tolle, report of a spontaneous awakening, for most of us, waking up starts with a clear recognition of the True Self. It then falls away, leaving a yearning to experience it again. This usually leads to a deep personal commitment to chip away at the ego-self until the True Self shines through like a beacon in the night.

Noah and I know the ups and downs of this awakening journey. We've stumbled along the spiritual path, laughing at the mind's antics, and gradually embracing the liberating truth: we are, at our core, pure Nothing! Absolutely NOTHING. And, believe us, it's magnificent!

It hasn't been easy, though. The mind, with its sticky narratives and emotional dramas, can be a tough adversary. But through self-enquiry, open communication, and a shared commitment to living as the Stillness, Silence, Peace, Love and Joy that we KNOW we are, we've found a way to dance beyond the drama and rebel in all our luminous glory.

We can affirm, through our own experience, that these four elements of the True Self never fade away, regardless of the bullshit that may appear to overshadow them. Discovering this is part of the Joy of waking up in stages. It allows us to BE the awakening, to live it fully, to trace its unfolding, and to share it with those who are equally dedicated to experiencing it.

We have no hesitation in saying that the desire to wake up and "die" the ego-self is the ONE true desire that every human has, whether they realise it or not. This is not a fickle want created by the mind. It's not a desire to avoid suffering. It's the longing to face the suffering full on and let it go, knowing that it doesn't define the True Self "You".

We repeat, waking up is the true Game of Life. You're ultimately here to experience yourself AS Conscious Awareness and that's IT! Anything else is just the mind-self's elaborate playground. So, ditch the drama, ditch the bullshit, and dive inwards. Let your attention settle on the True Vast Eternal Nothing that is your eternal being.

That, dear reader, is the real, eternal, secret to your genuine, gradual, and delicious In-Lightenment.

Inner Peace Is Not Complicated

We know we've said that waking up isn't always obvious, but it is an exciting ride. One moment, you're stuck in the angst, and the next, you're bubbling over with Joy.

Long before our paths intertwined, Noah and I had independently trekked the trail of awakening. We'd peered into the True Self's blinding brilliance, only to find ourselves stepping back into the muck of bullshit. Despite glimpses of divinity, we continued to identify with the ego-self's drama, spinning intricate webs of self-importance and judgment. We clung to the illusion of progress, mistaking flashes of insight for lasting transformation. In reality, our world remained stubbornly unchanged, a stark reminder of the gap between intellectual "enlightenment" and authentic being.

We realised this when we got to Pune, India. We were taken aback when the Zen Master said: *"Don't ask me any questions directly, and respond only with 'Yes' and 'No' answers if I talk to you. Write down any questions and they'll be answered by the time you leave."*

She finished that session by adding: *"I'm not here to like you. I don't care how you feel and you shouldn't either."*

It was a confronting thing to hear but she was right! As we delved deeper into self-enquiry, we recognised that she was correct in dismissing our feelings. There are no feelings when you KNOW yourself as an eternal expression of Nothing.

This is what happens when you start to wake up – you truly understand that you are NOT your life story, or the labels used to define "you". The True Self "You" extends far beyond those limiting constructs.

Spiritual growth, or waking up, happens in the blink of an eye. It's a mission of devotion – to break free from the bullshit of the mind and just BE.

The process unravels in weird and wonderful ways. And it's certainly not linear. It's not something you do; rather, Consciousness does you. It claims you. The more you commit to exploring its depths, the vaster those depths become. There are no limits to experiencing yourself as this pure Awareness. You cannot control it, but you must surrender to it. You have to build a relationship with it, and you do this by paying attention within to what always IS.

So many people ask us what happens when you start to wake up. We tell them that, actually, NOTHING happens, you just experience yourself more and more as profound Stillness, Silence, Peace, Love and Joy. In other words, you become aware of the Awareness that you ARE. You become fully present to life in every moment, finally living more in the NOW.

Waking up entails the gradual elimination of the mind-self and its demands. There are fewer "I" thoughts, and the need to create separation from others softens. There is less mind chatter about "you", fewer judgments about people, and a diminished urge to defend yourself. Fear about the future fades, as does your attachment to sadness and anger associated with the past.

We understand why the Master told us not to ask questions, and you will too. As you awaken, you'll realise that there are no questions. In Consciousness, words simply don't exist. Awareness is always silent. It's only the ego-self that ever asks, *"Why?"*, seeking explanations. The awakening individual stops asking because the answer to any question is always, *"It just is!"* There's no need to pacify the mind by dissecting why something has or hasn't happened.

Moving your focus away from the bullshit and waking up is not rocket science, but it does require discipline. Sitting with a teacher helps. It will give you the signposts to follow, but it's you who must do the work. You must turn inwards and recognise the True Self.

No one can wake you up, and nobody can predict how long it will take for you to wake up fully either. Nevertheless, each time you consciously push through the bullshit and recognise yourself as the True Self, a chunk of the ego-self dies, unravelling more Joy. It's this Joy that keeps you going, propelling you forward, chipping away, confident in the KNOWING that Grace will eventually lift you out of the bullshit, and place you firmly down in eternal Bliss.

In the meantime, let's turn inwards together and expand your recognition of the inner knowing that ALWAYS resides deep within.

Wake-up Call: Snap Back to Awareness Fast

This is a powerful tool for navigating the bullshit when it occurs. It builds on the Awareness exercise from ***Chapter 4*** *(practice No.8 on becoming more present).*

Start by acknowledging your surroundings. Take a moment to observe where you are, whether you're sitting or standing, and whether there are others around you. Without judgment, simply experience yourself in your physical environment.

Next, imagine a part of you is either moving behind you or floating above you, looking down at you reading. Keep observing the scene as if it were a film, watching yourself and anyone else who's there. Notice how quickly your Awareness expands to encompass it all.

Continue watching until you inherently recognise that "You" are not confined to the body. You're everywhere – behind the body, above the body, and around the body. Notice that there's no dialogue with Awareness, only silent observation.

If you're unsure, focus again on the sensation of Awareness moving behind you. Ask yourself: *"Does this Awareness ever talk or think?"* The answer is a resounding *"NO."* Keep asking until you feel this truth resonating within you. Observe how Awareness expands as you acknowledge it. This expansion is Awareness in action.

Continue doing this exercise until you're clear on what it feels like to snap back to Awareness. It's an important one to master because it will help you to step out of the bullshit when you slip into it. As soon as you become aware of Awareness, you'll expand straight back into the Bliss of being "You".

This is what Violet learned to do, and we're going to discuss her story in more detail now.

Client Case: Violet Moves Beyond Overwhelm

There are no wrong decisions in life, only experiences woven into the tapestry of becoming. This liberating truth was the start for Violet, 39, whose constant overwhelm stemmed from obsessing over what other people thought about her. Second-guessing became her default, leaving her unfulfilled and stuck in a hamster wheel of anxiety.

As part of her treatment plan, Violet recognised the need to drop the incessant mind chatter. To help herself, she began to shift her focus within, adopting a powerful mantra: *"I AM NOT my worrying thoughts. I am Stillness, Silence, Peace, Love and Joy. I KNOW that everything's working out for me, always has and always will. I therefore release the need to control and embrace the expansiveness of the True Self instead."* She also used her imaginary "white noise" button (see **Chapter 4)** to distance herself from the bullshit.

To gain a deeper understanding of her mind and emotions, Violet began to question their origins. Through first-hand experience, she acknowledged that intuition manifested through subtle, neutral sensations in the body, like a flutter in the heart or tingling in the legs. In contrast, more intense feelings such as jealousy were narratives crafted by the mind – an interpretation of her raw emotions filtered through the lens of her experiences and beliefs.

At first, this challenged Violet, causing some unease. However, she persevered, cultivating a deeper Awareness of her underlying feelings. Reminding herself of the distinction between the True Self, vast and open, and the ego-self clinging to familiar bullshit narratives, she started to practise discerning her intuition from her mental noise.

Two questions echoed in her mind:

1. *"Who is this 'I' who believes that my thoughts are true?"* And
2. *"Who is this 'I' who assumes that my gut feelings must be correct?"*

Repeating these fuelled her self-observation, exposing her reliance on her feelings, a trait mirrored by many. She soon realised that even her "gut" instincts weren't always reliable. In fact, they sometimes caused a lot of unnecessary drama. This inspired a new approach: facing and transmuting uncomfortable feelings, and choosing to shift internally to Peace instead.

As Violet trained herself to disengage from the bullshit, she embraced Consciousness. No longer driven by conditioned patterns and limiting beliefs, she glowed with newfound clarity and authenticity. Her relationships blossomed, nurtured by her genuine and empowered presence. In Violet's journey, we see the transformative power of recognising Awareness, not as a distant goal, but as the ever-present groundedness of BEING.

One of the most profound moments in my own awakening rebellion occurred after Noah and I had finished hosting a one-to-one retreat a few years ago.

Sam's Story: Losing The Story I Was Addicted To

Noah and I had just spent 10 days helping our client Immi, 35, start to let go of the grief she'd been carrying after losing a child.

By teaching her how to transmute her pain, and shift her attention to eternal Stillness, Silence, Peace, Love and Joy instead, she was able to step out of her suffering for a few minutes.

Immi had been convinced that she would never be able to let go of her grief. However, after just one day of facing the inner turmoil and purposefully focusing within, she acknowledged that she was feeling more peaceful.

Even traumatised people CAN detach from their psychological anguish. Yes, it IS painful, no one can deny that. However, if you can learn to let go for one minute, then you can learn to let go for good!

After Immi left, I experienced the "death" of another chunk of my own ego-personality. Noah had said something to me that triggered my sense of insecurity. However, instead of succumbing to my usual negative self-talk, I experienced a profound moment of Awareness. I stopped and heard myself say: *"I don't need to keep playing this role."* In that moment, the energetic pull to engage in my critical thoughts vanished. It was liberating because I'd been defaulting to that self-defeating mindset for most of my life.

One of the most challenging things to do is to observe your ego-self from outside of yourself, but that's exactly what you must do if you want to wake up to it. You have to know in every cell of the body that the True Self "You" is NOT who or what the mind thinks it is. It's not your bullshit thoughts or beliefs. It's not your feelings. It's not your melodramas. It's not your past. It's not your gut feelings, and it's not your aches and pains. It's way vaster than all of that bullshit.

As you experience yourself more as the True Self and the True Vast Eternal Nothing, you'll come to know inherently that you really can BE and vibe as anyone you want to be – not just the version of "you" that the mind has identified as being "you".

In my own case, I recognised that I had three options to consider in terms of my self-perception:

1. I could continue seeing myself as a "wounded" human and remain stuck.
2. I could wake up and decide to focus on FEELING the best about my ego-self. I could perceive myself as an attractive, successful, intelligent, and loved woman, etc. Or,
3. I could take it one step further and stop identifying with my mind-self altogether. To do this, I could train the mind to stay focused within and experience myself as expansive Stillness, Silence, Peace, Love and Joy.

Choosing to break free from the crippling limitations of the old "me" was a no-brainer. I longed for liberation, and mere intellectual understanding wasn't enough. My journey of transformation has been both blissful and challenging. On some days, I bask in extended periods of Peace, whilst others require me to constantly redirect the mind's focus back to Awareness. But through it all, I remain steady, knowing that each intentional step brings me closer to a life permeated by the radiant Joy of being.

When You Wake Up, You See Yourself Differently

As you delve deeper into recognising pure Awareness, you'll start to accept that this Awareness definitely doesn't think or speak. As a result, you'll come to the natural conclusion that ALL your thoughts must be "made up" by the mind.

This truth is universal. Every word, every passing feeling, is a product of the mind. They don't originate from the True Self, which exists before, during, and after the mind's ever-churning story. There's no inherent emotional meaning to any of your thoughts, only the meaning the mind assigns to them through its lens of experience.

Imagine your beliefs and thoughts as puppets dancing on a stage built within your psyche. No divine authority dictates their script; they merely reflect your interpretation of your life's grand play. This is why you think and feel the way you do – not because the mind holds some universal truth about "you", but because it's playing within the confines of your unique story.

Left unchecked, this limited perspective traps you in a cycle of "seeing life as you are" instead of experiencing it for what it truly is. But there's another path, a secret door hidden within the muddle of the mind. It unlocks the gateway to recognising that you are the True Self – infinitely vaster than the mind-self and its fabricated narratives.

Here's the magic trick: as you repeat to the ego-self that the true "You" is Stillness, Silence, Peace, Love and Joy, a transformative shift starts to happen. Your Awareness sharpens, and the ego-self begins to glimpse the space between its habitual play of bullshit and the radiant "Self" that shines out. It sees that pure Awareness resides backstage, observing the limitations, not bound by them.

This newfound understanding of your thoughts as your own creation empowers you to perform differently in your unique play of life. It boils down to two profound questions:

1. *"If I'm going to think until I experience myself permanently as the True Self, then why not train the mind to focus on the most joyful thoughts I can in the meantime?"* And,
2. *"If it was 'me' who unconsciously trained the mind to focus on the bullshit, then can't the same 'me' retrain it to focus on more vibrant, positive thoughts instead?"*

As you ponder these questions, remind yourself: *"I know that my default thinking stems from my perception of my life story. I acknowledge that it's my mind-self that labels situations as good or bad. Consciousness passes no judgment. Therefore, I can choose to reframe my perception of life in any way I desire. I can't change the past but I can alter the lens through which I view it, and release any attachment to it.*

"If I can accept this, I can also accept that I have the power to focus on any thoughts I desire. I don't have to listen to the negative ideas that automatically arise. If I KNOW this, then I KNOW I can bypass the bullshit and revel in abundance instead."

Let these words resonate within you, and feel your expansiveness and Peace blooming as you do. When you're ready, ask yourself another vital question: *"Why would I continue to suffer when I can choose to live more within and focus on the True Love that I AM?"*

As you awaken further to the incessant bullshit that you tell yourself about your ego-self, you'll realise that the only answer that holds any truth is, *"I wouldn't!"*

These powerful questions are catalysts for self-discovery, inviting you to embrace the expansive space within. Remember, the mind is not out to sabotage you; it wants to support you. Once it rationally comprehends the truth behind these questions, it will stop arguing and begin to step aside.

Waking up is a delicious journey, one that unfolds with each "mind-less" step that you take. It's a process of deconstruction, whereby you SEE the lies that you weave about yourself and others. With this realisation, you'll inherently KNOW that you can reframe life, and all its experiences, in any way you choose – seeing challenges as opportunities, setbacks as stepping stones, and ordinary moments as shimmering with magic.

When You Wake Up, You See Others Differently Too

Let's recap:

- As you recognise yourself more often as the True Vast Eternal Nothing, you'll understand that there are no fixed thoughts or beliefs about yourself or anyone else.
- There's nothing external that confirms your identity as "you". However, you can trust that you ARE always the True Self, embodying the four elements of Stillness, Silence, Peace, Love and Joy.
- The truth is that ALL your thoughts and feelings are products of the mind, shaped by your life story and your perceptions of it. And,
- Consequently, this means that your thoughts about yourself and everyone else are ALL arbitrary and fickle, created solely by the personality known as "you".

Once you grasp this, you'll realise that you have the ability to focus on positive thoughts about anyone or anything. Keep in mind that negative thoughts and feelings about others may arise, but you don't have to engage with them or believe them.

This means you can consciously decide to think positively about your noisy neighbour, neurotic spouse, irritating parent, or unfaithful partner. Remember, no one else "God" put those particular thoughts and beliefs in your head. You judge people based on your expectations and your perceptions of life. It's NEVER about the truth of who those people are. Similarly, when others judge you, it's always based on their perceptions too!

Other people can only meet you emotionally based on where they're at emotionally. If they're primarily critical, self-righteous, or intolerant to themselves, that's how they're going to treat you. They're going to allow their underlying perceptions of life to influence their reactions towards you. Likewise, your emotional encounters with people are a reflection of your emotional state. Thus, if you're predominantly angry, sad, or fearful, this is how you're going to meet other people.

However, as your Awareness expands, so do your interactions with others. As you awaken, you'll start to see that you can be as unconditionally loving as you want to be. You can opt to see every perceived flaw in others as a reason to love them more. You don't have to wait for someone to love you in order to love and accept them.

It really does take only one person to become more unconditionally loving for a relationship to shift into one that's genuinely more loving. If this feels challenging, remind yourself that the Joy derived from your relationships is down to YOU.

So, what are you waiting for? Sometimes, though, you may need a kick to understand how you're acting towards people. Let's see how Noah started to wake up to his own reflection!

Noah's Story: Seeing My Behaviour Was A Real Gift

By the time I landed in Pune to sit with the Zen Master, I knew I was ready to shake off the fog that had been clouding my understanding. Despite sticking to my spiritual practice, my ego-self was still holding the reins, creating drama, especially when it came to my relationships with women.

After the disintegration of my third marriage, I found myself indulging in the world of online singles, hunting for fleeting pleasures. It was exhilarating and I met some incredible women. However, I wasn't looking for anything serious, and even though I thought I was being honest in conveying this, I can see why some of them labelled me deceitful and selfish. It was a bitter echo of a truth I'd refused to face: my love was like a flickering flame, dimmed by the insatiable monster of my sexual desires.

It was clear that I needed to change my approach. I'd met a woman after bowel cancer, and we shared our struggles. However, I couldn't commit to her in the way that she'd wanted. Despite my desire for connection, emotional intimacy remained elusive, a recurring ghost in my relationship graveyard.

Sitting with Sam and the Zen Master a few years later marked a turning point. It triggered a profound moment of Awareness regarding the ugly truth of my behaviour. This understanding deepened when an email from the past landed in my inbox – it was from a woman I'd had a passionate relationship with two decades before. Her words stated how unheard and invalidated she'd felt during our five years together. Emotionally, she'd never felt secure with me.

In an instant, I realised how arrogant I'd been with most of the women in my life. I'd habitually regarded my partners as temporary, succumbing to the allure of any attractive woman who showed even a bit of interest in me. Regardless of how ardently I would profess my love for my partner at the time, I would allow myself to be distracted – flirting and pushing boundaries until I eventually enticed the other woman. The distraction might have been fleeting, but the damage to my relationship had already been done.

There's a famous quote by the Scottish poet Robert Burns that hit me like a thunderbolt. *"Oh the gift that God would give us to see ourselves as others see us."* That email became a brutal mirror, forcing me to confront the pain I'd caused those I care about, including Sam.

This Awareness has transformed me. Fuelled by recognising my own True Love, the thought of dishonouring myself, or any woman, has become unthinkable. All I care about is being the best version of myself that I can be, loving in the intense way that I know I can.

I used to say that I would never allow one woman to confine me. However, I've come to understand that it wasn't commitment that caged me; it was the chains of my ego and the fear of shedding the persona I'd constructed. This realisation has resulted in the demolition of the fragile bullshit foundations that I'd built my ego-self on.

As I continue to wake up, I've discovered that the grass is NOT always greener, and leopards can change their spots. But, first, I had to acknowledge that I wasn't the leopard. I had to drop my ego-fuelled beliefs that I was an insatiable sexual animal, and recognise that I was a humble human who wanted to experience genuine, authentic Love.

After so many failed chances, the message had become crystal clear – I had to recognise my bullshit behaviour, cultivate integrity, and experience myself as the True Love within. If I was truly intent on waking up, I had no other choice.

This is my story, not a finished masterpiece, but a brushstroke on the canvas of self-discovery. It's a testament to the transformative power of Awareness, the everlasting flame of True Love, and the intimate journey of becoming the man I was born to be – no more Mr Mitty for me!

The Mind Will Resist When You Start To Awaken

Remember the "untrained puppy" we mentioned earlier? Without proper training, it WILL run wild, believing it's the leader of the pack, even though it's not. So, when you first try to put it on a lead, it might dig its heels in. You can expect a few playful nips and defiant barks – it's all just part of the process.

All minds, like puppies, will resist the lead until they understand their role. It takes patience and consistency to guide them to a place of surrender, where they step back and await instruction from the true leader – "You".

The real work is in the daily practice. The key is to gently bring the mind back to the NOW as soon as it starts chasing squirrels of worry, digging up bones of regret, or barking at imagined threats. Remember, it's not about controlling the mind's antics; it's about choosing not to engage in its drama. Instead, you turn inwards, redirecting your attention to the Peace and Love at your core – in other words, the True Self that you ARE!

However, although we are all for surrendering to True Love as your guiding force, we're not saying you have to muzzle your thoughts or shove them in a cage. The mind still has a valuable role to play. It's like a sharp tool – incredibly useful when handled correctly, but dangerous if wielded impulsively. It's our analytical powerhouse, the planner, the problem-solver. Just remember, though, it shouldn't be the captain steering the ship of your life, but rather a skilled assistant waiting for your command.

Awakening is not a tug-of-war between mind and Consciousness, a battle to crown the stronger force. This internal conflict misses the point entirely. The mind is an integral part of Consciousness. Awakening, then, seeks not dominance, but unity. It's a return to wholeness, where the mind embraces its role as the loving servant, whispering insights and executing tasks, while Consciousness guides with wisdom and compassion.

Therefore, if the mind feels a bit "off the lead", like a playful puppy testing boundaries, it's simply a reminder to offer yourself gentle understanding. It's not a sign of failure, but a natural part of the journey. This is an opportunity to practise redirecting your attention away from the habitual narratives and back to the present moment, where True Love shines bright.

When the mind has a tantrum with its bullshit dialogue, remember, you have an immediate choice. You can either get entangled in the drama, or take a deep breath, and step back. Then, say to yourself slowly, *"I am Stillness, Silence, Peace, Love and joy."* With each word, FEEL the resonance. Observe the tension melting away, replaced by a sense of spaciousness. This is the gateway to your own Love, which is always present when you choose to turn towards it.

If, after connecting to this Love, a bit of noise resurfaces, ask yourself, *"Who is this 'I' who's witnessing the drama unfold?"* And *"Where is this 'I' who gets so caught up in the story?"*

As you search, notice the absence of a solid entity claiming ownership of the narrative. There is only Awareness, holding the drama without judgment. In this recognition of the small "self", the pain surrounding the bullshit will start to lose its grip. So, breathe deeply, and feel the true essence of your BEING, radiating Peace and Joy.

Wake-up Call: Quick Process To Return To Love

The next time you find yourself getting tied up in the drama, try this exercise to push yourself beyond the bullshit story of "you" and return to Bliss.

First, take a few deep breaths and acknowledge that even if life feels challenging, you're OK. Remind yourself that you KNOW you can handle it because the True Self "You" is way vaster than the bullshit story of "you" that you're buying into. This realisation alone should help you to create more inner space.

Now, take another breath and, regardless of your thoughts, clap your hands, and say aloud, *"NO! I'm NOT going there. I KNOW that everything's working out for me, always has and always will. I therefore release the need to control and embrace the expansiveness of the True Self instead."* Put the emphasis on the word "know" and recognise how empowering it is to say "KNOW" instead of "hope". Repeat this statement to yourself a few more times.

Next, picture that zip running through your eyebrows and see yourself closing it. From now on, you're going to refuse to give into the pull to engage in any thoughts about what's happening in your life. Instead, you're going to focus on transmutation and presence.

Begin by turning within and acknowledging what's present (any form of sadness, anger, or fear). Imagine the feeling or sensation growing like a balloon until it becomes so big that it bursts. Alternatively, you can see it as a vast pool of emotions that you dive into.

Facing it will be challenging, but stick with it. You may feel sadness or anger. You may cry or tremble. Whatever you experience, simply allow it and become it fully. Layer upon layer of discomfort and emotional pain may arise, but remain perfectly still, with your eyes fixed straight ahead. Even if it's uncomfortable, resist the urge to move the eyes or body.

If you still feel bad after a few minutes, remind yourself again that the reason you're feeling like this is because you're identifying with your story, and your thoughts and feelings about that story. This is what feeds the emotional discomfort. Talk to the tension or tightness directly. Say: *"I know that I'm feeling bad because I believe that what I think about X, Y, Z (fill in your own words) must be true!"*

Repeat this a few times and observe what happens internally – the discomfort should begin to dissipate. You don't need to understand why you're feeling the way you are, but you do need to recognise that your emotional pain is demanding your presence. So, talk to it and acknowledge it. Remember, you're not trying to avoid feeling the pain; instead, you're allowing it to move through you and touch you with as much grace as you can muster. This is the gift of presence that you give to yourself when you do this.

If you need more support, repeat to yourself slowly: *"I'm aware that I'm experiencing this uncomfortable sensation, but I still know that I'm NOT it. No matter how real it feels, I still recognise that I'm the True 'Me'. I KNOW that the True Self is way vaster than the small 'self' that feels upset."*

Sit with it, FEEL it, repeat it, and transmute any emotions that pop up. Remind yourself often that you're not doing this to change how you feel. You're doing this to get intimate with what IS. You'll instinctively know when you've pushed through another layer of bullshit because you'll suddenly feel the expansive Peace and Love that you ARE. They're waiting just beneath the bullshit to embrace you.

Tap Into The Overflowing Love Within

Remember, awakening isn't a privilege reserved for spiritual masters; it's the birth right we all share. But true freedom demands a trade-in: your attachment to the ego-self and its drama for the radiance of the True Self. It's a commitment to crafting a life of Joy.

Imagine your current reality, defined by its familiar echoes of sadness, anger, and fear. Now, envision a landscape bathed in the golden light of True Love, a limitless experience where you really can soar. This, dear reader, is the potential Joy at the very core of your being.

Believe us, you CAN experience this profound Joy. It is safe to shed the cocoon of limitations and transcend the fabricated story of a "you" that craves external validation. The key lies within. As you delve deeper, paying attention to the True Self more often, your awakening unfolds, revealing the most fulfilling Love of all – the Love that "You" truly embody.

However, the idea of "love" comes with many masks, not all of them divine. Some, draped in the ego-self's warped desires, resemble clinginess, offering a suffocating embrace instead of Joy. True Love, however, whispers liberation, not limitation. It doesn't shrink "you"; it ignites a supernova within.

So, how do you understand the whispers? Ask yourself, *"Who is this 'I' who IS Love?"* And *"Who is this 'I' who believes 'I' need the love of others to feel whole?"*

These questions will pierce the veil of the mind-self, urging you to step beyond its boundaries and experience the Bliss of BEING – a state that words can never truly, accurately, describe.

With each enquiry, your Awareness unfolds, revealing the truth: you ARE Love, overflowing and complete. You never need validation from another; the True Self radiates warmth and acceptance. As you dance with your own True Love, you'll discover that unconditional love with another comes naturally, a harmonious echo of the harmony within your own being.

So, keep asking the questions. Let them be your compass on this magnificent journey. For every answer offers expansion, freedom, and a path that ultimately leads you home – to yourself, to True Love, and to the boundless possibilities that await.

Now, as we turn the page, dear reader, let's explore the next chapter together, delving into the multifaceted dimensions of love.

CHAPTER 6

LOVE AND ALL ITS DISGUISES

"When it comes to love, you really do have to know your own True Love first before you can experience deep connection with another. Therefore, if you're in a relationship right now in the hope that the other person will 'complete you and make you happy', this is NOT authentic love. It's an ego-love attachment."

True Love Vs. Ego-Love. What Sets Them Apart?

Forget the fairy tales and Hollywood romcoms. True Love isn't a whirlwind romance, a laugh a minute, or a knight in shining armour. It's a luminous state of being that starts within, radiating outwards, and drawing to you authentic connections.

Contrary to popular belief, True Love isn't a gift bestowed upon you by another. It's a symphony playing within you, a silent chorus of Love and Joy that exists independent of your relationships. It's NOT a verb, or a feeling. It's the essence of the True Self, a vibrant core that shines regardless of external circumstances.

This essence of being is synonymous with Self-Love, which is the embrace of the True Self. Therefore, we use the words True Love (Love), True Self-Love, and Self-Love interchangeably to refer to it. This Love transcends the ego-self's fickle desire for approval. It's a steady flame, nurtured within you, fuelled by silent acceptance and understanding. It's an intrinsic Love that forms the bedrock of true, fulfilling relationships.

Unlike the steady beacon of Self-Love, romantic love often dances in the shadows. It can be intoxicating, a rollercoaster of emotions fuelled by attachment and desire. While captivating initially, this type of love is driven by the ego-self, seeking recognition and fearing loss. These "relatingshits", as Noah and I call them, can often leave an emotional trail of destruction, jealousy, and insecurity.

Many of you believe that your romantic relationships (and even platonic friendships) are grounded in authentic, or unconditional, love. However, this is frequently not the case. More often than not, these relationships are fuelled by ego-love (i.e., love for one's ego-persona). This so-called "love" always demands something from another, no matter how subtle. It's a love that's primarily driven by attachment and the need to satisfy emotional "needs" (or fill an aching inner emptiness).

Ego-love is a hungry ghost forever seeking external validation. It's based on the belief (or deep feeling) that you are incomplete and need others to make you feel whole. However, these relationships are a hollow echo of True Love, masquerading as affection, but ultimately leaving everyone unsatisfied.

In contrast, authentic love between two people blossoms from a foundation of individual Self-Love. It recognises the inherent wholeness of each person, and celebrates the happiness of others without seeking anything in return. This altruistic Love prioritises the well-being of another, offering support and acceptance without judgment or the need for change.

Authentic love isn't about finding your missing piece (or person); it's about sharing the abundance you already possess. It allows you to relish life with others, offering mutual respect, genuine care, and unfettered Joy. This is the Love that transcends momentary entanglements and feeds your being.

Most people long for genuine romantic love, asking us how to achieve it. The answer lies in experiencing your own Self-Love first. This intrinsic recognition of wholeness liberates you from depending on other people for happiness. The more you bathe in this radiant Self-Love, the more authentically loving you naturally become towards others.

Of course, the inevitable question then arises: *"So, if knowing my own True Self-Love can make me feel so complete, why would I want to be in a relationship with anyone else?"*

To which we reply: *"Because true connections fuel your life's journey. Prioritising filling up on Self-Love allows you to live more as the Awareness that exists beyond egoic limitations. This will enrich all your relationships, transforming them from ego-driven exchanges to meaningful expressions of Love. Remember, you cannot truly offer this love to another without first exploring and embracing your own. They really do go hand in hand."*

Their eyes widen when they hear this, a flicker of understanding ignited. In this shared space, bathed in the warm glow of acceptance, we stand poised on the precipice of a radiant landscape. Let's peel back the layers of Self-Love now, unveiling its transformative power.

Demystifying The Hype

Self-Love has become the buzzword of the moment. It's everywhere – on social media, podcasts, online courses, and more. Every client we encounter is on a mission to find it. *"It all comes down to Self-Love,"* they tell us when we ask them what the root of their problems is. We agree. Then we ask them if they've ever experienced it and what it feels like.

Their response is often a blank stare. And this is the main block when it comes to Self-Love – most people have no idea how to access it, or what it FEELS like in the body to experience it.

They think it's something they can make themselves feel. They can't. The Love we're talking about cannot be contrived. It's NOT a function of the mind and it has nothing to do with what you think. It's a profound Love that slaps you awake with startling clarity.

However, it's not always obvious, and it's no surprise that most people mistakenly place Self-Love under the same umbrella as self-care. From the standpoint of Conscious Awareness, this is incorrect. They are definitely NOT the same thing.

Self-Love Is NOT A Quick Fix

It isn't:

- A temporary Band-Aid for low self-esteem.
- A self-improvement project for your image.
- A prize for finding "the one".
- A reward for reaching a fitness goal.
- A by-product of society's validation.
- A trophy for career success.
- A fleeting high from fame. Or,
- Purely endorphin-driven euphoria.

It's also distinct from:

- Loving the ego-self known as "you".
- Liking the ego-self known as "you".
- Defending the ego-self known as "you". Or,
- Praising the ego-self known as "you".

The crux of the matter is this: True Self-Love is not about treating yourself to a manicure, pedicure, massage, or therapy. Nor is it about repeating affirmations, seeking orgasmic pleasure, going for a run, or getting an early night. These are all self-care. While they may help you to relax and focus beyond the bullshit of the mind, none of them are prerequisites for experiencing the Love of the True Self.

Hear us clearly when we say: *"True Self-Love is NOT the same as self-care. It never has been and never will be."*

In fact, your ability to experience True Self-Love has got nothing to do with how you see yourself or your material 3D world.

True Self-Love Is Experienced ONLY In The Body

The truth about your own Love is quite simple: *"True Self-Love is a delicious sensation experienced in the body, and that's IT."*

This Love dwells beyond the mind's reach (via the body), yet it's not distant or conditional. It resides deep within "You", always ready to be discovered. It's not a fleeting feeling dependent on external circumstances, or emotional states. It's a constant well of nourishment, ready to be tapped into, even in the middle of life's challenges.

To experience it, all you have to do is stop searching for it in the 3D world and recognise that it's already attainable internally. It's a physical experience that's available to you NOW.

My journey to discovering this inner sanctuary, this delicious sensation that transcends everyday struggles, wasn't straightforward. The following story shows the power of waking up to the True Self-Love that resides within all of us.

Sam's Story: Chasing Fairy Tales...

I spent years looking for love, clutching at fleeting sparks that offered warmth but never true fire. From my teenage days, it wasn't a specific prince I craved, but simply the embrace of a man's affection, any man. My father had left me longing for an emotional intimacy that he hadn't been able to offer, resulting in me feeling sensitive and needy for many years.

Like many daughters pining for a father's love, I bloomed too quickly under the harsh sun of neglect. By 13, I sported the armour of adulthood, masking my vulnerability with a string of boyfriends. Ed, the first, offered a stolen glimpse of paradise, heady moments of shared secrets and laughter punctuated by the gnawing fear of abandonment. The inevitable goodbye felt like a death knell, although we were only kids stumbling through a clumsy waltz of hormones and misunderstanding.

However, this first heartbreak seemed to set the stage for my romantic play of life. As I aged, love became a whirlwind, a desperate lunge for connection fuelled by nano-seconds of attention. Days, hours, sometimes even the ghost of a smile online – it was all it took to send me tumbling into the compulsive whirlpool of ego-driven infatuation, mistaking brief validation for the embers of genuine love.

In one case, I didn't even need to be loved back. I was seeing a man in Hong Kong who kept blowing hot and cold with me because he hadn't let go of his last relationship from years earlier. Had I been feeling fuller on my own Self-Love, I would have walked away earlier. Instead, I kept myself on an emotional rollercoaster, deluding myself into believing that I had enough love for both of us. I thought I was being spiritual, but I was just being a masochist!

After years of disappointment, I learned that I didn't have to stay with a man who wouldn't meet me emotionally just to prove to myself that I was good enough. I realised that:

- I can't force another person to be open to receiving my love if they don't want it. Attempting to persuade or convince them is a pointless task.
- I can't stop someone from cheating on me. If they choose to betray my trust, it's entirely their responsibility.
- I was so identified with my bullshit that I only ever believed I was loveable when a man told me that he loved me. Before that, in any new relationship, I would be an emotional wreck,

waiting for him to say those three little words. This is the tyranny of ego-love – an external dependence that blinded me to the fountain of True Self-Love that's always available and abundant within me.

- If I desired more meaningful relationships, I had no choice but to go within first and recognise and embrace myself repeatedly as True Self-Love. And,
- If I wanted to stop the excruciating sting of rejection, I had to prioritise filling up on that True Love rather than incessantly seeking approval from others.

Fed up with feeling shit about myself, I resolved to break free. I began delving into the arsenal of tools at my disposal, starting with self-hypnosis. Twice a day, every day, I would repeat a suggestion to myself with as much feeling as I could muster.

It went like this: *"I'm the sexiest woman on the planet. I love ME. Men love me. I'm so popular and busy. I'm happy, peaceful, successful, and with a man who loves and adores me."*

At first, repeating these words before I fell asleep at night and when I woke up in the morning helped. However, the positive effects didn't last long because, at the heart of it, I just didn't feel good enough. I was still buying into my own bullshit narratives. I had yet to truly grasp that I was the True Self – an expansive being and the embodiment of Stillness, Silence, Peace, Love and Joy. Consequently, my mind rejected the affirmations. Instead of feeling uplifted, I found myself feeling even worse.

I realised that trying to convince the mind of something it didn't believe at a core level was pointless. It was not conducive to feeling better about myself nor to finding authentic love.

It was time for a wake-up call – a resounding SLAP of Awareness. Through self-enquiry, I realised that I'd been trying to escape my loneliness by "filling up" on other people's love. I instinctively understood that I had to stop looking for love outside of myself and recognise its presence within. I had to embrace what I called "the pain of lonely existence", whilst also letting go of the sad "abandoned-woman" story that I'd been clinging onto.

To do this, I sat with my pain for hours, allowing it to really move through me. I also made myself pay attention within and experience myself as Conscious Awareness on an hourly basis. The results came quickly, and I soon felt more peaceful and at ease in myself. Finally, my preoccupation with trying to get Mr X, Y, Z to fall in love me began to fade.

Recognising myself as Conscious Awareness has allowed me to KNOW, in every fibre of my being, that True Self-Love is always available to me – it's the essence of my authentic "Self". I didn't need to tiptoe around others, or be on my best behaviour to experience it. It was the SLAP that I'd been waiting for, finally shattering the belief that I needed a man to feel good about myself. The truth was that I could feel great just by experiencing my own Love. And what a liberating moment that was!

The evolution of my True Love story has surprised me. I recognise that creating a profound connection with Noah would not have been possible had I not realised the expansiveness of the True Self. I had to turn away from the limiting ego-self known as "Sam" and experience True Self-Love first.

Today, I share this wisdom with others: *"You don't need the validation of ego-love to discover your own True Love. But recognising and nurturing your own Love is the essential foundation for experiencing authentic love with another. Without this inner sustenance, relationships can often feel like temporary exchanges rather than fulfilling connections. However, the beautiful truth is that cultivating your own Love opens you up to the possibility of genuine connection, a love that you can truly rely on."*

This is a profound truth that stops people in their tracks and pushes them to delve within. It's time to dive in and unravel the baggage behind "I love you".

What Does Saying "I Love You" Actually Mean?

We adore the feeling of being in love, but let's be clear: when your priority is to experience yourself as the True Self, hearing *"I love you"* from your partner or anyone else becomes insignificant. This is because you're more interested in knowing your own True Love than depending on someone else's attention to feel good about yourself. Revelling in the Stillness, Silence, Peace, Love and Joy that you ARE is now more important (see **Chapter 7**).

We understand though that people on the journey of awakening, including recognised gurus, often say, *"I love you."* But what does it even mean? Let's explore it within the context of any close relationship (romantic, family, friends, etc).

When you start to awaken and know your own True Love, it's not unusual to feel so blissed out, and vibe so much Love, that all you want to do is share it with others. The most obvious way to do that is by telling them that you love them.

In this case, saying *"I love you"* is about sincere adoration and gratitude for the other person. It's a liberating expression, with no hidden hooks or expectations. You say it to express the delicious expansive Love that they evoke within you. As a result, you have no burning need to hear it back from them to feel good and happy. See if you can recognise this truth the next time you say *"I love you"* to someone.

The Dysfunction Of Ego-Love Attachment

However, things start to get murky if you tend to engage in the controlling ego-love model of relating. If this resonates with you, recognise that this type of attachment doesn't feel good for long. If you want to connect on a deeper level, you have to wake up to your bullshit first, and then evolve your relating style into one that's more genuinely loving. Let's focus on two examples:

1. If you tend to feel more emotionally insecure, or "needy", you're likely to have an underlying narrative that sounds something like this (it may help to recall how you've related to people in the past): *"I long for emotional connection and only feel loved when you reciprocate my affection. I rely on your love and approval to feel good about myself. Being with you means I can 'fill up' on your love, which is great because I don't know or trust my own. Please never leave me; I need your attention to fill a void within me. I fear the emptiness and insecurity that I'd experience if you were to go."* Or,

2. If you're usually more emotionally reserved, or "avoidant", the inner narrative might sound something like this: *"For someone like me, expressing vulnerability feels overwhelming. You make me feel comfortable when you respect my boundaries, but my own discomfort holds me back from embracing the full depths of your being. Expressing and processing emotions, both my own and others', leaves me exposed and uneasy, pushing me to maintain emotional distance. Opening my heart fully is a foreign concept that I've never explored, a skill I haven't yet mastered. Distractions are my life raft, offering a false sense of security. Should we drift apart, I'll quickly find another relationship to serve as a quick-fix bandage for my unhealed wounds."*

In all cases, the underlying dynamic is one of seeking validation and fulfilment through the other person, rather than filling those needs internally. This imbalance, where True Love takes a backseat to attachment, can lead to unhealthy dependence. Both partners risk losing touch with the authentic "Self", and one may often end up holding more emotional sway due to factors like insecurity within the relationship. Ultimately, this leaves both individuals vulnerable to the pain of separation, even if it's just temporary.

However, recognising this pattern can be a powerful catalyst for growth, inviting you to cultivate self-reliance and discover your own source of Self-Love and security.

Knowing The "True Self" Leads To Deeper Relating

To feel safe in any relationship, you must first acknowledge the pain of existence that resides within "you". Once you've faced it, you must build your recognition of the True Self. You achieve this by deliberately turning your attention inwards and focusing on the Stillness, Silence, Peace, Love and Joy that you already ARE.

To deepen your Awareness of the True Self, ask yourself: *"Who or what is this Stillness, Silence, Peace, Love and Joy?"* Take a deep breath and keep asking until you experience a sensation of spaciousness in the body that feels like, *"It's ALWAYS 'Me'."*

As you observe yourself as this more frequently, you'll begin to recognise that you CAN rely on yourself. This is because you KNOW deeply that you already have a True Love that never wavers. It never betrays you. It never compares you. It never flirts with other people. It never sex-texts or online dates behind your back. It never blows hot and cold. It never stops talking to you, and it never dumps you. All it does is nourish and support you. It strengthens you and enables you to be unconditionally loving with others.

When it comes to love, you really do have to know your own True Love first before you can experience deep connection with another. Therefore, if you're in a relationship right now in the hope that the other person will "complete you and make you happy", this is NOT authentic love. It's an ego-love attachment.

If you seek an authentic love story (or to go deeper into relating with people), you must let go of expecting others to act in certain ways to make you happy. It's not their responsibility to make you feel wanted and secure, even if they want to. It's your responsibility, especially if you're on a mission to wake up spiritually. You achieve this by realising that you are way vaster than the limiting version of "you" that you believe to be true. As you embrace this notion, it becomes easier to transcend the bullshit and fill up on the Love that "You" already ARE.

However, while nurturing your own True Love forms the bedrock of fulfilling relationships (with yourself and others), it does lead to the question of how to approach attachment…

The Importance Of Healthy Attachment

In the realms of spiritual awakening, a common misconception is that the process requires detachment – that true In-Lightenment means soaring above the messiness of human relating. But what if this isn't the whole story? What if awakening doesn't mean severing your ties, but actually transforming them?

Healthy attachment isn't about clinging to rigid labels or striving for an elusive ideal. It's about weaving genuine connection, threads spun from honesty, respect, and mutual growth. The craving for strong, supportive bonds is woven into our human fabric. Nurturing these bonds, awakening or not, enriches our journey.

True Love, in its luminous essence, is the understanding that we mindfully choose the relationships we cultivate. This empowerment allows us to feel anchored in our connections, rather than trapped by obligation or fear. When resentment creeps in, whether in partnerships, families, or friendships, it often signals that we're clutching onto limiting narratives about ourselves or the relationship. These stories – "I can't be happy without them," or "This is what love is supposed to look like" – keep us buying into patterns that no longer serve our highest good.

Awakening, in its truest form, isn't about silencing emotions or denying the human need for connection. It's about embracing a profound understanding of the interconnectedness of all beings. It's about recognising that even as we move towards self-realisation, we can honour the transformative power of relationships. Healthy attachments become not obstacles, but mirrors reflecting our growth and humanity. They are sanctuaries for shared learning.

So, challenge yourself to start viewing your relationships differently. Consider these two questions:

1. *"How can I shift my perception of my relationship(s)?* And,
2. *"Can I push myself to change my internal dialogue about them right now, even if it feels awkward to do so?"*

Again, take a moment to reflect. Keep asking the questions until you inherently KNOW the truth, which is the recognition of the Vastness within. If this spaciousness were to communicate in words, it would say something like: *"Of course you can change your perception of any person at any time. It's only 'you' who's judging, comparing and/or blocking that person. If you change your inner dialogue about them, you'll change the way you feel, which WILL change how you relate to each other. Try it and see!"*

Similarly, when you feel irritated by people, recognise that it's the mind-self that experiences the discomfort, not the True Self. When you shift inwards and recognise your own Peace, you'll naturally feel more expansive and liberated. Therefore, any feelings of irritation indicate that you're temporarily buying into your own judgments and expectations of others.

To deepen this Awareness, ask yourself: *"Who is this 'I' who's irritated with X (fill in your own words)?"*

The more you ask, the quicker your focus will shift from your usual bullshit to the True Love within, melting away any trace of anger. So, trust the process and keep diving further into your own inner revolution.

Ultimately, when you prioritise your connection to the True Self, you'll radiate more True Love to others. This is the real magic that will transform your life and relationships.

How Do You Know If You Love Him Or Her?

Several clients have asked us this and we have two answers:

1. *"If you have to ask that question, you're not in love."* And,
2. *"If you haven't yet recognised yourself as True Love, you're not going to be able to recognise authentic love when it's offered to you by another."*

These responses can be surprising and we understand why. Nobody wants to admit that they haven't experienced their own True Love, or that they don't know what it feels like to love or be loved by someone else.

If you haven't yet recognised the depths of your own Love, you're likely to find yourself trapped in an ego-love cycle for most of your relationships. It's an endless push-pull dynamic where you believe that the love you feel for your partner is dependent on them, and that the love you receive from them is external to you! But the truth is that the Love you experience is always dependent on YOU! It comes from you. It is YOU!

The bottom line is this: if you want meaningful relationships, you must first taste the sweetness of True Self-Love. You have to experience it somatically to know that it's a Love that never falters. It's always there, it's ALWAYS you, and it's ALWAYS others too!

Take a moment to digest the truth of these words. FEEL them in the body. Ask yourself:

1. *"Who is this 'I' who believes that True Love is something external to me?"* And,
2. *"Who is this 'I' who thinks 'I' can ever be rejected?"*

These may seem like trick questions but their answers will lead you deeper into the Vastness of being. So, keep asking them and recognising the True "Self". You'll be so glad that you did, particularly the next time someone rejects you (even if it's just for a few minutes).

Wake-up Call: Understanding Rejection

Even without an aura-reading degree, you can feel it when someone's energy screams "closed for business". It's a palpable shift, a chill in the air, a whisper that says, *"Not today."* And when it's directed at you, the frost can be brutal.

Rejection hurts more when you're dependent on someone else's attention to feel good in yourself. If you're more attached to them than to your own True Love, rejection feels like tearing a bandage off a raw wound. It hurts deep down.

The ego-self believes it needs external validation to make the wound feel better (i.e., dim the pain of emptiness). However, the only attention you actually need is your OWN. You achieve this by acknowledging the pain of being rejected, not distracting yourself from it. This is the only balm that heals. Sit with the emptiness, feeling the sharp edges of rejection without flinching. This isn't about wallowing; it's about a radical act of self-awareness.

Do NOT torment yourself with the "what ifs" or "maybes". We know it's harsh, but who cares if "they come back to you". The truth is, it's NEVER about their return, it's about your homecoming. When it comes to the person who rejected you, try to hold your heart open to them, but with the gentle detachment of a branch swaying in the breeze. Remember, your thoughts shape your inner world, and what you think about them is down to you! So be loving, and be wise.

The golden key to breaking free from the cycle of rejection is to face it squarely, surrendering to the pain, rather than resisting it. Visualise yourself sitting on a chair in the middle of it, allowing the waves of sadness, anger, and fear to pass through you and over you. FEEL it. BECOME it. Experience it all without replaying the bullshit story of what happened.

If the discomfort becomes unbearable, speak to it directly. Tell it that you're hurting because you still believe you need the other person's attention to feel good. You believe you won't be OK without it. Acknowledge this belief, but see it for the bullshit that it is. You are Love, complete and limitless, even if you haven't yet learned to swim in its depths.

To help yourself further, observe yourself as being distanced from the drama. Notice the thoughts that swirl in the mind, and that clinging to them intensifies the pain. Let go of the narratives, zoom out of the details, and focus on the raw emotions underneath. Breathe into and expand them until they dissolve like mist in the morning sun.

Remember, beneath the layers of rejection lies a deeper truth: a real fear of being alone. Acknowledge it. Don't judge your own Love as being inferior to another's. It's not, you just don't recognise or trust it. This realisation is a big step forward in your awakening journey.

Focus on the breath and pay attention to what occurs when you can experience the physical sensation of "being hurt" without immersing yourself in the story that triggered that hurt. Something magical will unfold, and suddenly you'll find yourself on the other side – not just experiencing Love, but radiating it. Finally, you're home.

This is the process, the exploration that Cassie undertook as she turned her attention inwards. Let's delve into her story, which shows the healing power of embracing rejection as a good wake-up call to experience True Love.

Client Case: Cassie Began To Process Her Pain

Cassie, 37, was the more emotional one in her relationship. Her partner, 39, on the other hand, was more avoidant. Despite their differences, they both had a real desire to love each more authentically, even though they had some challenges to work through. If they ever argued, Cassie would often cry, release the emotions, and find her centre again. Her partner, however, struggled to cope with her outbursts, and was inclined to close down.

As part of her treatment plan, Cassie learned to recognise the early signs of an escalating argument, like her rising heartbeat and clenched fists. In those moments, she would excuse herself and find a quiet space to practise calming her nervous system. Focusing on the breath, washing her face with cold water, and swaying her body helped to dissipate the tension.

Empowered by her growing Awareness, Cassie embarked on a quest to accept her emotions, allowing them to flow freely through her. This radical acceptance was in stark contrast to her old habits of suppression and overanalysing.

She also adopted a potent mantra, repeating it with conviction: *"I am Stillness (pause)... Silence... Peace... Love... And Joy."* Saying these words pointed her to the eternal space that always exists between and beyond them. The mantra became an anchor, which she recited almost reflexively whenever tension arose around her partner.

The more Cassie dedicated herself to this emotional alchemy, the easier she found it to be silent and present to her uncomfortable emotions. She learned to catch herself in the quicksand of blame, reminding herself that her emotions were nothing to do with her partner. In shattering the belief that he was "making" her feel anything, she accepted her feelings, and freed herself from the drama she'd been weaving in the mind.

Cassie's journey is proof of the liberating power of emotional ownership. In claiming her feelings, she paved the way for more openness between them. This transformed their relationship into one built on a lot more authenticity and kindness, which was exactly what they'd both sought.

Stop Defending Your "Mindfool" Indignation

When the heart hardens towards another, it whispers a profound truth about "you": you've become entangled in a web of thoughts that you've mistaken for reality. You cling to them, defending your right to feel wronged, justified in your actions and words, even when they hurt those you love the most.

This self-righteous indignation, while seemingly protective, is a block to the freedom and connection you crave. True Love offers a different path: owning your emotions, not to fortify walls, but to transform them into a bridge of understanding. It's in this alchemy that the attachment to bullshit stories loosens, and your heart feels open to others again.

Awakening to this Love is like opening a window to a world bathed in a softer light. Even from a distance, you'll perceive others through a lens of compassion, recognising their struggles as reflections of your own. There's a sense of inner spaciousness, a release from the burden of constant defence. Your actions will become steeped in Love, not because you're striving for it, but because you recognise it as your essence. In embodying it, the Universe responds in kind, mirroring back the Love that you've cultivated within.

Noah used to struggle to drop his righteous indignation, but now he finds it much easier to soften and return to being Love. He knows that he's come a long way for a man who was once deeply identified with painful, demanding ego-love.

Noah's Story: From Ego Clashes to Inner Peace

As writer Kimberley Jones wisely said, *"Don't let people pull you into their storm. Pull them into your peace."* This philosophy has become my guiding light, replacing a life once defined by the dramas of ego-driven love and conflict.

In my younger years, I clung to the belief that arguing was the only way to protect myself and ward off scrutiny. The irony, however, is that I loathed arguments and had absolutely no clue how to handle them. When confronted, my ego-self tactic was to raise my voice, fervently hoping the other party would just go away.

Embracing peaceful conflict resolution has been transformative. I no longer shut down out of helplessness. Instead, I embrace the moment and try to see things from the other person's perspective. I view every argument as an opportunity to transmute my own reactions.

These days, I let it all just BE – the anger, the fear, the need to be right. My mission is not to engage in a battle but to go within. With Awareness, I now take a deep breath, and transform into the Stillness, Silence, Peace, Love and Joy that I KNOW I am. This centring allows me to beam True Love to others.

And it genuinely works. The art of "pulling someone into your peace" involves consciously moving beyond the storm and turning inwards to radiate AS true Peace. Gone are the days of getting caught up in the whirlwind of my bullshit thoughts, such as:

- "I'm done with this."
- "She's intentionally pushing my buttons."
- "I don't deserve to be treated like this."
- "She's weak and pathetic."
- "I can do better than her." And,
- "I've had enough and I'm going to leave."

Thoughts and beliefs like these kept me light years away from experiencing myself as the abundant, In-Lightened "Self". It took a while, but I finally understood that if I was going to think at all, I might as well choose to think the best about everyone. Even if they were acting horribly, I could still decide to love them.

I don't relish conflict, but I've come to see it as a mirror reflecting my own potential. Now, when faced with a heated situation, I pause to consider whether I might be contributing to the tension. Instead of reacting, I turn my attention within, observing my "self" and the dynamics of the situation.

This shift from defensiveness to "mindless" listening has been an invaluable part of my inner rebellion, fuelling my growth, and allowing me to live more as True Love. I've finally learned that Love is always a choice, even in the choppiest of seas!

And so, inspired by Noah's journey, let's turn inwards and explore how self-reflection can lead you to the eternal Love that defines you.

How Self-Enquiry Leads To True Self-Love

As we've said before, everyone CAN wake up, including YOU. All you need to do is realise when you're stuck in the bullshit, step back, let it go, and pivot inwards to experience yourself as an ocean of Peace, where you own Love dances on the waves of eternity.

You don't need to be a guru to do this, but you do need dedication, especially at the start when it can feel mechanical. Don't let this discourage you. Like yoga or working out, any new lifelong practice takes time to become a habit. So, trust the process because it's unlike any other. The more devoted you are to knowing the "Self", the more your Buddha Nature will reveal itself to you. To experience it, consider these steps:

1. As soon as you become aware that you're engaged in the bullshit, make the decision to give yourself a SLAP (reminder, SLAP stands for Self-Love Awakening Process). Then make yourself focus on more uplifting thoughts.
2. Remind yourself that you were born to experience yourself as True Self-Love.
3. If you find yourself wobbling, ask: *"Who is this 'I' who has any doubt that I CAN recognise myself as True Love?"* And,
4. Keep asking until you feel an inner shift that translates into: *"There's no doubt because there's no separate 'I' entity known as 'me'. I AM a true, vast, eternal expression of Love."*

No matter what you may think during times of emotional suffering, True Self-Love is ALWAYS available to you. It doesn't ever depend on external circumstances. It's the truth of who you ARE and it all begins with one fundamental question, *"Who Am I?"*.

This question forms the foundation of your daily SLAP and, in the next chapter, we're going to guide you through the entire process.

CHAPTER 7

MEETING "WHO AM I?"

"The process itself is disarmingly simple: ask yourself 'Who Am I?' relentlessly, with a fierce curiosity that burns through the stories you've been telling yourself about yourself and others. Don't overthink it, don't analyse it. Just feel it. It's a repetitive practice that points you deep inside, well beyond the narratives that you believe define 'you'."

A SLAP Reminds You That Self-Love Is There

When people ask us how to genuinely FEEL Self-Love, our response usually surprises them: *"You can feel your own Love every day, often in less than a few minutes. You can do it anywhere, and it doesn't require years of convoluted meditation to recognise it!"*

We stand by this statement. This practice is about stripping away the layers of bullshit and directly experiencing the boundless Stillness, Silence, Peace, Love and Joy that reside within.

Imagine living beyond the mental chatter and stepping into a cathedral of Silence. The Vastness of this space offers a deep sense of KNOWING that fills your being. It's the Awareness that you're aware of everything, an observer witnessing the dance of life.

This isn't magic; it's the raw power of presence. And the best part? You don't need any special training. All you need is a willingness to let go of the bullshit, shift inwards, SLAP yourself awake, and revel in the miracle of being "You" in its purest form.

Yes! It's that simple and that real. As you start, you might not realise what you're experiencing, but as soon as you've gone through the process and recognised yourself as Love and Joy, you'll want to experience it again and again. Such is the power of this practice.

Ultimately, True Self-Love manifests as a sweet sensation in the body that FEELS like an opening or spaciousness (some people report of heat in the chest and tingling sensations in the body as well). It's not a warm, fuzzy emotional reaction you get after telling yourself just how much you love yourself. It's crucial to remember this. You don't need affirmations, hypnosis, stories, or any other form of bullshit to feel it.

So, are you ready to meet the real "You"? Then, let the inner revolution continue.

Being *IshQ* And Basking In The Indescribable

As you've already glimpsed, words tumble and stumble when you try to capture the experience of being the True Self. The Joy that shimmers within (we call it *IshQ)* transcends language, yet somehow, we must attempt to bridge the gap.

Think of *IshQ* as a cosmic lullaby sung by the stars. It's the overflowing cup of True Love, brimming from every cell of your being, flooding your heart with such an expansive warmth that tears of delight slip down your cheeks. It's the laughter that bubbles up from the core of your existence, unprompted, and unbridled.

Whilst *IshQ* translates uniquely within every individual, one common thread binds us all: an undeniable shift in Awareness. Suddenly, the boundaries between you and the world dissolve. You become the observer, the experiencer, nestled within the very essence of being.

Time melts away, thoughts fall silent, and all that remains is this exquisite, indescribable *IshQ*.

Yes, this state of radiant Joy might seem like a distant mountain peak, shrouded in mist and accessible only to the select few. But remember, *IshQ* isn't some exclusive prize reserved for the spiritual elite. It's your birth right, ever-present beneath the layers of anxiety, doubt, and bullshit narratives that obscure your true nature.

As you recognise yourself as the vast Awareness cradling Stillness, Silence, Peace, Love and Joy, the veil lifts, and *IshQ* reveals itself. This isn't just Self-Love; it's the Love of your most expansive SELF, your unique frequency, your inherent superpower.

When you vibe more as this expansive SELF, and detach from the limitations of the ego-self, you'll observe that the world around you begins to reflect it back at you. You'll witness deep connections blossoming everywhere – with family, friends, and even strangers.

The highpoint in relating occurs when you can experience yourself as *IshQ* and recognise the same in another's eyes. In such moments, you'll be able to meet each other in your most expansive state of Love. There's never any separation when you relate to people like this, just profound harmony.

To illustrate, imagine two young children giggling and enjoying themselves in a bubble bath. There's no judgment. No obligations or demands. There's not even a need for words. There's just Joy in being together. This is the purest form of intimacy.

These children are completely open to each other, free from neediness, or avoidance. Both are fully savouring the moment. They share the space, the bath, and the love. One doesn't take more than the other. Both give and receive and, unknowingly, in radiating True Love and presence to the other, they receive back even more.

This is where True Self-Love meets authentic love. As you awaken and live as the True Self, you'll gravitate naturally towards individuals who love more and criticise less. People who are both open to experiencing, giving, and receiving True Love.

Be gentle with yourself though. It takes courage to wake up to the bullshit and shift inwards. But it's not a quick-fix. As Noah discovered for himself, to live your best life, you have to make turning within a life-long practice.

Noah's Story: The Guru In Me Is The Guru In You

My first encounter with even a glimpse of the True Self happened when I was in my early forties. It was a challenging period; I'd just left my wife and daughter to be with another woman. I knew from the start that I'd made a big mistake, but this didn't stop me from plunging into a decadent cocktail of sex, drugs, and rock 'n' roll. I was also struggling financially and spiralling into a mid-life crisis.

I had no idea what to do. Sensing my turmoil, my new partner introduced me to the spiritual wisdom of teachers like Osho, Ramana, and Papaji, Indian sages who became my literary therapists and newfound allies. I devoured their books and soon became more centred. After six months of reading, I'd found a way through my internal hell to a state of more acceptance.

I was so grateful to be able to step back from the incessant bullshit that had been consuming me. However, I regrettably put my spiritual practice on hold once that relationship had run its course. I remarried, had another child, and settled into a life of successful middle-class mediocrity. Little did I know that a duck-egg-sized cancerous tumour growing in my bowel would be the catalyst to reignite that wisdom within me.

Desperate to stay alive, I sought the help of therapists, Reiki healers, lightworkers, kinesiologists, and sound healers. You name it, I tried it in a bid to purge the malignant blob from my body. I learned rapidly that fear wouldn't prevent my death, but it could hold me back from living.

My quest for healing also led me to embark on an eight-week stay at an Osho meditation centre in Nepal. My intention was two-fold: to observe the nature of the unique personality called "Noah" and, more profoundly, to experience myself as I truly AM.

When I first arrived at that remote and austere environment, my initial reaction was, "What the fuck am I doing here?" It was no plush resort by any stretch of the imagination. Yet, an inner voice urged me not to leave. I knew I had to stay; this was another pivotal step in my mission to break free from the bullshit ego-personality that I'd constructed over a lifetime.

Within a week, I was celebrating being there. The Love, the Peace, the Silence, the act of surrender, the daily practices, and the heartfelt bonds forged with kindred souls all seeking the True Self enthralled me. Every evening we would celebrate life with songs, laughter, and dance. Not even the bevy of beautiful women swirling around me like ecstatic angels every evening could distract me. My interest lay not in their physical allure, but in basking in the elevated states they were accessing. It was intoxicating – and I wanted it!

Before long, I too was in ecstasy. I finally understood that turning inwards and embracing the True Self was the most empowering thing I could do this lifetime. I was committed to delving as deeply as I could into that experience of eternal Love. I dedicated hours each day to introspection and started to release my pent-up emotional pain. It was a Herculean job, but I stuck with it.

With a heart brimming with Self-Love, gratitude permeated every aspect of my existence. My two precious children, cancer, my past marriages and relationships – I held them all in a warm embrace. Tears flowed freely as I welcomed both my shortcomings and achievements as a partner, father, artist, and filmmaker, as well as for all the other challenging and wonderful events that I'd been through.

As I experienced myself more as the inherent True Self, my innate understanding deepened. I came to the realisation that there was no one and nothing to forgive. Most crucially, I began to shed the layers of anger and self-recrimination that had imprisoned me for far too long. My stay at the ashram and my communion with the spirit of Osho marked a big turning point on my journey of awakening.

From that moment, my life started to transform. I ventured into the unknown, unsure of what would happen when I left the ashram, but determined to continue my spiritual practice and deepen my recognition of the True Self. Since then, it's been an ongoing journey of self-discovery. I've learned that the guru within me may not be perfect at living an In-Lightened life, but he IS certainly perfect enough.

You see, dear reader, In-Lightenment is all about realising that, at your core, you're not just "you", the personality. The True "You" that you're searching for is not some distant, hidden treasure. Shit no! It's right there, staring back at you when you look in the mirror. It's the one peeking out through your eyes, taking it all in. It's the "You" that's been there all along, watching, like a seasoned chef keeping a close eye on a simmering sauce.

This "You" is not some rookie in the Game of Life. It's deeply tuned into the world around you, soaking up every flavour and nuance. It's not distracted by the noise and commotion; it's the calm at the centre of the bullshit. With this understanding, it's time for you to tune into the guru within "You", give yourself a SLAP, and get intimate with who "You" truly are.

"Who Am I?"

If you're ready to rip off the mask of "you" and plunge into the depths of the True Self, then this question is your lifeline: *"Who Am I?"*. It's a relentless enquiry, a fiery SLAP in the face, a searing beam of light that pierces through the fog of bullshit drama you've been conditioned to call "life".

This True Self isn't some elusive spiritual entity hiding in the clouds. It's the vast Silence that cradles your every thought, every emotion, every experience. It's the unshakable Peace beneath the storm, the unconditional Love that holds "you" in its embrace. It's *IshQ*, the sparkling Awareness that knows itself as Stillness, Silence, Peace, Love and Joy.

Here's the deal: you definitely don't need to sit with a guru, or commit to years of meditating to go through the *"Who Am I?"* self-enquiry process and recognise the Bliss of the True Self. It's already here, pulsating within your being, waiting for you to focus on it. All you have to do is turn your attention inwards consistently, beyond the haze of bullshit, and the Joy of the True Self will unfold with increasing radiance.

The process itself is simple: ask yourself *"Who Am I?"* continuously and quickly. You don't need to spend hours, or even minutes, pondering it. Just BE whatever you experience in reply. Remember, you're not asking the question to engage the mind; you're asking it to transcend the mind and delve deeper into the True Vast Eternal Nothing, via the opening sensations in the body (usually the chest).

Every human is innately wired to recognise the True Self, to feel its presence beyond the bullshit mind chatter. So, let go of the need to get it right, or to achieve some imagined state of radical awakening. Just ask the question, tune into the sensations, and allow the transformation to unfold. As you start asking *"Who Am I?"*, however, you might find the ego-self stepping in and responding with "spiritual-speak". This may include answers such as "the divine", "light", "God", "source", "truth", or "energy".

None of these are accurate. This is because these words are created by the mind and exist only in the mind. They're not existential sensations that you can experience consistently in the body. Remember, the answer is ALWAYS a sensation in the body. It's NEVER a response heard in the form of words.

The journey from bullshit to Bliss begins with that simple question, a poignant moment of pivoting your attention inwards, and an opening sensation in the chest or body. This one question is going to push you to delve beneath the surface, revealing the delicious truth of who "You" really are.

Wake-up Call: Step 1 – Cracking *"Who Am I?"*

As we embark on this practice, we want to remind you that the answer to the question "Who Am I?" is always pleasant, even for those new to this enquiry. Thus, if you experience any discomfort, whether emotional or physical, such as anxiety, pain in the chest, tightness, breathlessness, dizziness, or bodily contractions, understand that this is NOT the response you're seeking. These sensations arise from the mind's resistance to the process. We recommend taking a break and working on transmuting your emotions (see ***Chapter 4*** *on Letting Go). If the pain persists, we advise you to seek medical attention immediately.*

Begin by sitting or standing in front of a mirror or visualise yourself doing so. Gaze into your own eyes and say, *"I love you."* Allow those words to sink in, then say it again, *"I love you."* Notice how you feel as you say it.

You're likely to feel uncomfortable. This is because the ego-mind doesn't usually believe it. Remember, True Self-Love can never be experienced in the mind – it's a sensation that arises in the body. Thus, saying *"I love you"* to yourself in this manner is an ego-driven statement that usually feels empty. It's not the same as experiencing yourself as the fullness of *IshQ*.

To know yourself as the True Self, and embody True Self-Love, you never have to say, *"I love you."* In fact, you don't need words at all to recognise it. All you have to do is turn your attention inwards and experience your "Self", beyond the mind's bullshit. Let's explore this practice further now.

Once again, look into the mirror and ask, *"Who Am I?"*. Do not dwell on the question or attempt to grasp its meaning. You're simply asking the mind as a gateway to receive the answer in the form of a pleasant physical sensation.

As you enquire, observe the body, particularly the chest and stomach. Initially, the sensation may be subtle, especially if you're new to self-enquiry. However, keep going and remember that the only correct answer is a feeling of spaciousness, tingling, or heat within.

Ask again and observe. Then take a deep breath and allow yourself to relax for a moment. What did you experience? Did you feel anything in the chest or body? Make a mental note of it. Then repeat the question, this time snapping the fingers as you go. The snap serves as a signal to the mind that the body has received a response.

If noticing subtle sensations feels challenging, or if your emotions are swirling and you need a moment to step back, don't worry. Sometimes, a gentle shift in focus can pave the way for deeper Awareness. Take a few moments to practise the following *Conscious Heart Breathing Technique*. This simple breathing method can help to centre you and invite a sense of spaciousness into your being.

For 2 minutes, allow your Awareness to track the breath as it journeys through the body. Begin with the cool air entering the nose, feel it move over the crown of the head, then down the spine, tracing its arc around to the front of the body. As it rises up through the legs, visualise it entering the stomach and chest, filling you with a comforting warmth. When it reaches its peak, exhale forcefully through the mouth, imagining a gentle surge of energy clearing through the heart centre.

Ideally, you want to do this in one breath, but if that feels challenging, start with two shorter ones. Find your own rhythm and simply observe the expansion that unfolds in the body as you go.

When you feel calmer, bring your attention back to *"Who Am I?"*. Then snap the fingers again, and repeat the question until you recognise a definite sense of spaciousness. Initially, you may need to focus on heart breathing and asking the question several times, but as soon as you become aware of that opening sensation, lean into it and become the Vastness. Recognise that this IS the True Self.

Remember, the mind can't guide you to this experience, so simply notice whatever you're experiencing. As soon as you recognise that slight opening, even once, you'll know – that's the True Self. Come back to this sensation often, let it fill you up, and feel the Vastness that you truly are. This, dear reader, is your answer. Take a moment to point it out to the mind – doing so repeatedly WILL encourage it to recognise that it's NOT the boss of "You".

Wake-up Call: Step 2 – Focusing On The "Self"

As soon as you've clearly recognised the inner spaciousness once, you can start to cultivate it like a beautiful garden.

Breathe through the heart, ask *"Who Am I?"*, and snap the fingers. Then say to yourself: *"I AM the space that exists between, beyond, and around all words."* As you repeat it, zoom in on your experience and recognise yourself as the True Vast Eternal Nothing that's present in every particle of that space.

Then gently follow with: *"I'm Stillness, I'm Silence, I'm Peace, I'm Love and I'm Joy. I AM Everything and I AM Nothing. I'm aware of it all. This is IshQ."* Let these words sink in and feel the space expand within you. Read the sentence again and, as you say:

- *"I am Stillness,"* focus on the Vastness within the chest and FEEL the Stillness that permeates your whole being. Imagine the anchor-like strength of a tree's roots, holding you steady no matter what the weather.
- *"I am Silence,"* acknowledge the inner spaciousness and become aware of the Silence that holds every noise, both internal and external. It's the silent space between musical notes.
- *"I am Peace,"* recognise the sense of Nothing inside and expand your Awareness to encompass everything around you. Remember, the Peace you ARE includes everything, not just the calm moments. And,

- *"I am Love and I am Joy,"* feel the Vastness within and the three other elements. Direct your attention to the heart centre, imagine yourself breathing in and out through it, fully embodying the Love and Joy that you truly ARE.

Go through the process a few times, noticing the distinct sensation of Vastness or spaciousness in the chest or body. As you do, allow yourself to melt into the experience of "You", the true YOU beyond all limitations.

Remember, *"Who Am I?"* isn't a mental puzzle. It's a doorway to experiencing the True Self in the present moment. Attempting to find the response mentally contradicts the essence of the practice. So, if your eyes start wandering, gently bring them back to centre. This keeps you out of the mind and anchored in the NOW. (However, if you're curious about the difference between mental searching and present-moment Awareness, try asking the question while moving your eyes. You'll feel the shift from spaciousness to mind chatter. Observe it without judgment, then return to centre.)

This is the process; this is the SLAP. This is how you'll experience yourself as the True Self every day. It will no longer be a moment of *Satori*. It's who you truly ARE. It's *IshQ*.

To KNOW it, dedication is the key, even if it feels mechanical at first. There are many paths that lead to truth, but only one "You" – the boundless expansion that transcends all words. So, keep breathing, keep asking, and keep giving yourself that SLAP of Awareness.

Wake-up Call: Step 3 – Deepening The Enquiry

Remember the sweet Vastness you recognised within? Let's go deeper into it. Keep asking *"Who Am I?"* and experience yourself as that expansive sensation in the chest or body. If it's still unclear, revisit Step 1. Ask, snap the fingers, and repeat the answer until you feel that spaciousness, tingling, or heat, etc.

Once you recognise the True Self, dive into these questions (answers given after Question 3):

1. *"Can anyone give me this Vastness (or the Stillness, Silence, Peace, Love and Joy that I AM)?"* Ask with your attention turned inwards, observing any physical shifts. Keep your eyes fixed ahead, asking until you receive a clear response. It won't be in words, but a clear KNOWING sensation within. Trust your intuition, for the mind plays no part here.
2. *"Can I lose this Vastness?"* Once again, explore the True Self, acknowledging the answer that arises as you focus on your bodily sensations. And,
3. *"Do feelings or emotions like jealousy, insecurity, frustration, self-doubt, anger, sadness, or fear exist within this Vastness?"* Use your Awareness of the True Self (or the True Vast Eternal Nothing) to recognise the accurate response. Then breathe deeply and sink further into the experience of the eternal "Self".

The correct answer to all three questions is *"No"*. A *"Yes"* means the mind has crept in, diverting you from the truth. Simply return to *"Who Am I?"* and keep going through the process. This is the essence of correct self-enquiry – you persist until you recognise yourself clearly as the expansive True Self, well beyond the mind's bullshit stories and pictures.

As soon as you intuitively sense that the answer to all the questions is *"No"*, ask yourself *"Who Am I?"* again. When you recognise the opening sensation, continue with these:

4. *"Does the Vastness have a beginning and end?"* Keep asking until you recognise the correct answer – *"No"*. It's boundless and limitless. And,
5. *"Was the Vastness present before my birth and will it persist after the death of my body?"* Allow your Awareness to explore the Vastness that "You" are until you KNOW that the right response is *"Yes"*. Consciousness is eternal, and the deeper you delve,

the more you'll feel it viscerally. It never ends and never moves in the rollercoaster cycles that the mind-self is so addicted to.

These five questions and answers (Q&A) are powerful signposts on your journey within. They'll guide you to know who you truly ARE. Eventually, though, you won't need them – you'll go directly to the body and its answers. You'll find yourself dancing to a silent mantra: *"Who Am I? I am Stillness, Silence, Peace, Love and Joy. I AM IshQ."*

Repeat the Q&A now. FEEL each word and KNOW the truth of who "You" always ARE. Then, take a deep breath and contemplate Henri's journey of awakening to the True Self.

Client Case: Henri's Senses Shifted Beyond Sounds

Henri, 32, was determined to wake up fully. One day, she asked us what she would hear if there were no external sounds at all?

We said: "*You would hear the internal hum of Conscious Awareness. When external noise fades, and the mind is quiet, you'll hear the sound of life-force energy much clearer.*"

To attune herself to the True Self's subtler frequencies, we advised Henri to give up anything that contributed to her inner noise. We recommended limiting her time on social media, reducing TV consumption, listening to only select music, and even moderating her reading habits. Above all, we told her to do her best not to engage in automatic, default thinking.

Curiously, Henri asked us why. We replied: *"Because the True Self is ALWAYS silent. Although you don't need Silence in the external environment to inherently KNOW it, surrounding yourself with Silence will enhance your ability to recognise it, especially as you begin the process."*

Knowing yourself as Stillness, Silence, Peace, Love and Joy is what this transformative journey is all about. We explained to Henri that turning her attention inwards repeatedly, breathing through the heart, and focusing on these existential elements is the catalyst to experiencing herself as the True Self that she always IS.

Eager to deepen her recognition, Henri dedicated time every morning to sit in front of a mirror and repeat the self-enquiry process. It took her a few attempts to notice a clear, opening sensation in the chest, but she found it. Then she focused on conscious heart breathing and experiencing herself as pure Love and Joy. Of course, there have been moments when she's slipped into the bullshit, but she's committed to pivoting her attention away from it, and going within to know the True Self whenever she can.

As with Henri, experiencing myself repeatedly as expansive Peace and Joy is my true calling in life. The following story offers a glimpse into my first real taste of emotional freedom.

Sam's Story: Finally "Filling Up" On Self-Love

The first time I became aware that I'd filled up on my own True Love was after I'd spent a day with Noah in Rishikesh. We'd been hanging out a lot as friends, and even though I genuinely didn't want anything romantic to happen between us, I still had a perverse ego-longing for him to tell me that he "liked" me. Alas, it never happened and, despite enjoying our time together, each encounter left me feeling rejected.

On the last day, however, something interesting happened. Whilst attending a talk on spiritual philosophy (*Satsang*), instead of fixating on the lecture, or dwelling on feeling unwanted by him, I started my own self-enquiry.

I began by inhaling through the nose and exhaling through the mouth, envisioning the breath pouring out through my heart centre. This simple breathing exercise helped me to soothe my nervous system and detach from the distracting narratives I'd constructed about what he was thinking. Once I could feel the warmth radiating from the chest, I widened my focus to the surrounding sounds. Imagining myself as a giant ear, I just listened, causing my Awareness to expand. I then tuned into the teacher's voice, observing the Silence that enveloped each word. This amplified my Awareness even more.

Next, I became aware of my body sitting on a chair, and of all the other bodies in the room as well. By experiencing the room exactly as it was, without trying to analyse anything, I felt profound Peace. I recognised that I wasn't separate from any of the people there. I could feel myself becoming more aware that I was the limitless Consciousness that unified us all.

As I experienced myself as a formless, eternal being, I started to say to myself, *"I AM the space that exists between, beyond, and around all words. I'm Stillness, Silence, Peace, Love and Joy."* The more I repeated this slowly and focused on the heat emanating from my heart centre, the more I felt my Awareness expand.

Two hours later, as we walked to dinner, I noticed a feeling of "fullness" inside. No longer did I have any feelings of not being good enough. I actually didn't care what he thought about me. I just felt full on being "me". Remarkably, I also found myself unfazed by his imminent departure – there was no sadness at the thought that I might never see him again.

For the rest of the night, I kept noticing that "it" hadn't gone away. There was no emptiness inside that screamed for his attention. Nothing, and I really do mean NOTHING, mattered.

In that revelatory flash, I grasped something crucial: by directing my focus inwards to experience myself as Stillness, Silence, Peace, Love and Joy, I'd attained a state of profound presence. This marked a big milestone in my awakening journey. I'd discovered a conscious, repeatable, method to transcend the bullshit and experience myself as True Love. I finally knew what being "full" on my own Love actually felt like – and it was glorious. It's a Love that's always more blissful than the external love that another person can offer you.

As we parted ways at the end of the evening, I hugged Noah goodbye, and walked back to my guesthouse with a genuine inner smile. I felt free. I finally KNEW that I didn't need his approval. I didn't need it from anyone, not even from the ego-self known as "me".

In that moment of self-realisation, I KNEW I'd shed another layer of bullshit. With it, I heard myself ask: *"Why would I ever believe that I need the attention of a man, especially one who doesn't desire me, when my own Love is so much more fulfilling?"*

The True Self Is Unbreakable

Knowing your own sweet Love initiates a profound transformation. You become more focused on "filling up" on this own internal Joy, and less preoccupied with external, ego-driven infatuation and validation. You also start to exist more in the NOW, and less in the painful past or fearful future.

The more you live as Love, the more you have to offer others. Love becomes your daily experience. You begin to vibe as Love, live as Love, and laugh as Love. You smile more and vibe less sadness, anger, and fear (or any version thereof). You finally glow more from the inside out and your whole life really does start to transform.

However, what happens if you lose your centre and find yourself entangled in another bullshit drama? Or when an argument with a loved one upsets you? What if illness strikes and worries about the future creep in? And what about those times when you react to life's inevitable losses?

None of these experiences imply that you have lost the True Self. If you ever feel that you're losing your recognition, ask yourself this question immediately: *"Who is this 'I' who believes that I could ever lose my connection to who I truly AM?"*

As soon as you ask it, zoom in on the body. You WILL experience an opening sensation, a subtle reminder of the True Self. Repeat the question if necessary, then go through the *"Who Am I?"* process. This will help you to relax back into the True Self "You".

Remember, awakening to the True Self is not a fluke. Regardless of what life throws your way, you CAN maintain your connection to the True Vast Eternal Nothing that you always are. To do so, simply recognise the bullshit when it arises, and pivot your attention inwards, reconnecting to the Peace that is buried deep within.

In the following chapter, we'll delve into how to remain grounded in the True Self when faced with some of life's most challenging situations.

CHAPTER 8

STAYING GROUNDED IN LOVE AMID THE BULLSHIT

"Relief comes when you incorporate ultimate spiritual truth into everyday reality. The mind won't argue when it hears truth. The following steps will remind you that no matter how bad you feel, True Self-Love is ALWAYS waiting just beyond the bullshit to embrace you. You don't have to suffer any longer!"

Radiant Self-Love Is Always Accessible To You

"*That's bullshit!*" our clients say when we drop this truth bomb on them. "*Never lose it?*" they repeat, their voices thick with doubt. "*Yeah, right. Like the ego would ever let go of its drama-queen status.*"

But we stand firm, knowing their resistance is just another ripple on the surface of their ever-present Self-Love.

We then say: "*You can NEVER lose your connection to the True Self or your own Self-Love. No matter what's going on in your life, or the world around you, you can always turn inwards and experience it again. The secret is in knowing that you CAN.*"

If you ever find yourself caught in the ego-self's bullshit whirlwind, you might feel you've lost your connection to the radiant True

Self. But this is an illusion, a temporary haze obscuring your inherent brilliance. So, take a deep breath, and pivot your attention inside. Drop the heavy cloak of drama and resume heart breathing. Inhale Silence, exhale Peace.

Ask yourself *"Who Am I?"* and snap the fingers. Then feel spaciousness expand within you, filled with Stillness, Love and Joy. It's not a treasure to reclaim, but the foundation of your very being. Even a single shift inwards builds trust – the trust that your Bliss is unquenchable, a flame no outer storm can ever suppress. It doesn't matter how dire your circumstances may seem, nothing you do will ever make the *IshQ* that you are go away. It cannot be lost, for it is who you truly ARE, always and eternally.

We guess-estimate that 99.9% of spiritual seekers who are waking up have experienced the Bliss of the True Self, and then seemingly "lost" it again.

Here's what typically happens: you have that first, intoxicating sip of awakening and realise that you're way vaster than the ego-self and its bullshit. You transmute every chance you get and turn within often to experience yourself as True Love and Joy. You feel lighter. Irritations dissipate rapidly, and you're living more in the present moment. Life becomes more enjoyable because you're less fixated on the momentary aspects of your 3D reality.

But then, without warning, you recognise that you're buying into the familiar story of the ego-self known as "you". Here we go again. You find that you're easily triggered and flying off the handle. Perhaps you feel inadequate and withdraw into isolation. Maybe you snap at other people due to loneliness, or shed tears because of perceived rejection. Whatever the reason, your connection to the True Self now seems like it's a million miles away.

"Why has it disappeared?" you ask us, a flicker of panic in the eyes. *"It hasn't,"* we smile reassuringly, knowing all too well the dance of forgetting the radiant "Self". Then we say: *"Don't fret. After believing*

the bullshit story of 'you' for so long, it's all too easy to start believing it again. It's no wonder that you feel like you've lost it and will never get it back."

If this resonates with you, take a breath and remind yourself that you can NEVER lose it. Understand that all that's happened is that you've resumed playing your role in the drama. This is a result of not having practised living as the True Self for long enough to build a neural pathway that automatically shifts your attention beyond the story. You just forgot that Bliss is generated "within" and started looking for it on the "outside" once again.

Welcome to the human playground, where the mind, that mischievous puppy, still sees itself as the Master. You try to train it, oh yes, but its old habits die hard. It craves the ego-self's drama, the thrill of being in charge. You see, its default setting is to control; it has no interest in surrendering to the Vastness of the True Self. Remember, dear reader, the mind is just a tool, a servant, not the king. So, keep training that puppy, and remind it with each breath that its leash leads not to the ego-self's throne, but to the boundless freedom within.

It may take patience and practice, but the mind-self can learn to pay attention. All you have to do is repeat the *"Who Am I?"* self-enquiry, and the heart-breathing technique, until you clearly recognise that opening sensation (or heat or tingling) in the chest or body.

Then deepen your experience by repeating the following: *"I am the space that exists between, beyond, and around all words. I AM the Awareness that recognises that I'm ALWAYS Stillness, Silence, Peace, Love and Joy, no matter what's going on in my world."*

Next, ask *"Who Am I?"* again. As you observe the opening sensation, enquire: *"Can anyone give this Awareness to me? [Reply to yourself] NO. Can anyone take it from me? NO. Can I lose it? NO. Can I find it? NO. Does it start and does it end? NO. Was it there before I was born? YES. Is it a memory? NO. Is it happening now? YES. It's who I AM right NOW."*

Keep breathing through the heart and repeat the words to yourself slowly, allowing the expansiveness of the True Vast Eternal Nothing to envelop you. As its presence becomes apparent, allow yourself to relax, and go deeper into it.

Continue with: *"True Self-Love does not reside in the mind. To experience myself as this Love, I have to SLAP myself awake, step back from the story, and shift my attention back to the body. I now commit to repeating the 'Who Am I?' self-enquiry process throughout the day. I promise myself that I WILL keep going until I break the habit of diving into the library of painful memories and fearful expectations of the future. I vow to move beyond the bullshit consistently by turning inwards to live as the True Love that I KNOW I always am."*

Remember, no words can accurately describe *IshQ* and the In-Lightened state of being. However, certain words can point you in its direction. By continuously asking yourself *"Who Am I?"*, you WILL experience that opening sensation more frequently, deepening your recognition of the True Self and True Self-Love. You just have to make it a priority and keep bringing your attention back inside, even when you really don't feel like doing it.

It was this devotion to the True Self that ultimately supported both Noah and I when the Covid nightmare struck.

Sam & Noah's Story: Love In The Time Of Covid

Covid cast a shadow on my relationship with Noah. He was in Bali, recovering from surgery, whilst I chased a dream – a 200-hour yoga teacher training course in India. Four weeks of yoga and self-discovery – that's what I signed up for. Life, however, had other plans.

Three weeks into the course, India slammed the door shut on the rest of the world. My serene yoga practice dissolved overnight, replaced by the walls of my Rishikesh hotel room. We managed to finish the training, but it did little to ease my growing anxiety. Despite my knowledge of Zen principles, I was really struggling.

The situation became even more harrowing when I received the news of my mother's sudden death. It hit me like a rogue elephant, leaving me in shock, and thousands of miles away from both Noah and my family. I was drowning in grief, separation anxiety, and emotional bullshit – and boy, did it rear its ugly, destructive head.

My inner turmoil was off the scale. Could I watch my mother's funeral online without breaking down? Would Noah support me or find comfort in the arms of another woman? How would we survive financially without our planned Conscious Awareness retreats in Asia? Fear gnawed at me. Even the thought of leaving my room felt risky, given that the police were cracking down on lockdown "violators". My trauma triggers were on high alert, and nothing soothed my troubled mind. I ate little, lost weight, and couldn't face talking to many people. I was trapped in grief and despair.

It was an overwhelming experience, and even though I KNEW I had to rise above the bullshit and turn within, it took me a while to consciously shift out of my suffering. Noah tried his best to support me, but as someone who finds it difficult to deal with emotional outbursts, it wasn't easy for him. We had some tense conversations. All I craved was reassurance that we'd be together again soon., but Noah saw my neediness as a lack of trust in our love story.

Eventually, though, we found a rhythm. Some days, we were hand-in-hand, confident in the love bond that kept us together. Others were harder, and we flung around hurtful words. And yet, amidst it all, I knew the separation was pushing me to look deep within. It was time to stop relying on Noah's love and SLAP myself out of the bullshit I'd been wallowing in.

To help myself, I dove into the Zen teachings I'd learned in Hong Kong and India. I spent hours each day soothing my nervous system, transmuting my fears through the repetition of the *"Who Am I?"* self-enquiry and Q&A, and practising other techniques (like EFT) to ground myself. I also began a conversation with Conscious Awareness (which is another name for the Universe). I asked it to reveal to me how my reunion with Noah would unfold.

The answer came through a friend who connected me to a Delhi angel – a wealthy woman who rescued me from Rishikesh and offered me a haven. In return, we sat together every day and I coached her, and her beautiful friends, on how to experience themselves as the True Self and True Self-Love.

It was like a dream, a manifestation of possibilities. None of it would have happened had I not followed the inner wisdom that guided me to go to India, regardless of the Covid threat.

To some, it might have seemed like it was a very bad time to go. However, living as True Love, and guiding others on how to experience it for themselves, is my life's work. It was exactly what I'd needed, even amid the challenges of losing my mother and being separated from Noah. The call to awaken to Love eclipsed everything else. It pushed me through the darkness, urging me to ditch the bullshit, and bathe in my own Bliss. In the face of heartbreak, I grew – a testament to the power of surrendering to the Love within.

Noah's Bali sojourn was different. His "soft" lockdown was more of a gentle suggestion. He savoured the solitude, his recovery aided by serene landscapes and villa-pool swims. Days were spent exploring Ubud, capturing its essence in photos and paintings, and sculpting stories from lava stone. He reconnected with old friends and forged new bonds.

However, it wasn't all laughter and ease for him. Some days he also felt lonely and desperately missed me too. And then there was the frustration of being locked out of Australia and not knowing when he could get back to see his children.

Nevertheless, he approached it all as an opportunity for growth – the school of life. It allowed him to recentre himself in his own Zen teachings and experience himself as the True Self on a daily basis. Strengthened by this inner exploration, he became a support for others grappling with the stress of the pandemic and loneliness.

The days of separation turned into weeks, and weeks into months. However, despite moments of insecurity, my commitment to transmutation and living beyond the bullshit as the True Self never faltered. Neither did my faith in KNOWING that we would manifest a joyous reunion. And manifest it we did. Six months after I'd left for India, Noah and I reunited in London. A month later, we got married, despite lockdown!

Perhaps we'd both needed the time apart, to turn inwards and experience ourselves as the True Self, whilst also realising the depth of our authentic love for one another.

Wake-up Call: The *"Who Am I?"* Journey

By following these steps, you'll be able to recognise yourself as the True Self, regardless of what's going on in your life. Take the time to read the words slowly and FEEL them in the body. You definitely don't need words to wake up but repeating these frequently will encourage the mind to step back. Furthermore, feel free to tweak any words if necessary. Sometimes, a simple word swap is all it takes to provide the insight needed to shed more bullshit. Trust your intuition. We also recommend revisiting ***Chapter 4*** *on Letting Go. As you become more familiar with the process, you can go straight to the transmutation steps and the "Who Am I?" self-enquiry and Q&A.*

1. **Address the noisy mind.** If you're stuck in the bullshit, start by repeating this to yourself: "*I'm lost in the mind but I don't need to get sucked into it. I KNOW that it's simply the ego-self taking a victory lap, replaying the 'tired-me story' of judgments and concerns. I know, though, that I'm not trapped in this drama. I AM the whole damn theatre! The silent observer. Those loud thoughts? It's just the mind-self whispering, not the roar of the True Self. So I breathe and remind myself: 'Sadness, anger, and fear – these are the costumes the mind wears, but beneath them lies the unshakable Peace of who I always AM. The more I see through the mental masquerade, the closer I am to living fully as pure Stillness, boundless Joy, and eternal Love. So, I keep watching,*

KNOWING that The True Self remains untouched, no matter what the drama raging in the mind."

2. **FEEL the words.** Once again, take a moment to experience where the words are guiding you to. As you relax into a life beyond the story of "you", you'll start to see how attached you've been to the false "self". Recognising this attachment is the beginning of your everlasting freedom.
3. **Practise conscious heart breathing.** If the mind remains active, practise breathing in through the nose and out through the heart for a few minutes (see the *Conscious Heart Breathing Technique in* **Chapter 7**). After 2 minutes of breathing like this, recognise that the chest area feels warm, or tingly, and that you can tangibly feel Love radiating from you. This is what we mean when we say, *"We get high on true Self-Love."* We can feel it emanating from us like a ball of Love in the chest. You can use this breathing method any time you want to (In-)lighten your mood or situation.
4. **Express your emotions.** If you're experiencing any form of sadness, anger, or fear, express it. Shout out the anger, cry out the tears, or jump up and down and vigorously shake the body to release the fear. You need to shift the energy associated with these raw emotions. Continue this practice for a few minutes until you feel lighter. You'll know instinctively when you've cleared another layer of blocked emotional energy because you'll feel more spacious inside.
5. **Use your imaginary "white noise" button.** If necessary, another effective method to transcend the false "self" and its bullshit is to imagine that you're pressing a button that transforms all the stories, pictures, and words in the mind into white noise. Try this now. Begin by repeating your story aloud, then press that imaginary button and notice that everything has turned into a background hum. Try to tune into this hum for at least 2 minutes and observe how the mind relaxes.

6. **Find sensations in the body.** By now, you should be experiencing more Peace. For the sake of this practice, though, scan the body and find five sensations, such as an itch at the end of the nose, or tightness in the buttocks. Count them off on one hand. Then find another five and another. Recognise as you do this that it's getting easier for you to shift your attention away from the bullshit of the mind.
7. **Transmutation or self-enquiry?** If you're feeling calm, you can move straight to Step 10. However, if you're still entangled in any drama or unresolved emotional response, use the following steps to transmute it (also see **Chapter 4**).
8. **Use the Direct Transmutation Method.** Begin by visualising yourself sitting in a plane, or on a chair, in the middle of your emotions. Alternatively, blow up your emotions into a giant pool and dive into them. Whichever method you pick, allow your emotions to move through you and around you. Observe the mind-self with gentleness. Remember, you're not trying to change anything. Your goal is simply to acknowledge what you're experiencing with a sense of curiosity. (Note: You can also do this with positive emotions. The aim is to transmute all emotional attachment).
9. **Or try the "Library" method.** Envision yourself dropping all thoughts and walking out of a library door into space. Out there, thoughts do not exist – there's only the True Vast Eternal Nothing that's everywhere, within the space and encircling it. As you walk out, say: *"I am the True Vast Eternal Nothing. I am the space that exists between, beyond, and around all words."* Repeat this to yourself so slowly that you're slurring it. This will allow you to FEEL the words in the body and experience yourself as Vastness. Realise the truth of what you're saying and point it out to the mind often. If you notice any contraction in the body, recognise that this is the mind's resistance. Keep dropping the book and walking out of the library until any

discomfort dissipates. Remember, you're not trying to change anything; you're just observing what IS.

10. **Time to self-enquire.** Now that the mind is quieter, start the self-enquiry process. Ask yourself *"Who Am I?"*, breathe through the heart, snap the fingers, and continue asking the question until you feel that sensation of Vastness or tingling. Once you recognise it, say to yourself: *"I'm Stillness, Silence, Peace, Love and Joy."* Keep your attention on the spaciousness as you repeat it and your experience will deepen.
11. **Repeat the "*Who Am I?*" Q&A**. Ask *"Who Am I?"* again. As you recognise the opening sensation, observe your Awareness expanding. Then say: *"Can anyone give this Awareness to me? [Reply to yourself] NO. Can anyone take it from me? NO. Can I lose it? NO. Can I find it? NO. Does it start and does it end? NO. Was it there before I was born? YES. Is it a memory? NO. Is it happening now? YES. It's who and what I AM right NOW."*
12. **It's ALWAYS within "You".** Then say: *"So, if no one can give it to me and no one can take it from me, this must mean that it comes from within me. It also means that I don't need anyone external to me to experience it. I KNOW that no one else can give me a Love that fulfils me like my own can. Therefore, the only way to experience it is to recognise that it's ME and that it dwells only within ME."*
13. **Embrace your SLAP.** As you ask yourself the questions and repeat the answers, keep focusing on the sensations in the body. The truth of being reveals itself through these sensations. Don't just repeat the process with the mind; tune into the body and truly FEEL the answers. And,
14. **Finally, stay committed to your awakening.** To do this, set an alarm on your phone. These *"Conscious Creation Calls"* will help you to maintain your inward focus during the day. Set five alarms at different times for 1 minute practice runs. When the alarm goes off, take a breath and imagine yourself instantly dropping all thoughts (i.e., the book). Then walk out of the

library. Once you can step out without engaging in thoughts for 1 minute, increase it to 2, 5, 10, and so on.

That's the process. Incorporate it into your day and use it often. The more dedicated you are to your own awakening, the deeper your recognition of the True Self will become. You'll soon realise that NOTHING in the material world can satisfy the yearning to know who "You" truly ARE.

The following pages will guide you on how to transmute and apply the *"Who Am I?"* self-enquiry and Q&A to navigate some of life's most challenging situations. Relief comes by incorporating ultimate spiritual truth into everyday reality. The mind won't argue when it hears truth. These steps will remind you that no matter how bad you feel, True Self-Love is always waiting just beyond the bullshit to embrace you. You don't have to suffer any longer!

Wake-Up Call: Find Your "Self" After A Fight

1. **Notice what you're thinking.** Begin by examining the nature of the mind. What are you saying to yourself about this argument? If you're not actively thinking about it, tune into your current vibe. For instance, if you have a knot of tension or tightness in the stomach, acknowledge that you're vibing as "tense and heavy" in this moment.
2. **It's not the True Self "You".** Reaffirm to yourself that it's the small "self" that's having the psychological reaction, NOT the True Self "You", which is silently observing it. If you're experiencing an intense fight-or-flight response, remind yourself that the True Self ALWAYS just observes the bullshit narratives that the ego-self is buying into. Try to step back and watch yourself even if you're crying or shaking. What happens when you do? There's more calmness, right? Repeat this process often, noticing how the recognition starts to loosen the tension in the body.

3. **"I feel bad because I believe what I think."** Then, say: *"I see that I believe my thoughts about [X]. I believe that he or she has let me down, disrespected me, been unkind to me, betrayed me, or [insert your own words]. I'm uncomfortable because I think that what I feel about this argument must be true. However, no matter how intense it feels, I remind myself that this isn't the trauma of the past repeating itself. This is NOW, and I know how to soothe myself and return to Peace."*
4. **No one can take your own True Love away from you.** Continue with the following: *"I'm aware that if no one can give me True Love and no one can take it from me, then nothing anyone says or does can change that. Even after this argument, I'm still Love. The reason I'm upset is because I believe what the mind thinks about the situation. It falsely believes that the only thing I need to feel OK is that person's love and attention. This is the greatest lie of all. What I really need to do is recognise my own True Self-Love. This self-enquiry process is leading me to experience an unwavering Love that never criticises, blames, or abandons me."*
5. **Say it until you relax.** Repeat and FEEL the truth of these words until they begin to melt the sadness, anger, or fear that you may be experiencing.
6. **Find out why you're angry.** Next, ask yourself why you're angry or sad with yourself. In most cases, the answer will be because you feel like you've put yourself in an unwanted situation. Often just reading that will free you up internally.
7. **Vent the emotion.** If you sense that there's emotional energy that needs to be expressed, allow it to flow. Scream it out, shake it off, or let the tears run. Noah and I refer to this as "dynamic release". Continue until you feel like you've shifted a layer of energy within you. You'll know when this shift has happened because you'll feel more spacious inside. When you're doing this process, train yourself to focus only on what you truly desire. Do NOT rehash the story as this will make you feel worse, and keep you feeling stuck (**Chapter 9** delves further into this topic).

8. **Face the fear of being alone.** If you're feeling upset and desperate to hold onto a relationship, whether it's romantic or otherwise, recognise that beneath the raw emotion, there's usually the chilling prospect of being alone. This is why you twist yourself into knots, replaying the argument, defending every inch, all to avoid the unsettling emptiness within. Remember, accepting the reality of the situation DOES NOT mean you'll be dumped, friendless, or alone for the rest of your life. It simply means that, right now, the person needs space to process their own emotions. This leaves you facing your own need for attention. Be brave and look inwards. Stop pushing yourself away and offer yourself the warmth and understanding you crave. Your own company is a haven, not a wasteland. Teach yourself that it's safe to dive in and you'll never fear your own internal space again.
9. **Learn to remain open.** Your responsibility to yourself is to keep your heart open to the other person, regardless of whether you believe you're in the "right" or not. Remind yourself that no matter how upset you may feel, you KNOW that you're not the sad or angry person that your ego-mind thinks "you" are. You're way more expansive than that. Repeating this to yourself will create internal space, allowing you to step back from the drama a bit more. You can also ask: *"Do I want to radiate True Love and be in harmony with X [insert their name], or do I want to remain unhappy and keep proving myself right?"* If you don't need to be right, you'll have nothing to defend. It then becomes much easier to reach out to the other person. Remember, it's only EVER the ego-self that needs approval and validation!
10. **Challenge your perceptions.** Instead of defending your irritation towards someone, look for what you appreciate about them. Remember, your thoughts are shaped by your own experiences and biases, they are not absolute truths. As you awaken to this, you'll realise it's all a reflection of your own perception, and has absolutely nothing to do with the other person!

11. **Choose kindness.** Regardless of how you feel after an argument, you can still decide to be kind to the person that you've argued with. Don't get caught up in mental justifications – trust that you can choose to think positively about anyone. Remember, criticising them is like criticising yourself. Start cultivating more loving thoughts, even if it feels forced at first – you'll soon find that it creates a more open, peaceful feeling within you.
12. **You get what you vibe.** Remember, if you don't release your underlying bullshit (i.e., what you've made your trauma and life story mean about you), you're likely to continue attracting the same types of relationship and reacting to them in the same manner. For example, if your core belief is that you're broken and needy, you'll manifest relationships that reinforce that perception (this is not limited to romance). Whatever your vibe is, if you slip back into your bullshit ways of relating, it's going to come back to haunt you. You must recognise your behavioural patterns in order to transform them.
13. **"Fly" through your pain to transmute it.** To grow spiritually, it helps to master transmutation. One way to do that is to imagine yourself either sitting on that chair in the middle of your discomfort, or on a plane flying through clouds of it. Allow any form of sadness, anger, or fear to move through you and around you. As you do this, remind yourself that the True "You" is not the small "you" who's experiencing the pain. Don't dismiss it; that's resistance and will keep you stuck. Zip the eyebrows shut and pay attention to the Love within.
14. **Or amplify it to release it.** You can also let go by using your attention to expand the emotions you're experiencing. For example, if you feel anger or sadness, locate the sensation within, expand it as much as you can, then imagine either diving into it or bursting it. This places your Awareness in the centre of the emotional storm. Sit still, become your experience, and notice the Peace that unfolds within.

15. **Repeat the "*Who Am I?*" self-enquiry process**. Keep asking the question until you experience that sensation of Vastness (heat or tingling) in the body. Then, go through the Q&A (see the *"Who Am I?"* journey in **Chapter 8**). And,
16. **You possess the power to create peaceful relationships.** If you're resisting making peace after an argument, observe what you're thinking about the situation. Whatever is playing out in the mind, whatever defensive stance you're taking, recognise that it's bullshit. Tell yourself firmly that you no longer choose to believe any excuse that creates separation, and release the story. Then, reach out to make amends if needed, and open yourself to understanding. With romantic relationships, recognise that all your conditions around it, including your relentless judgments, are bullshit too. The idea that a successful relationship requires a so-called "spark" or specific physical attributes is a misconception. Genuine love thrives on shared values, growth, and mutual respect. Transforming any connection requires only one person's commitment to growth. Be the one to step into that commitment, cultivate your own spiritual understanding, and watch your relationships blossom with renewed grace and harmony.

Based on this template, we're going to explore Sarina's approach to overcoming her relationship issues and creating more harmony.

Client Case: Sarina's Relationship Revolution

Sarina, 43, wanted support because she found herself constantly arguing with her partner. Despite her efforts to keep their discussions neutral, they always seemed to escalate into a heated argument, leaving Sarina feeling upset and drained. Conflict was something she hated, and their inability to communicate effectively led to prolonged periods of emotional distance.

Their relationship had fallen into a cycle of disappointment where Sarina expected her partner to let her down, and he often did. Frustration mounted, resulting in emotional walls forming between them. Unsurprisingly, this also took a toll on their sex life, exacerbating the situation even further.

Over time, Sarina started to understand the difference between ego-love and authentic love. We explored how unrealistic expectations could be the kiss of death when it came to relating. It became clear to Sarina that she couldn't be unconditionally loving whilst also placing conditions on her partner's behaviour.

Emphasising the importance of keeping her heart open, we guided Sarina on how to rekindle their connection. Her treatment plan focused on the following key points:

1. **Internal reflection.** Instead of expressing her dissatisfaction to her partner, we encouraged Sarina to turn within. We guided her to ask herself: *"In what ways am I disappointing myself?"* This led her to realise that she often felt out of control and was projecting her expectations onto her partner. While this understanding didn't bring instant change, it did bring some relief and helped her to accept her emotions.
2. **Personal responsibility.** We explored why it was Sarina's responsibility to address her own blocks within the relationship. Whilst it was valid for her to feel angry in certain situations, she needed to work through it and let it go in the understanding that not all battles are worth fighting. As she practised accepting her emotions, she found that she was able to keep her heart open for longer, gradually breaking down the protective walls that had built up between them.
3. **Cultivating compassion.** This became Sarina's secret weapon. In the heat of an argument, instead of letting frustration engulf her, she would silently repeat a mantra: *"We're both doing our best."* This simple shift helped her to see beyond her immediate reactions and recognise the bigger picture. We explored the key distinction between disliking a person's behaviour and still holding space for the person behind it. It wasn't about

condoning the act, but about understanding that behaviour often springs from past experiences and individual narratives. Sarina fully embraced this concept, committing to viewing her partner through the lens of his unique life story even during the harshest moments. This conscious effort to see things from a wider perspective proved liberating, paving the way for greater empathy.

4. **Transmuting emotional responses.** We explored the letting-go techniques from **Chapter 4**, including transmutation, to help Sarina release resentment in real time.
5. **Self-connection.** Sarina started repeating the *"Who Am I?"* self-enquiry and Q&A in order to recognise her connection to the True Self. This inner work enabled her to strengthen her relationship with herself and, subsequently, her partner. And,
6. **Nurturing intimacy.** Our discussions extended to the topic of sex and affection. Sarina recognised that knowing her partner's love languages was not enough if she didn't actively use them. Withholding affection because she didn't like her partner's behaviour had turned their relationship into a transactional arrangement – in other words: *"You do what I want to keep me happy (like cook the dinner sometimes and tidy your office) and I'll stay emotionally open and be intimate with you."* To foster genuine harmony, Sarina committed to using her partner's love languages whilst also practising gratitude for him. This shift helped her to become more forgiving and open to deeper relating.

Sarina was relieved to have an action plan. Initially, embracing her emotions and staying open to her partner made her feel vulnerable, but she persevered. A crucial breakthrough came when she learned to separate her partner's behaviour from the overall quality of their relationship. She realised that if he burnt the dinner, this didn't mean that their relationship was doomed. This insight, coupled with the knowledge that everyone handles life's bumps uniquely, helped her to navigate those challenging moments.

Sarina also discovered the transformative power of proactive love. By deliberately choosing to offer more affection, she began to receive an abundance of love in return. Over time, their previously cycle of conflict transformed into a virtuous cycle of love and respect.

Wake-up Call: Return to "Self" When Feeling Stuck

Feeling stuck is like psychic quicksand, sucking the life out of all possibilities. It's the suffocating belief that you're trapped, helpless to make changes. If you find yourself clinging to this quicksand, the first step is to shake the sand off your feet – literally. Move your body to feel lighter (see **Chapter 4** on Letting Go). It's a potent way to shift the energy of stagnation. Then, dive into these steps to reclaim your eternal Peace:

1. **Reframe the bullshit story.** Don't let "stuck" define you. It's just a mental state, one where solutions are temporarily obscured. The absence of an immediate answer doesn't equate to its non-existence. Maybe it's beyond your current grasp, or you're not quite ready to take the leap. To unstick your "self", first acknowledge the quicksand. Then, remember who you truly are. Ask yourself *"Who Am I?"*, and recognise that the radiant "Self", untouched by circumstance, is always there. Remember, even prisoners locked up in cages have found the path to freedom. They have learned to turn their gaze inwards, away from the bars, and discovered a deep spiritual awakening. You too have that power. It starts by affirming your intention to break free, no matter how daunting the task may seem.
2. **Create inner space.** Now, repeat this truth to yourself: *"I'm making space for inspiration to unfold. No matter how shitty things get, I KNOW I'm not the mind replaying this stuck tape. I'm the silent Awareness that's observing the anxious ego-self. The worry-wart, the overthinker – that is not the True Self. I'm the Awareness that sits just behind these thoughts. The more I repeat this, the quieter the mind gets. Even on death row, prisoners can find Peace. And if they can do it, I can too. I'm not*

the ego-self trapped in this drama; I'm the Awareness knowing it's all temporary. To help myself, I'll stop feeding the bullshit and turn my focus within to live as Stillness, Silence, Peace, Love and Joy. This recognition is my key to liberation." Observe the internal shifts that occur as a result of repeating this mantra frequently.

3. **Embrace acceptance.** The next step in getting unstuck is to consider whether you can accept your current situation. Remember, resistance arises when our expectations don't align with our reality. Even if full acceptance seems difficult at first, ask yourself whether you can accept that you're resisting. Recognising your resistance will naturally lead you to a place of greater acceptance. Try asking that now.
4. **Explore your alternatives.** If, however, there's no mental space to budge right now, ask yourself whether you're willing to leave the situation – and then imagine or sense yourself doing just that! Sometimes, seeing yourself going is almost as empowering as actually doing it. When you realise that you CAN leave, you'll also recognise that you'll be OK if you do. This usually makes it easier to stay for now.
5. **Release the mental struggle.** Keep pushing yourself until you reach a level of acceptance (or can at least accept that you can't fully accept your situation). At this point, it's time to face your inner struggle, and start letting it go. If you're constantly reiterating how stuck you are, all you're doing is feeding the feeling of being stuck! By accepting the situation to the extent that you can, you'll create more internal space to find a way forward. To help yourself, train the mind to tune out of the story of stuckness, and focus on one tiny aspect of progress, even if that's simply having the energy to go for a walk!
6. **Shift emotional energy somatically.** Whenever you find yourself crying, shouting, or feeling fearful, channel that emotional energy towards manifesting a better situation. As you experience any form of these emotions, say to yourself: *"I'm now creating internal space to draw to me happier circumstances,"* or

something like that. We recommend that you try this at least once to understand the power of releasing emotions while focusing on moving forward (see **Chapter 4** on Letting Go and **Chapter 9** on Manifesting).

7. **Reject the bullshit story.** At the same time, whenever you feel sadness, anger, or fear regarding the situation, clap your hands, and say: *"No, I'm not going there. I KNOW that everything's working out for me, always has and always will. I therefore release the need to control and embrace the expansiveness of the True Self instead."* Don't allow yourself to fall back into the bullshit. Whether you fully accept it or not, life IS unfolding in your favour. Never forget, you embody Conscious Awareness (the True Vast Eternal Nothing) and you're the creator of your own life (within the framework of your karmic story). There are no coincidences or wrong decisions! As you start to internalise this truth, you'll begin to sense freedom permeating your being.
8. **Transmutation.** Sometimes, shifting the energy physically is enough, whilst other times, focused transmutation may also be necessary. As you start this process, again imagine yourself sitting still on a chair in the middle of your raw emotions, observing them. It's crucial to approach this without any intention of wanting to change what you're experiencing. If you try to transmute in an attempt to avoid your emotions, this will only exacerbate the inner turmoil. The secret to transmutation is to observe without expecting anything to be different.
9. **Ask *"Who Am I?"*.** Next, breathe through the heart a few times, and repeat slowly: *"Who Am I? I am the space that exists between, beyond, and around all words. I'm Stillness, Silence, Peace, Love and Joy."* Even if it feels awkward initially, keep saying the sentence until you experience that sensation of Vastness in the body.
10. **Question it all.** Once you've recognised that opening sensation (or tingling or heat), repeat the following Q&A to yourself: *"Can anyone give me True Peace? [Reply to yourself]* NO. *Can*

anyone take True Peace from me? NO. Can I lose True Peace? NO. Can I remember True Peace? NO. Is True Peace always present in the NOW? YES. Is there any helplessness here? NO. Is there any fear? NO. Is there any anger? NO. Is there any sadness? NO. Is there anything here other than Stillness, Silence, Peace, Love and Joy? NO. So, if this is the case, how can I be stuck?"

11. **And the answer is...** *"I'm NOT, it's just the ego-self that's convinced I am. I KNOW that if I can change the way I perceive the situation, I'll feel more peaceful and the circumstances around me will eventually shift as well."*
12. **Read it again.** Repeat the process a few times, embodying the words with your entire being. As you go through the *"Who Am I?"* process and Q&A, trust that the truth will come to you via that opening sensation in the body.
13. **Freedom from stuckness.** Next, ask yourself, *"Do I still feel stuck?"* Feel the question resonate in the core of your being. Then, with unwavering conviction, reply: *"I can't be. I am the True Vast Eternal Nothing. I AM that which doesn't start and doesn't end. I am limitless. No prison can exist here."* Stay alert and observe any internal shifts as these words wash through you. Feel the truth of your inherent freedom dissolving any remaining traces of stuckness.
14. **Welcome Awareness.** However, if you're still feeling contracted and buying into the story, take another breath through the heart, and gently enquire: "*Where does this belief in being stuck arise from?"* And *"Who is this 'I' who clings to this idea?"* As you recognise the transient nature of this limiting "I", another layer of the ego-mind will crumble away. In its place, you'll start to feel the Vastness of the True Self unfold. It's a subtle shift, like sunlight warming the heart. Embrace this expansive Awareness, knowing that your liberation cannot be confined. And,
15. **Gratitude and transformation.** Finally, even if your situation seems dire, challenge yourself to feel grateful for it. There's magic in gratitude. Try to express gratitude for every

circumstance in your life – the shittier the better. Say to yourself: *"I bless everyone and everything that's ever made me suffer."* As you do this, you'll notice more inner Peace, and often the situation will transform as well.

Wake-Up Call: Count On Your "Self" Despite Money Woes

1. **Release emotional energy.** If you find yourself feeling concerned because you've lost money, a job, or made a bad investment, start by trying to move the internal energy associated with it. Take some time to vent your emotions by shouting, crying, or shaking them out. This can be particularly helpful if you're feeling fearful about the future. However, remember not to release raw energy while worrying about your current situation, or any other bullshit story, as that will just make you feel worse. The secret to shifting fear around money is to release the energy while focusing on aligning with something new and empowering.
2. **Sit and observe.** To transmute, imagine again that you're sitting on a chair in the middle of your emotions. Allow yourself to experience them fully, but do NOT allow the attention of the mind to wallow in the *"Why did it happen?"*. You can also focus on the raw feelings inside, expanding them until they get so big that they pop like a balloon. Either way, remember there has to be no motive of wanting to change how you feel.
3. **Address fearful thoughts.** To encourage the mind to step back even more, have a conversation with the ego-self known as "you". Say to yourself: *"I know it's easy to focus on the fear because it feels so real. I know that having no money and no job is scary. But I also KNOW that fear is ONLY a sensation in the body, it's NOT reality. Deep down, I know that I AM the True Vast Eternal Nothing from which everything in life flows. This means that every reality is already available to me in energy form. I KNOW that there's a direct correlation between embodying this and drawing to me more abundance in my 3D world. ALL I have to do is focus on what I want to manifest, rather*

than on what I don't, and pull that to me by becoming the vibrational version of the person who already has it (i.e., BE it now). I KNOW that everything's working out for me, always has and always will. I therefore release the need to control and embrace the expansiveness of the True Self instead."

4. **Self-enquiry.** When you're ready, breathe through the heart, and ask *"Who Am I?"*. This will expand your Specific Energetic Love Frequency (SELF). When you notice the spaciousness inside, say: *"I am the space that exists between, beyond, and around all words. I am ALWAYS Stillness, Silence, Peace, Love and Joy."* Observe what's happening within as you repeat this. More spaciousness right?
5. **Repeat the *"Who Am I?"* Q&A.** Then ask yourself: *"Can anyone give this Awareness to me? [Reply to yourself] NO. Can anyone take it from me? NO. Can I lose it? NO. Can I find it? NO. Does it start and does it end? NO. Was it there before I was born? YES. Is it a memory? NO. Is it happening now? YES. It's who and what I AM right NOW."* And,
6. **Continue to shift focus and embrace Stillness.** When the next wave of fear hits you, remind yourself that you know what to do: consciously breathe through the heart, and ask *"Who Am I?"*. Then redirect your attention inside to experience yourself as Stillness, Silence, Peace, Love and Joy. By making this conscious shift, your vibration will expand naturally, drawing new people and prospects into your life. TRUST that regardless of how things appear right now, you really have nothing to worry about.

As you live more as the True Self and cultivate a deeper trust in life, you're going to find that you're worrying less about money and survival – even if challenging situations occur. This doesn't mean that you're going to end up living under a bridge (unless you want to). You're still going to take action; you're just going to take it from a space of greater inner expansion.

Your commitment to BEING the True Self is going to support you, especially when life gets tough. So, if the bullshit rears its ugly head, remember the tools you've learned:

1. **See through the story.** Notice when you're caught in a web of fear. Acknowledge that these narratives aren't "You", they're just clouds passing across your inner sky.
2. **Step out of the drama.** Even though fear feels real, it's just a constructed story you can choose to leave behind. Shift your focus to a different narrative, one fuelled by Love and courage.
3. **"I am Nothing."** You are way vaster than the ego-self's limiting bullshit. Connect with the expansive nature of the True Vast Eternal Nothing that you ARE. Say to yourself, *"I am Nothing. I AM the True Vast Eternal Nothing from which all of life flows."* FEEL the expansiveness within as you repeat this.
4. **Be present to the discomfort.** When pain arises, don't resist it. See it as a messenger, pointing you inwards. Either transmute it, or if that's too challenging right now, talk directly to the tension in the body. Say: "*I know that I'm feeling this way (i.e., sad, angry, or scared) because I believe what I'm telling myself about the situation must be true.*" Repeat it until you feel the contraction start to ease.
5. **Breathe and enquire** Return to heart breathing, and repeat the *"Who Am I?"* self-enquiry and Q&A until you expand into *IshQ*. Remember that knowing yourself as True Love speeds up your vibrational frequency, drawing to you experiences that resonate with the authentic "Self". Abundance and success naturally follow when you deeply recognise your worth. And,
6. **Question the illusory "I".** Finally ask, *"Who is this 'I' who feels like I don't have enough?"* And "*Who is this 'I' who feels separate from others?*" See through the illusion. The answer is simple: *"There's no such 'I'."* You are an interconnected part of the vast, vibrant tapestry of existence.

By embracing these steps, you'll cultivate emotional resilience, and evolve into a more empowered version of "you". Whether facing daily tasks or life's unexpected curveballs, you'll navigate them with a newfound grace, mirroring the unruffled spirit of a Zen master, who still *"chops wood and carries water."*

This connection to your inner wisdom paves the way for ongoing transformation and a more fulfilling life, where Joy blossoms alongside growth and acceptance. But the key to unlocking your limitless creative power isn't in "doing" more, it's in simply BEING.

I Am "Everything" – And Anything Is Possible

As you shed the ego-self's limiting cloak and embrace the True Self, the Universe becomes your canvas, and your limitations, just brushstrokes ready to be transformed. Realising your Oneness with everything ignites a power within you. You are both "Everything and Nothing", the infinite source from which all of your desires emerge. Within this sacred space, the bullshit falls away like a withered leaf, revealing the glistening potential that awaits your creative touch.

This awakening unlocks the secret to Conscious Manifestation. It's not hidden in doing endless techniques or franticly striving; it's discovered within the depths of your being. By anchoring into the True Self, that unshakeable Awareness of the True Vast Eternal Nothing, you become the artist who effortlessly paints your dreams onto the landscape of reality.

So, are you ready to manifest your dream life? The next chapter unlocks the secrets of inner alignment, conscious choices, and unwavering belief – the essential tools for turning your desires into reality. We'll delve into practical techniques and real-life examples, making Conscious Manifestation as natural as breathing. Flip the page and let's start to co-create the dream life you so desire.

CHAPTER 9

THE BOUNTY OF BLISSFUL MANIFESTATION

"Remember, dwelling on limiting narratives while trying to manifest is like wearing flip-flops to a mosh pit. It doesn't work. To transform your life, you have to crank up the vibration of who you're BEING as much as possible, for as long as possible.
That's the way it works."

Unleashing Your Inner Architect

While moving beyond the trappings of the mind and embracing the Great Unknown is a key part of awakening, we're not going to tell you that you shouldn't have material desires. Of course you're going to have desires. It's only natural to have aspirations and dreams – they're the flames of your potential! Instead, dear reader, our purpose, is to provide you with the tools and wisdom to harness the power of the mind, enabling you to draw more of those desires into your reality.

Conscious Manifestation starts with accepting your role as the creator of your Universe. What you draw into your life depends on the energetic vibration (and frequency) that you emit to the world. This is based on your thoughts and, specifically, how you feel about those thoughts. We call this your Specific Energetic Love Frequency (SELF), and your thoughts, feelings, and emotions direct it (in other words, who you're BEING most of the time).

Think of the Universe as a cosmic dance floor. You're either vibing high and light, like the IT crowd at a concert, or slow and heavy, like that guy who keeps knocking over the drinks. As you consistently gaze inwards and connect with the True Self, your vibrational SELF amps up naturally. Once it becomes your new groove, life shifts into a whole new reality. The beauty? No fancy footwork is required – just redirect your focus from the outside world to your inner disco party.

But here's the catch: if you cling to your limiting story and feed yourself with ongoing bullshit, this will keep you stuck in the slow-dance zone. As a result, you'll continue to manifest slow, heavy experiences that mirror your dense, low-vibe energy. Sorry, there's no escape unless you actively up your game and expand your vibration.

Think of your SELF as the currency of manifestation, the direct "remote controller" of your desire-attracting superpowers. It's not some external hard drive; it's "you", radiating 24/7. From a spiritual perspective, no cosmic puppeteer pulls the strings. You orchestrate your own life, no punishments, no rewards, no "deserving" involved. You simply attract what you vibrate (with a sprinkle of past-life karma thrown in for good measure).

This means that if you're jiving as True Love, supportive situations and people will gravitate towards you. But if sadness, anger, or fear are your go-to tunes, frustration and drama become your regular dance partners. You attract things with a similar frequency to your vibe (aka WHO YOU'RE BEING).

Remember, dwelling on limiting narratives while trying to manifest is like wearing flip-flops to a mosh pit. It doesn't work. To transform your life, you have to crank up the vibration of who you're BEING as much as possible, for as long as possible. That's the way it works.

1. I had to actually stop buying into the bullshit story that I wasn't good enough (and not just pay lip service to the idea) and clear any stuck energy around it.
2. I had to see myself more often as the True Love within. And,
3. I had to start expanding into the version of myself who KNEW that this profound love was already a reality. In other words, I had to begin feeling like a woman who was ALREADY deeply loved. I had to ask myself, *"How would I feel if I had this love right now?"* then BE her as often as I could.

This was no easy task, especially as I was still thawing from the pain and loneliness of my final few years in Hong Kong. In all honesty, it was hard initially to move beyond my negative narratives and make myself believe (i.e., FEEL) that I was already loved by this wonderful man. Nevertheless, I was determined to transform myself.

To accelerate my growth, I signed up with some great coaches and learned a lot about energy. I discovered that the quickest way to transform myself into a "loved-up" woman was to work directly on shifting the heavy energy that I was still lugging around with me. Here are the steps I integrated into my daily life:

1. **Start with beginner's mind.** The first thing I did was drop any beliefs that caused me to doubt my ability to draw to me a deep and meaningful new relationship. This included several personalised astrology predictions that I would never get married (see **Chapter 4** on Letting Go).
2. **Active, not passive, meditation.** I practised a form of dynamic meditation taught to me by one of my coaches. Every day, for at least 30 minutes, I allowed my body to move and express itself, while simultaneously venting my emotions. I gave myself permission to moan, cry, scream, or shake, as needed, releasing a lifetime of trauma-related pain. Most importantly, though, I did this without paying any attention to the old stories of "me" that surfaced in the mind.

3. **Reframe experiences.** I consciously used any emotional release as an opportunity for transformation. Whenever I cried, shouted, or expressed any emotions, I repeated a mantra that came to me: *"With every molecule of sadness, anger, and fear that I release, I create energetic space in my life to manifest X, Y, Z."* This consistent shift in perspective kept me firmly focused on what I wanted to draw to me, rather than on rehashing my painful story and staying stuck in the past.
4. **Understand the deeper layers of letting go.** I acknowledged that every time I cried over the end of a short-lived romance, I was actually releasing deeper layers of emotional pain associated with my father abandoning me. Realising this correlation felt liberating; there was no reason to be so distressed by the end of a brief romantic encounter.
5. **Recognise the metaphors in body sensations.** The more I made this dynamic mediation my own, the deeper my understanding that every physical sensation was a metaphor for how I felt emotionally. For example, whenever I experienced discomfort while standing still, I recognised it was reflecting the frustration I felt when faced with rejection. A shooting pain in my head, meanwhile, mirrored the emotional pain I experienced when being too hard on myself. The insights kept coming and I kept moving. I was literally "pulling out" my old-story energy and "sending" it to what I wanted to manifest instead. As a result, my relationships with men started to improve.
6. **Persist and affirm.** When I began this practice just after arriving in India, I was having a fling with a man in Rishikesh who was happy to have sex with me but not a coffee. His rejection stung but I kept moving the body and releasing. I also reaffirmed to myself often that my new love was on his way. Any time I cried or got angry, I said to myself: *"With every molecule of sadness, anger, and fear that I release, I KNOW that I'm creating energetic space to draw to me a loving, adoring, affectionate, fun,*

conscious, committed, sexually satisfying, emotionally available, and generous life-long relationship with my most-compatible, awakened partner." Repeating this always brought me back to the KNOWING that I would get what I desired.

7. **Appreciate gradual inner shifts.** As I persisted in clearing out old energy and rebuilding my self-perception to align with what I desired, I met a man who was interested in both sex and a coffee. Albeit espresso! This was a big improvement on that last fling, but I still wanted more. So, I focused on what I desired and continued to do the energy work, creating space for something bigger to manifest in my life.
8. **Spot the signs.** Within a few months, I'd met yet another man and the connection felt immediately more fulfilling. Although it didn't last long, I knew that he'd loved me. I was delighted. Despite shedding a few tears when he disappeared, I recognised that this was the Universe celebrating my progress and indicating that my true love was definitely around the corner. Why? Because the vibration I was emitting was changing frequently enough to move me away from one individual, towards another.
9. **Reiki, energy work, and other manifestation techniques**. To balance my energy-clearing practice, I also started doing energy-building work to establish a connection with my future life-long partner. I "called in" this man energetically and talked to him telepathically every day. I wrote petitions to the Universe, burning them at night in a symbolic release. I also used Reiki to expedite my manifestation process and started teaching it. I was doing everything that I truly loved. Furthermore, I made deep self-enquiry a part of my day, filling up on my own delicious Self-Love and radiating it out to the world as often as I could. Life was definitely vibing a lot more cheerfully.
10. **Relax into Self-Love.** As a result of my commitment to "Self", I began to experience a true sense of fulfilment. I was finally happy on my own. So, why was I so determined to draw

to me a new partner? Because I could, and it was fun. I sought an awakened man who would walk next me, not someone to save me. Two very different things!

11. **Available to all possibilities.** As I embraced a deeper connection to the Love that I AM, I felt a growing openness to receive my next lover. I could feel the momentum building within me. Every time I thought about him, I felt a spark of positive expectation. There was no doubt; I KNEW that my new man was moving closer towards me. And,
12. **Stay open to surprises.** Indeed, he was. No one was more surprised than me that the profound new love I manifested was Noah, someone I knew and considered just a friend. The Universe operates in mysterious ways, and by trusting and allowing the pieces of the puzzle to fall into place, I was led to a remarkable romantic connection.

Reflecting on my journey, I attribute the turning point to clearing my dense emotional energy consistently, practising and teaching Reiki, immersing myself in self-enquiry, and FEELING full of Self-Love every day. This combination allowed me to bypass my fears and expand my personal vibration.

In moments of doubt, and there were a few, I would shift my attention to the loneliness within, observing it until it transmuted. Then I reinforced my commitment to what I desired by repeating to myself: *"With every molecule of sadness, anger, and fear that I release, I KNOW that I'm creating the energetic space to draw to me a loving, adoring, affectionate, fun, conscious, committed, sexually satisfying, emotionally available, and generous life-long relationship with my most-compatible, awakened partner."*

By embracing these practices to the best of my ability (and at no time was I ever doing them perfectly), I gained a deeper sense of clarity. I also came to realise that experiencing my own Love somatically was generating a positive ripple effect throughout my life. Even when nothing was shifting in my 3D reality, I didn't entertain the idea that the process was taking too long because "there was something wrong with me". Instead, I remained excited and in the absolute KNOWING that my loving new man was on the way, without being attached to how, when, or where he would show up.

As I continued expanding, I could feel the transformation happening within me. I was no longer tense and heavy. Nor was I trying to persuade myself that I was aiming for something that I didn't believe was possible. More often than not, I was BEING the woman who already knew that she IS expansive True Love. I had infused my vibrational energy with lightness, softening from within, and becoming more trusting, patient, and calmer. I was smiling more, laughing more, and frowning less. I was BEING Joy a lot more of the time (at least 51% of my day).

My lens on life had widened immeasurably. Within eight months of committing to my Conscious Manifestation process, and living as a more expansive being, I'd begun my big-love relationship with Noah (Note: shifting my self-perception and expanding how I felt about life took time; I won't sugar coat it. I've seen clients manifest deep love stories faster than I did. It all comes down to how fast you can consistently focus more on the Joy of receiving what you want rather than clinging to the version of "you" who doesn't have it.)

Wake-Up Call: Shift Your Vibration In Minutes

Because your vibrational frequency (or SELF) is at the heart of your manifesting ability, it's crucial to know whether you're vibing as expansion or contraction. Remember, inner expansion is the secret sauce that draws to you more lovers, money, and magic, while contraction is the root of your misery.

Let's begin with the former. The simplest way to recognise inner expansion is to think of someone or something that triggers a profound sense of Love within you. It could be your partner, friends, children, parents, a wonderful experience, or even your beloved pet.

Take a few moments to think about that person or animal until you notice that you're feeling lighter. You don't need to think too much about why you love them, just pay attention to how you feel inside as you expand into that experience of Love. You may notice a lightness, tingling, or warmth in the chest or body.

Observe and acknowledge that this comfortable sensation is the physical manifestation of Love and a gateway to the True Self (remember, if there's any discomfort, this is not Love but resistance. In this case, refer to **Chapter 4** to transmute your emotions before continuing).

Now, affirm to the ego-self: *"This expansion, spaciousness, warmth (or whatever you're experiencing) is how I physically experience Love."*

FEEL it. BE it. Notice how expansive you are within. Repeat this statement to yourself several times while breathing out through the heart. Really emphasise the words so that the ego-self begins to associate them with what expansive Love feels like somatically – notice that it's all happening within "You", even if it initially seems to be triggered by another.

Take a deep breath and let it go. Now, let's focus on contraction. Recall a situation where you felt sadness, anger, or fear (or any form thereof). Fully immerse yourself in that memory. Pay attention to how the body experiences denser emotions. Point out to the mind the bodily sensations that you're experiencing.

Say: *"This contraction, heaviness, tightness (or whatever you're experiencing) is how I physically experience any form of sadness, anger, or fear."*

Notice the contracted or heavy feeling within. It may not feel pleasant to experience this in the body but allow yourself to FEEL it anyway. Don't try to change it.

Spend a few moments fully acknowledging this contracted state. Then, take another deep breath and shake it off. Now, quickly shift your thoughts back to the person or pet that triggers Love within you. Continue focusing on them until you feel lighter again. Notice how much better it feels inside when you're in a more expansive state.

Appreciate the truth of this and recognise how swiftly you were able to shift from expansion to contraction. In just a few moments, you transformed from BEING Love, to BEING angry, to BEING Love again.

It's truly as quick as that. Ultimately, if you strip it back and look at it from the perspective of Consciousness, what keeps you stuck is your attachment to justifying, or denying, your emotional pain and limitations. So, if you're still holding onto dense emotions and convinced that you can never let them go, guess what? You've just proven to yourself that you can!

Now, let's explore the life stories of Sadie and Arti to grasp how their ways of being have affected the course of their lives.

Client Cases: Sadie And Arti Shape Their Reality

Sadie, 51, and Arti, 48, both grew up in affluent families, one in India and the other in London. While they'd both married into wealthy families and had children, this was where their similarities ended.

We tried to help Sadie, but she struggled to shift her feelings and inner dialogue concerning her situation. This was understandable given that she felt trapped in a loveless marriage. No matter what strategies we discussed, she couldn't let go of her anger at being stuck with a man she didn't like. This kept her on edge, and on the verge of snapping most of the time.

Sadie said that her husband often criticised her and her extended family was rude to her. She recognised that she felt resentful most of the time and couldn't see how to move past it. In Sadie's case, all we could do was support her to accept and transmute how she was feeling, as well as helping her to stay open to the possibility that things could change eventually.

Have you ever been in a similar situation? If so, take heart because the tide can change. Your reality isn't some random movie; you're the screenwriter and hold the power to rewrite the script. Each feeling, thought, and action ripples out as your unique energetic frequency (SELF), attracting experiences that resonate with it. So, when resentment, frustration, or insecurity fill your days, you can expect similar echoes in your reality. Conversely, if you're predominantly BEING peaceful and calm, life will reflect that back to you. Your external environment serves as the most accurate gauge of how you're vibing.

Remember, the goal is to release the ego-self's need to defend, and then pivot inwards more often to vibrate as the True Self. Even when this seems challenging, persist, because you WILL receive more appreciation from your environment. Knowing yourself as True Love NEVER hinges on the actions of other people; it always stems from your own source of Love. So enquire, explore, and discover this truth for yourself. The journey starts with a moment of Awareness, and the destination is a life bathed in the radiant glow of true Being.

Now, let's journey with Arti. Her story serves as a strong confirmation of the principles we have discussed, a living example of how embracing the True Self can transform reality.

Arti's life hadn't always been peaceful but she was committed to waking up regardless of her circumstances. She recognised the importance of dedicating time every day to experiencing her own True Love and engaging in activities that expanded her. She also understood how to use her imagination to experience Joy even if she wasn't feeling it from the people around her.

As a result of her consistent efforts, Arti began to vibrate at a more expansive frequency, and life reflected that back at her. People became friendlier and more helpful. Her business flourished, and she found herself with more orders than she could handle. Most importantly, her relationship with her husband improved. As Arti relinquished her attempts to control the situation and embraced her own inner Love, a sense of tranquillity permeated their connection.

In exploring such transformative journeys, dear reader, it becomes evident that embodying Self-Love can manifest profound changes. While turning inwards to know yourself as the True Self isn't the only way, any experience that expands your inner world, be it creative expression, mindful movement, or exploring your passions, can expand who you're BEING and draw to you better-feeling experiences.

However, this inner expansion doesn't require spirituality or "niceness"; it operates on neutral energetic principles. For many people, ambition, confidence, and determination is the dominant force fuelling their buzzing expansion, creating thrilling opportunities and resources. Ultimately, the process of Conscious Manifestation accommodates anyone willing to align their thoughts and actions with their desired reality, whether through True Love, ambition, or any other potent (not necessarily ethical) driver.

So, are you ready to map your own route on this expansive journey? Buckle up and let's unlock the secrets to accelerating your flow towards a life you truly adore.

Three Stages Of Manifestation: Where Are You?

The more Noah and I have committed to living beyond the bullshit and "dying" the mind, the more open we've become to receiving. Being able to recognise ourselves as the True Vast Eternal Nothing (i.e., the True Self) has allowed us to experience inherently that life is full of infinite possibilities. The more we expand, the more we draw to us a life that we adore.

However, to get to this point, we've had to pass through three distinct stages of creation. These stages provide insight into the direct correlation between knowing yourself as True Self-Love (i.e., living with more inner expansion) and Conscious Manifestation. They offer guidance for those seeking a more fulfilling and empowered reality. Let's discuss each stage now.

1. Negative Unconscious Default Manifestation

At this stage, most people are oblivious to the power of their thoughts and emotions. In fact, they have very little self-awareness at all. It's for this reason that we call you a Random Unconscious Manifester (RUM). You remain identified with the ego-self, unclear about your intentions, and easily influenced by your habitual, negative thinking patterns and your external world. The RUM is SURE that any bullshit thought or feeling that pops into their mind must be true.

If you resonate with this stage, you'll recognise that you often focus on lack, worrying about what you don't have, and struggling with how you perceive many areas of your life. You often feel contracted about your reality and find it hard to receive. You may find yourself stuck in unsatisfying relationships, facing financial challenges, or often defending your righteous indignation. When people ask you how you are, you say "fine", which really means: *"I have nothing much to celebrate but thanks for asking."*

If you continue along this route, not much is going to transform in your life. Your default vibration will stay the same and you'll get more of what you've always had.

We know, however, that this isn't what you really want. To break free from the cycle, it's time to step into the mindset of positive transformation. Instead of wrestling with your inner critic, choose to invest your attention in a different direction. Start by noticing your internal dialogue. Is it dominated by pessimism? Can you shift your focus towards kinder, more uplifting thoughts?

Imagine turning your gaze towards a sunlit inner garden, where seeds of Joy begin to sprout. As you practise this shift, you'll feel your worries dim, your vibration speed up, and positive momentum build around you. Read on to discover how the manifestation journey unfolds.

2. Awakening To More Focussed Manifestation

This is the second stage of manifestation. If you're a Purposeful Awakening Manifester (PAM), you're starting to wake up and realise that the only person who's manifesting your life is "you". This is happening via your thoughts and emotions, and more importantly, how you FEEL about your life. While you may not fully recognise yourself as the abundant True Self yet, you grasp the significance of allowing people and circumstances to come and go, and that your general vibration (or how you feel most of the time) shapes your overall experience of life.

As a PAM, you've unlocked the secret: you're taking more responsibility for who you're BEING. You're doing your best to observe any negative mind chatter from a distance, choosing instead to dance with more uplifting thoughts and vibrant emotions. This conscious shift isn't about ignoring the mind's bullshit – it's about stepping into your inner power and aligning yourself with the flow of life.

Think back to that radio. When you focus on what's wrong with your world, you're stuck on a scratchy station, filled with static and conflict. But by choosing empowering vibrations, you turn the dial towards more abundance. Suddenly, the airwaves crackle with the laughter of kindred spirits, the hint of exciting opportunities, and the promise of uplifting experiences.

You're on the right path, PAM, but the adventure doesn't end here. There's an entire orchestra of abundance waiting to be heard. So, keep exploring, keep honing your focus, and keep radiating your empowered being outwards. Remember, the more you dance with Joy, the more the Universe joins the rhythm, painting your life with true magic and fulfilment.

3. Embracing Conscious Manifestation

The Conscious Awakening Manifester (CAM) is what you are when you find yourself at the third and transformative stage of manifestation. At this point, you're able to recognise the True Self and are revelling in living a more inward-focussed life. You make it a daily practice to know yourself as Love and Joy.

As a CAM, you realise that the more you live as the True Self, the more your vibration expands automatically. At the same time, you find yourself clinging less to material desires and releasing any attachment to them.

Because you're experiencing yourself as an expansive being, you're starting to understand that you can "manually" tap into the power of the mind to manifest what you desire. To get the best results, you focus on asking *"Who Am I?"* and knowing that you ARE the True Vast Eternal Nothing. This realisation reminds you that every reality already exists in the realms of energy. Therefore, to get what you desire, all you have to do is align with it energetically by FEELING like the person who's already received it.

Throughout your process, you maintain a relaxed and trusting outlook, regardless of the circumstances in your 3D world. Because you KNOW that you are the Universe, you have faith that this Universe will deliver your desires at the most opportune moment. In the meantime, however, you embrace the NOW, doing more of what you enjoy and vibing as Stillness, Silence, Peace, Love and Joy as much as you can. You KNOW in every cell of your body that what you desire IS on its way, and you're happy to sit back and enjoy the waiting with positive expectation.

In summary, therefore, this transformative inner revolution from RUM to CAM involves the following steps:

1. **Quiet the chatter.** Become aware of your bullshit narratives and gently shift your attention to the Love within.
2. **Embrace the *"Who Am I?"* question.** Turn inwards and repeatedly ask yourself *"Who Am I?"*. As you do, observe that opening sensation (tingling, or heat, etc) in the body, guiding you towards your infinite being.

3. **Lighten up within.** Support your inner expansion by engaging in activities that uplift you, like spending time in nature, or doing energy work. And,
4. **Start from a place of abundance.** As you consistently live from a space of inner expansion, your vibration naturally attracts experiences that align with your desired reality.

Remember, you ARE capable of moving through these stages and experiencing the blissful manifestation of your desires. Embrace the journey, expand your Awareness, and connect with the power of the True Vast Eternal Nothing from which everything in life flows.

Noah's journey serves as an example of this transformation. Through a humbling encounter with a wise man in India, he learned to trust that life always has his back and that abundance starts as a state of being. We now share this wisdom with you.

Noah's Story: Awakening To The Riches Within

In the wake of receiving a second cancer diagnosis in the prostate, I sought solace at another ashram in India, buying myself some much-needed time to regroup and heal. It was here that I crossed paths with a local street "guru". This man, residing under a tree, not far from Osho's ashram, caught my eye with his constant smile. All his possessions (a brush, cup, plate, and neatly rolled-up blanket) were visible for all to see, evidence of his minimalist lifestyle.

One morning, I approached him, chai in hand, and struck up a conversation. My curiosity was piqued. I wanted to learn more about his life and how he'd come to live in a shack beneath that tree. He smiled and shared his story. *"I'm a devoted follower of Osho's teachings,"* he said, placing his hands gently on his heart and offering a nod of acknowledgment. *"In life, I possess all the riches one could ever hope for."*

As I looked at him, he pointed to a crippled beggar on crutches. *"You see,"* he continued, *"I'm rich in so many ways. I'm blessed with good health, capable hands, and legs that allow me to walk the world. I'm content and know who I truly am."* With that, he handed the chai that I'd given him to the beggar.

His words struck a chord deep within me. For the first time in my life, I truly felt the immense wealth that resided within me. Not only had I been given a second and third chance at life, but I also had enough money in my pocket to buy a chai or two. I could even afford to live in a "proper" home. Gratitude swelled within me as I reflected on the wisdom offered by this inspiring man.

I'd spent far too long bemoaning my financial situation, worrying about my investment-and-crypto losses, and constantly FEELING like a man who was afraid that his money might soon run out. Little did I realise that I'd been trapping myself in a self-induced trance of perpetual stress and perceived poverty.

However, standing there next to this beaming human, a significant realisation hit me. The feeling of poverty was a product of the mind, a phantom idea bearing no correlation to the contents of my wallet. Here was a man who radiated a vitality of being that no amount of money could buy. His boundless smile and generous approach to life was an electrifying revelation.

"I AM RICH," were the words that echoed within me. *"I am rich by the virtue of being alive. I am rich because life-force energy is coursing through my veins. I am rich because I am aware of the True Self, the Conscious Awareness that I AM. I am rich because I am Love. I am rich in gratitude for it all."*

From that moment, I stopped telling myself that I was "working on myself". I recognised that most spiritual seekers often fooled themselves into believing they were evolving when, in reality, they remained trapped in their (usually negative) internal bullshit. The only work I needed to do was to recognise myself as the True Self more often. I knew that by tapping into this rich vein of abundance, I had finally started to shift beyond my feelings of lack.

It was time to breathe deeply and open myself up to receive more of life's hidden treasures. I realised that receiving and giving were the same thing. I wanted to give myself everything, to savour every experience that life had to offer. Over the years, I'd succumbed to just existing, suppressing my authentic voice, and becoming a shell of a man who'd compromised his needs and allowed himself to be manipulated. I'd spent far too long feeling victimised.

What a sack of bullshit I'd been buying into! I was entitled to receive as much as anyone else. And what's more, I no longer needed to prove my worth. All I had to do was stop the relentless self-criticism and allow myself to embrace my own Joy. By doing this, I knew that everything else in life would flow.

I stood amid the humble richness of my surroundings, gazing into the eyes of my new friend. There was no need for more words. We basked in the Stillness and Joy that enveloped us. In that timeless moment, I understood that true wealth was the recognition that I could live happily without most of the material things that I had in my life. It was all just external "stuff" that I desired yesterday and would tire of tomorrow.

With a heart full of gratitude, I stepped back into the world, carrying the wisdom of my years with me. I was no longer Noah, the man haunted by the fear of financial loss or failure. I had become Noah, the embodiment of gratitude, Love and Joy, choosing to live as an example of the abundance I'd experienced. In that moment, I knew I'd taken a significant step, discarding a big chunk of the limiting story of "poor me". I was finally ready to give life another chance and live in the inherent wealth of being. Now it's your turn.

Are You Ready To Receive?

Reflect on this for a moment: *"Am I truly open to receiving what I desire or am I just going through the motions?"*

Genuine openness unlocks an inner spaciousness that is reflected in your vibration and 3D world. If this resonates, you might be a PAM as CAM. Unlike the RUMs, who stay entangled in negativity, you're likely to find excitement and enthusiasm in life, regardless of what's going on in your current circumstances.

Your trust in the Universe runs deep, knowing that you're interconnected and supported. This leads to more patience and a deep understanding that your desires WILL arrive at some point. As a result, you refuse to settle – that's like telling the Universe you'll accept "crumbs" instead of the feast that you're waiting for.

As you connect with the limitless "Self", possibilities light up within you. This Awareness ignites an inner smile and strengthens your resolve to declare all of your desires, knowing that they are truly, already, yours.

On the other hand, those struggling with receiving might get fixated on their grievances. This focus often leads to accepting less than they want, like a job that pays too little, or a lover who offers inadequate attention. These people vibrate in a state of lack, perpetuating their seemingly, never-ending cycle of scarcity.

So, where do you stand? Are you a RUM, trudging through life, defending your limiting beliefs? Or a PAM, taking responsibility for manifesting and receiving? Or perhaps a CAM, primarily focused on experiencing the inherent Peace and Joy within, while surrendering to the Great Unknown?

In other words, have you consciously started to shift your Awareness, KNOWING that by becoming more spacious inside, you WILL naturally receive more of what you desire? Or are you still feeling mostly doubtful and convinced that nothing good will ever happen to you again?

If you relate more to the latter, it's time to step back and acknowledge that how you're feeling, and more importantly vibing, is shaping the course of your life.

Wake-up Call: Expanding From Doubt To Delight

Let's go deeper. Imagine the scenario where you crave a more-loving partner, but feel tense whenever the thought arises. Recognise that this discomfort is your sign – it's telling you that you're vibrating with contraction around the idea of finding fulfilling love.

So, what should you do? Acknowledge it. Then, consciously shift your focus inwards and tune into the spaciousness within. This expansive feeling of Vastness is synonymous with the Joy of receiving and being deeply loved. Next, jump into that feeling and "wear" it like a warm cloak, replacing tension with expansion. This shift is the basis for manifesting not only love but all of your heartfelt desires.

If, for example, you find yourself worrying about how money will arrive, immediately interrupt the pattern. Do this by shifting your attention to self-empowerment instead. Clap your hands, breathe through the heart, and say to yourself: "*No. I'm NOT going there. I refuse to entertain these thoughts. I KNOW that I AM the True Vast Eternal Nothing from which all of life flows. I KNOW that everything's working out for me, always has and always will. I KNOW that abundance really is mine.*"

Next, push yourself to transmute any lingering emotions relating to lack. Once you have imagined yourself sitting in the middle of the emotional discomfort, and feel lighter, focus on repeating the *"Who Am I?"* self-enquiry process and Q&A. This will expand your vibration and get you in tune with the sensation of receiving.

Take each day as it comes, staying alert to your inner state. And if you wobble, don't fret; it happens to all of us. Ultimately, if you're committed to manifesting what you desire, your main job is to notice when you're feeling contracted around it (or in the fear of not getting it), and consciously shift your attention to focus on the expansion that comes from the Joy of receiving it. Remind yourself often that you ARE the True Vast Eternal Nothing and that you can vibe as ANYTHING you choose.

If doubt creeps in, whisper: *"Fear is just a sensation in the body, it's not reality. I choose trust and Joy. I remind myself again that everything IS working out for me, always has and always will. I therefore release the need to control and embrace the expansiveness of the True Self instead."*

If you still feel uneasy after that, challenge the ego-self by affirming: *"I KNOW that good things can and do happen to me. If they happen to other people, they can absolutely happen to me. It doesn't matter how old I am, how much money I have, or what I look like."* Repeat this with feeling and make it a mantra for life – the magic will soon start to unfold.

"Knowing You Can Have It" Defined

When you really KNOW that you can have what you desire, it's much easier to focus on your target, rejecting any notion that suggests otherwise. This means concentrating on your prep work, not fears. Just as you wouldn't entertain thoughts of failing an exam, while diligently studying, so too you must refuse to engage in any doubts when consciously manifesting. Ultimately, you must have "zero headspace for failure" – that is your prep work.

Another way to look at it is that you trust wholeheartedly that your desires are on their way. It's like embodying the confidence of having your dream job before the interview, while still mastering the necessary skills to secure it. Remember, doubt vibrates lack, while trust vibrates abundance.

To boost the feeling of having already achieved it, recall a situation when you received a gift you adored, the thrill of an unexpected bonus, or better-than-expected exam results. Hold onto that feeling of Joy, and fill up on it NOW, replacing fear with excitement. Challenge yourself to stay in this expansive state for as long as possible.

Doing this feels great, so keep going. However, if progress feels slow, it's time to ask yourself:

1. *"Am I truly grateful for what I have right now?"*
2. *"Do I trust the Universe to unfold my desires perfectly?"* Or,
3. *"Do I just spend most of my time dwelling on what's missing?"*

Be really honest with yourself. If you want to open yourself fully to receiving the best life has to offer, you have to expect it in every cell of the body. You cannot entertain thoughts of delays, hardships, crooked politics, poverty, suffering, war, etc. Worry manifests lack, Joy manifests abundance. So, scan the body to see where your focus is. It won't lie. If you're tense in any area, this means you're worrying, or complaining – so change it. It's time to relax into life instead!

The True Self Never Complains

One of the key points to remember when it comes to manifesting a bigger home, deeper love, or more financial freedom, etc, is to ditch the grumbling, even the silent whispers. Abundance and complaining simply don't vibe together.

Remember, the True Self doesn't complain. Why would it, when it knows it's the Universe, the True Vast Eternal Nothing from which everything flows? All possibilities already exist there. Your job is to draw them to you via your vibration (or who you're BEING).

Patience is vital. Let's say you declare to the Universe (i.e., Conscious Awareness) that you desire something in particular, say a new job. Most people fail to understand that certain pieces of the puzzle always need to fall into place before you can get what you want. These pieces might not always seem "positive" to the ego-self – for example, being forced out of your current job or relationship. Try to embrace the bigger plan, even if it means your jobless for a moment. The more gracefully you can surrender, the smoother everything unfolds.

A good example of this "pieces of the puzzle" process was my experience of going through the Covid lockdown alone in India. Despite feeling raw, stuck, and miserable at times, I knew that this was a pivotal moment in my journey. Those pieces needed to drop into place so that future pieces could align later on. I had a choice – I could either accept it, transmute my fears and go with the flow, or I could resist and suffer.

To help myself, I reminded myself often that there are no "good" or "bad" pieces in Consciousness. I pushed myself to shift my angst through somatic release and emotional transmutation, and anchored my attention on the *"Who Am I?"* self-enquiry process. It wasn't always easy, especially when anxiety overwhelmed me, but I knew that's what I had to do.

I allowed myself little headspace for thoughts of failure and reminded myself often that Noah and I would reunite soon. From past experience, I knew that if I were to put too much energy into the fear of a painful outcome, a happy reunion would have been unlikely.

If you need an example of what not to do, I once spent five intense weeks in tears, fearing that my then-lover would end our relationship when he got back from holiday. My mind-self was drowning in sadness and fear, fuelling that negative scenario. I wept as if it had already happened, vibrating as a woman who'd already been dumped. Intuition? No, that was FEAR. Intuition is calm and neutral (unless physical danger is involved).

Crying over potential pain rarely leads to happy endings. But expecting the best? Who knows what wonders will await! Here's the bottom line – complaining…

- Is the ego-self's negative pity party. It criticises you and others. It's self-doubt, worry, inadequacy – anything that clings to the bullshit story of "you".
- Traps you in the vibration of lack. Money won't grow if you focus on its absence.

- Blocks your awakening to the True Self, the source of infinite Love.
- Sabotages your love life – jealousy won't attract a new partner.
- Shrinks your abundance – even if you're just grumbling about the wealth of known criminals. And,
- Is the kiss of death for manifesting anything you want – but great at pulling in what you don't!

Instead, it will help you more if you can:

- Breathe through the heart and reconnect with the *"Who Am I?"* self-enquiry process.
- Remember, complaining is a mind-made habit.
- Recognise that as infinite Awareness, there's no vibrational wavelength for complaints. And,
- Realise that "You" are the True Vast Eternal Nothing that creates it all – everything you have and everything you haven't manifested yet.

So, how do you consciously draw your desires to you? That part is coming up next...

Wake-up Call: The Steps To Manifest Anything

1. **Thank life often.** Wake up in the morning with words of gratitude. Thank the Universe for the gift of life. Then, pivot inwards, and go through the *"Who Am I?"* process, moving deeper into Silence. Feel the answer to the question resonate within. Speak to your deepest KNOWING: *"I am the space that exists between, beyond, and around all words. I Am the True Vast Eternal Nothing from which all of life flows."* Say it slowly and experience yourself as the Vastness. Then, repeat: *"I am Stillness. I am Silence. I am Peace. I am Love and I am Joy."* As you recognise that opening sensation in the body, focus on experiencing yourself as each element, and feel the abundance of who YOU truly are!

2. **Know what you want.** Next, get clear on your intentions and concentrate on them. Don't focus on what you don't want. Remember, directing your attention towards your goals creates expansiveness, while dwelling on the undesired contracts you. Use the time as you wake up in the morning and just before you fall asleep to FEEL like someone who already has what they want. Affirm to yourself that you have zero headspace for thoughts of failure. Recall a past situation when you concentrated on what you desired, took decisive action, and successfully obtained it. Allow this energy to permeate your being. Remember, the mind doesn't distinguish between past and future experiences, so your energetic vibration is always in the present moment. When you vibrate at a fast, expansive frequency, you manifest experiences that align with it. And the same goes for when you vibrate slowly (and heavily). The bottom line is that you draw to you anything that matches the frequency of your vibration.
3. **Expand to align with what you desire.** If finding a new partner (or anything else) is your goal, recite the following power statement that I've used at various moments in my life. The last time was the most effective because I started from a place of deep knowing that I AM the True Vast Eternal Nothing. I KNEW that I was limitless and available to all possibilities. I KNEW that I could have it ALL.
4. **Repeat this power statement for a new lover.** Saying this will expand your vibration during the manifestation process – so learn it and repeat it often: *"I KNOW that the limitless power of my Conscious Awareness knows exactly how to bring me and my next awakened life-partner together. I KNOW that if millions of people can meet their ideal love-partner every day, then so can I. If good things can happen to them, they can absolutely happen to me. I'm not special in that regard. We all come from the same pool of Consciousness, and if they can do it, I can too. I KNOW that I have nothing to worry about. All I have to do is savour the delicious waiting for this lover to arrive and take inspired action when it pops into my mind. I KNOW that I'm so loved by*

this man. He's funny, emotionally available, conscious, committed, smart, sexy, successful, sweet, kind, loving, wise, calm, patient, and positive. He's so generous with his time, money, and body. He's a man with whom I have a deep spiritual, physical, mental, sexual, emotional, and money-making connection. We have so much fun together. We love doing life together. He loves and adores me too. He KNOWS that I'm the sexiest, kindest, smartest, most beautiful woman on the planet. I LOVE that I'm so happy, relaxed, confident, and obviously deeply loved by this man." Remember, you can change the words to any that resonate with you (shorter or longer). Just make sure you recite it at least twice a day for 5 minutes each time.

5. **Embrace the KNOWING.** As you repeat the statement, try to emphasise the words "KNOW" and "LOVE". Really feel the power of saying these words in contrast to the word "hope". Remember, when affirming your power statements, it's vital to KNOW (or feel) that you've already achieved what you want. To do this, you must eliminate hope as it implies doubt. Expand into the KNOWING and LOVE instead!
6. **Tweak the words to pull in something else.** Customise the wording of the statement to manifest anything you desire. For example, if you want more clients, reword it to start with something like this: *"I KNOW that the limitless power of my Conscious Awareness knows exactly how to bring me and my ideal clients together [and then change the rest of the words to align with what you want to manifest]."* Repeat the statement to yourself with as much excitement as you can. The key is to experience an expansive state while reciting it and to maintain that vibe for as long as possible each day. You can also record it and listen to it for 5-10 minutes morning and night. As you listen, imagine the seeds of your desires being sown in the field of infinite possibilities. If you "water" them properly, they MUST grow.
7. **How to water your seeds to make them bloom.** Nurturing your desires correctly involves: a) starting from a space of expansive receptivity, b) KNOWING that you can have them,

c) being excited about them, d) FEELING as if you've already received them, e) staying in the abundance of having them, knowing that they will materialise at the right time (so, no complaining about the wait or anything else), and f) being ready to take inspired action to manifest them. Continue reading the statement, listening to the recording, and expanding your vibration until your desires turn up in your reality.

8. **Move the body to release emotional energy.** If you find yourself vibing feelings of lack (i.e., sadness, anger, or fear), it's essential to clear any related emotional energy (as discussed in **Chapter 4** on Letting Go). Give yourself permission to express your emotions – whether it's through shouting, crying, or shaking off the negativity. As you vent, say to yourself: *"With every molecule of sadness, anger, or fear that I release, I KNOW that I'm creating energetic space to manifest X, Y, Z."* Work on three intentions until they materialise, then pick three more to focus on.
9. **Tune into the hum of the expansive SELF**. Close the eyes and turn inwards, seeking the pulse of your Specific Energetic Love Frequency (SELF). Imagine, or even feel, a warm light igniting within your core. As soon as you sense it, use each breath to amplify this light, letting it wash through every cell of your being. Linger in this space, sensing the tangible vibration of your expansive SELF. It has a resonance that is pure potential. Can you feel it? When you recognise this energy, focus on it – and remind yourself that this IS your unique energetic love frequency!
10. **Find the frequency of your desires.** Next, close your eyes and journey inwards, where each intention awaits. They are as individual as stars in the sky. Are they orbs of warmth, pulsing with energy? Do they gleam with colours, hinting at their essence? Perhaps they hum with textures, inviting your touch. Trust your intuition as you scan each with your Awareness. When you align with their unique signature, a spark might ignite, a rush of KNOWING sweeping through the body, or a

gentle click confirming your connection. Make a mental note of what each intention FEELS like.

11. **Bridge the gap between the SELF and your desires.** Now, dive back into your own source of Love, using the breath to fill every corner of your being. Hold this Vastness and savour it. Then, turn to your desires, and feel the contrast in frequencies. With each exhale, bathe them in the golden light of your SELF, igniting them with each tantric breath. Then inhale their unique vibration, weaving them deeper into your reality. Five times a day, repeat this Tantric dance, KNOWING that your desires are moving closer to your physical reality.

12. **Cut off doubt.** If you feel worried during the day and can't remove yourself to vent it out fully, spray your face with cool water, clap your hands, and repeat to yourself: *"NO! I'm not going there. I refuse to entertain these thoughts. I KNOW that everything's working out for me, always has and always will. I therefore release the need to control and embrace the expansiveness of the True Self instead."* Do this any time you start worrying about the timing of your manifestations appearing in your life.

13. **The obstacles to manifesting...** Fear of not getting what you desire, feeling tense about it, complaining about the lack of it, grumbling about your life in general, comparing yourself to others who've obtained it, and refusing to believe in its eventual arrival are the main blocks when it comes to manifestation. These behavioural patterns are ALL forms of lack. If you don't genuinely believe that you can manifest your desires, you won't. But you WILL receive the opposite, which will be in alignment with the vibration of lack that you're emitting.

14. **Use sexual-attraction energy to ignite your intentions.** To do this, begin by thinking about any person you once had a crush on. Be as explicit as you can. You want to evoke that flip-flop/butterflies feeling of attraction in your stomach. Once you've fully tapped into this electrifying feeling, imagine it surrounding your intentions. For instance, if Noah and I want to

manifest a free table at a restaurant, empty parking space, or available taxi, etc, we "send" this high-vibe energy to it. This practice is remarkably effective. FEEL your intentions bathed in this vibrant energy as often as you can, especially if doubt starts to creep in. Keep your attention focused on them until you sense that they're being magnetically pulled into your future reality. Hold this state of excitement for as long as possible, repeating the exercise morning and night (and in moments of doubt) until your desires appear in your 3D world. Then, set your sights on new adventures, fuelled by the power of your own vibrant energy.

15. **Calm your impatience.** Linear time is an illusion when it comes to your manifestation abilities. Universal timing governs the manifesting process, and the only way to influence it is to accelerate your alignment with the version of yourself that already has what you desire. You also have to be prepared to make decisions and act on them. When you take inspired action, you're actively participating in your process. You're showing a commitment to your desires and sending them energy to manifest! And,

16. **Do this to boost clients and business.** Remember, you manifest by who you're BEING. So, if you seek more clients, increased financial abundance, a new job, etc, you must expand into (i.e., FEEL like) the person who's already enjoying it. As well as repeating the previous power statement, do this: recall a time when you were busy with work (any work that you enjoyed). Really feel the sensation of being happy and earning money. Now, imagine extending this energy to envelop a group of potential new clients, employers, or opportunities (you don't need to know who they are, just see or sense them as a concentrated ball of vibrant energy). Continue this practice twice a day, knowing that as you do, you're drawing your dreams closer to you.

The Conscious Manifestation process is an exhilarating journey of creation, and it's essential to embrace it with a sense of excitement. However, there's a delicate balance between being unattached to the outcome, whilst also knowing that you WILL receive what you want.

If you ever get stuck, remind yourself that your power is not in knowing that you can draw to you more "stuff". It's in the recognition that you are ALREADY the limitless True Self – the True Vast Eternal Nothing from which all of life flows. FEEL yourself as this often. The more you repeat the "*Who Am I?*" process, and embody this graceful of BEING, the more you'll be able to relax into life, trusting that the Universe will inspire you take action and deliver what you desire in perfect timing.

Noah and I used to be good old RUMs. Then we transformed into PAMs. Now, we are CAMs.

Our daily manifestation mantra is: *"Who Am I? I am Stillness, Silence, Peace, Love and Joy. I know that I AM the True Vast Eternal Nothing. I KNOW that everything's working out for me, always has and always will. Even in moments of sadness, anger, and fear, I still KNOW that good things can happen to me. I'm grateful for all the good stuff and I'm grateful for all the challenges. I'm grateful for it all. The only true desire of my heart is to experience myself permanently as the expansive Love that I always AM. This is my devotion in life. I am blessed every day, in every way. And so it is done."*

Breathe through the heart and repeat the words slowly, allowing them to expand your vibration. By saying this mantra, you're teaching the mind to surrender, prompting it to pivot within automatically. This is a key part of your inner revolution!

Peaceful Living Is Simpler Than You Think

It's like nurturing a garden within. The key to living a lighter life lies in turning inwards and expanding outwards. But this concept is so basic that most people overlook it. They think transformation requires that they work on themselves endlessly. This just keeps them trapped in the drama. The good news is that you don't have to wait to manifest a better life – you can do it NOW.

As soon as you commit to waking up, transmuting your psychological pain, and recognising yourself as True Self-Love, life will begin to shift for the better.

Words can't fully capture the Bliss of knowing the True Self. Yet, as you've begun to realise, the simple practice of asking *"Who Am I?"* is a fast track to living and radiating True Love.

So, ask again, *"Who Am I?"*. When you feel that clear opening sensation in the body, say to yourself slowly: *"I am the space that exists between, beyond, and around all words. I am the Stillness (pause), Silence, Peace, Love and Joy that is at the heart of everything."* Become aware that you are the Awareness that's aware of it all. This is *IshQ*, the divine union of True Love and Consciousness.

Breathe deeply and repeat: *"I AM Stillness, Sivcflence, Peace, Love and Joy."* Feel each element in turn (see **Chapter 7** to explore connecting with each of them). Notice how these words, combined with focused heart-breathing, lead you beyond, beyond the narratives of "you". Observe how the flicker of True Self-Love starts to bubble up within as you repeat them. This subtle spark of Love is the essence of the True Self, and gradually unfolds as the ego-self's grip diminishes. By nurturing this spark, you cultivate deep and abiding inner Love, a foundation upon which to offer inspired and In-Lightened Love to others.

This is the essence of awakening. It's subtle, not a blinding flash. No pearly gates or pot of gold, just a profound Joy that transcends your wildest dreams. Most expect a big deal, meticulously dissecting each step of the way. This very expectation can hold you back. To know the In-Lightened True Self, you MUST know that "You" are never the thoughts obsessing over it.

This Awareness is your true nature. No matter what's going on in your external world, you can choose to focus within on the True Self. You don't have to engage in the daily dramas.

To deepen this truth, ask: *"Who is this 'I" who's holding onto the belief that I can't awaken while living my life?"*

This question shatters the self-hypnosis that says In-Lightenment requires escaping from your reality. You CAN awaken here and now. Because if not now, then when? So, wake up and start living as an In-Lightened being today. The next chapter reveals the secrets to embodying this reality and making it your own.

CHAPTER 10

LIVING AN IN-LIGHTENED LIFE

"I may not be perfect at living In-Lightenment and that's OK. I KNOW the moment I realise I'm not present, I become present. As I read this, I recognise that the mind is reading the words but something way vaster is aware of them. This is Conscious Awareness. I'm 'dying' the ego-self as best I can and living as Love as much as I can. I'm waking up and all is well."

Embark On A Unique Journey

When the Buddha unlocked the route to In-Lightenment 2,500 years ago, he dedicated his life to sharing its secrets. He never intended it to be reserved for monks and mystics; it's for everyone, including YOU. Whether it arrives like a thunderclap in your face or a whispered breeze, In-Lightenment is yours to claim, a hidden oasis that beckons you deep within.

Remember, the desire to awaken is the only innate desire you were born with. It's not contrived by the ego. In fact, it transcends the indoctrination of the ego-mind. It's a profound, primal call to know yourself, unmasked and unbound.

The simplest path to In-Lightenment, we've found, starts with that single question: *"Who Am I?"*. Ask it with genuine curiosity, and allow the answer to unfold inside you. When you sense that opening in the chest, a subtle shift in Awareness, you'll know you've arrived. That's IT! This sensation is the gateway to In-Lightened living. Hold it close, let it ignite the flickers of recognition, and follow its gentle pull. Once you've sensed it inherently once, you can start to build on it, expanding further into the ultimate Bliss of being.

Living more as the awakened "Self" is an expansive journey. Your priorities will naturally shift. Instead of acting out the script of the bullshit "self", seeking external validation, you'll choose to shift inwards, experiencing yourself as Stillness, Silence, Peace, Love and Joy (see **Chapter 7**). You'll no longer feel any pressure to be anything other than who you truly ARE.

Consequently, life will become more peaceful. You'll find it easier to accept that you still *"chop wood and carry water,"* as the Zen quote states, and that life carries on. However, the petty annoyances that once triggered you will now melt away like snowflakes in the sun. The most important thing is BEING *IshQ* as often as you can. You're at a juncture where you know 100% that you can NEVER lose this *IshQ*. It's always there for you! It's always "You".

When you reach this stage, you'll KNOW that you've crossed another tipping point. However, be gentle with yourself. You ARE waking up in stages, so don't give yourself a hard time if you stumble sometimes and dip your toes back into the bullshit.

To help yourself stay alert, repeat the following every day (both looking into a mirror and without it): *"Recognising the True Self IS simple, even if it sometimes feels challenging. If I ever feel blocked, I know it's just the mind resisting and succumbing to the old story of 'me'. I KNOW that I'm way vaster than the limitations I impose on myself and fight so hard to maintain. However, I'm no longer willing to define myself by them.*

"I may not be perfect at living In-Lightenment and that's OK. I KNOW the moment I realise I'm not present, I become present. As I read this, I recognise that the mind is reading the words but something way vaster is aware of them.

This is Conscious Awareness. I'm 'dying' the ego-self as best I can and living as Love as much as I can. I'm waking up and all is well."

Some people adamantly believe that experiencing In-Lightenment in stages is impossible. They insist that it can only happen in a single moment, with the complete eradication of the personality-self, much like Eckhart Tolle's inspiring experience.

While we agree that it does happen in an instant, it doesn't have to be an overnight transformation. Every moment you're aware that you're experiencing yourself as the True Self, this IS In-Lightenment. It's not *Satori* if you KNOW inherently how to recognise yourself repeatedly as the expansive "Self".

This is the truth, and it can be your truth as well, whether you're a busy parent, working professional, or taking a break to recharge at a humble meditation retreat or luxury resort. You don't need your 3D world to be a certain way in order to live a more In-Lightened life.

The key to experiencing lasting Self-Love is to make each day a personal retreat, no matter where you are, or what your life looks like. You do this by committing to breathing through the heart and focusing your attention inside to live beyond your limiting narratives. You ask yourself *"Who Am I?"* every day and experience the SLAP of awakening. Then you revel in expanding your Awareness of the Stillness, Silence, Peace, Love and Joy that "You" ARE.

When you make this your daily practice, life itself becomes a retreat. You begin to realise that "You" are the retreat – the Last Ashram and the only guru you'll ever need to sit with. Living within, and experiencing yourself as Love, IS the fastest route to awakening.

You don't have to "work on yourself", physically "turn" anywhere, or "do" anything radical. The only thing you need to do is train your attention away from the mind's obsession with the external world, and live as the Bliss within. In summary then:

When You Live More As The True Self...

- You're less interested in defending your opinions or behaviour (in other words, your "self"). You realise that doing so only separates you from other people.
- You're more present to life in general, and less lost in thoughts about the past or future. There's no projection of fear. You're much more aware of your environment and live with a lot more clarity. There's no belief that "what happened before is bound to happen again". There's only the realisation that you ARE the True Vast Eternal Nothing and, as such, your life is perfect just as it is (because you KNOW that you are the Universe, and that your ongoing life story is conceived in "You").
- You no longer have a Plan B. You're totally focused on the NOW (Plan A) until life prompts you to take a different, inspired action. There's only ever one "right" action, and that's the action that you take in the NOW! Everything else is just the mind doing its crazy, erratic dance.
- You naturally enjoy spending more of the day "stretching" your Awareness and getting high on the Love that emanates from the True Self. You revel in filling up on it and beaming it out to the world.
- You're committed to chipping away at the ego-self, KNOWING that Grace will one day step in and deliver you into permanent Bliss. In the meantime, you're embracing your triggers as they pop up. You KNOW that when you react, the mind and its bullshit version of "you" has taken control. So, you do your best to transmute and return to centre, keeping your vital Universal Life-Force Energy flowing. And,
- You find pleasure in breathing simply for the sake of breathing. You KNOW that mind mastery and conscious breathing are interconnected. The more you focus on the breath, the calmer the mind becomes, and the deeper the breath flows. It's an immediate way to experience yourself as *IshQ*.

Ultimately, when you're living more as the True Self, you KNOW that you're BEING (or vibrating as) a person who radiates True Love. This is the greatest spiritual prize there is. You can be sure that as you vibe Love into this world, you're going to receive it back. This is precisely what happened to Noah and I.

Sam & Noah's Story: We Choose Love

No matter what chaotic scripts have unfolded in our life, Noah and I are committed to experiencing ourselves as we infinitely ARE.

Day in, day out, we dedicate at least 51% of our time to BEING (or feeling like) the True Self and embodying True Self-Love. We're no longer consumed with how we're going to achieve our 3D goals. We just KNOW that we will at some point in life. In the meantime, our focus is on turning within, and evolving beyond the ego-self.

By breathing through the heart and asking *"Who Am I?"* every day for years, our Awareness of the "Self" has sharpened. We revel in being NOTHING – the True Vast Eternal Nothing, where limitations don't exist. We choose to live each day experiencing ourselves as Stillness, Silence, Peace, Love and Joy as often as we can.

There's an undeniable playfulness in being and radiating Love to the world. And it hasn't gone unnoticed. Our joint vibration has expanded, and we continue to draw to us amazing people and experiences.

For the most part, we have "officially" relinquished our addiction to the dramas of life. However, we live an intense existence and sometimes the ego-self creeps in, leading to arguments. They don't last long though.

If we do get annoyed with each other, we take it as a sign that there's still more bullshit to face and release. We understand that our "job" is to transmute our own reactions; blaming the other person for them is futile and just keeps us stuck. Here's what we do now if we have an argument:

1. We recognise that we've been triggered. This is the first step in the process of calming down the mind and nervous system.
2. We then focus on the breath and remind ourselves frequently that the True Self is way vaster than the ego-self that's trying to butt heads. We KNOW that we are the Awareness that can observe the small "self" having a tantrum while recognising that we are NOT it. This creates more inner space to return to loving compassion.
3. We continue to practise heart breathing until we're able to stop the mind-self making the argument mean anything about the other person, ourselves, or our relationship.
4. Once we're calmer (and we continue to breathe through the heart until we are), it becomes easier to see that we're defending our own self-righteous indignation (i.e., locked into the mind and its bullshit interpretation of what happened). We then start to transmute any lingering emotional reactivity.
5. We don't deny what's happened, but we also don't engage in the heated story either. We discuss what needs to be discussed and then move on in harmony together.
6. To gain more perspective, we step into each other's shoes and ask: *"How does he or she perceive my actions?"* This helps us to see our bullshit patterns more clearly. It also invokes more empathy, allowing us to relax and open emotionally. And,
7. By this stage, if we're still finding it challenging to connect gently, we remind ourselves that the foundation of our relationship is Self-Love – this Awareness brings us back to presence. Even if just one of us can drop back into that Love for a moment, we both KNOW that the determination to express ourselves as Love ALWAYS conquers any anger! In that knowing, we both soon soften to each other.

As you make this practice your own, you'll find yourself laughing at how the "self" behaves, even if your worst scenarios seem to be playing out. When you're at this stage, you'll KNOW inherently that the mind is starting to "die", and the True Self is rising like a lotus from the mud. This is all the invitation you'll need to continue diving into the depths of the True Self.

Consciously using your will to pivot inwards to live more as Love is empowering. It's not just another technique to pacify the mind – it actually takes you well beyond the mind. The process is effective for all and will resonate deeply within you. It doesn't matter if you're single, married, divorced, bereaved, a parent, or child-free. It works because it IS the truth.

Living as an In-Lightened being isn't a distant star you yearn for; it's a hidden garden you unlock through self-enquiry. It beckons with open arms, pushing you to take proactive steps, beginning with that fundamental question, *"Who Am I?"*. This inner dive marks an important step in your self-discovery, which WILL unfold even amid the chaos of your 3D reality.

You'll find that life guides you towards awakening, with each breath, each step, each interaction becoming a meditation, a dance of present-moment Awareness. As we've said, this journey is not about years of formal, eyes-shut practice on a mat; it's about embracing the very real invitation to "In-Lighten" wherever you are, right here, right now.

To Meditate Or Not?

The question of whether passive meditation is a prerequisite for waking up continues to spark debate. While traditional meditation holds undeniable value as a practice, in our experience, it isn't the sole gateway to realising and embodying the In-Lightened True Self. Recognition CAN flower without it.

However, should you choose to meditate (even for 5-10 minutes a day), it will help you to witness the unique nature of the mind – and how easily it can pull you away from inherent Peace. The more aware you become of your thoughts, the faster you'll recognise that you ARE the distinct Awareness that's observing those thoughts.

Noah's early practice involved closing his eyes, breathing deeply, and letting go of the bullshit, as well as dynamic release. In focusing on the breath, he quickly reconnected to the Vastness of the "Self". Meanwhile, my process was to scan the body until I felt waves of Awareness flood through me, expanding me into eternal Peace.

There are many ways to quieten the mind, and it doesn't have to follow a fixed format. You really can use any situation in life as an opportunity to meditate. Let the ego-self's messy response to situations remind you that the True "You" is NOT the noisy "you". The True "You" is the Awareness that observes the small "self" – silently. Embrace this truth NOW, and start to taste the liberation it brings.

Then ask, *"Who's reading these words?"* This question will spark a shift in your perspective, a sudden knowing within. You might feel a sense of detachment from your limbs, like an observer witnessing your own experience. Continue asking until you recognise the opening sensation in the body – that calm ocean of tranquillity that exists well beyond the mind.

We understand that the journey to Peace through "normal" meditation practices may appear straightforward in theory; however, in the real world, various obstacles can surface. This reality becomes clear through Chandra's story, serving as a good illustration of how traditional meditation, on its own, often falls short in guiding people on the journey to tranquillity.

Client Case: Chandra Unlocks True Meditation

Chandra, 38, came to us feeling frustrated. She'd spent at least 15 years listening to mediations on how to control her thoughts and feel better about herself. However, she still believed all the bullshit she told herself. She presented as a woman who was very identified with her self-debilitating narratives.

Some days, she would spend hours meditating, only to get up and find herself arguing with someone or start crying. While meditation was a pleasant pastime, it hadn't improved the quality of her life. She wasn't more peaceful, or better able to regulate her emotions.

In her desperation to find a solution to her inner turmoil, she decided to sign up for a silent meditation retreat. It was there that she discovered the following practice:

1. Instead of criticising herself, she learned to label it as "judgment" and let it go.
2. When she found herself crying over a lost lover, or any other situation, she recognised it as "attachment" and released it. And,
3. If she noticed herself engaging in mental arguments, she identified it as "repulsion" and instantly dropped it.

By consistently challenging herself to stay alert to her incessant narratives, she finally managed to step beyond her cycle of bullshit thinking. And herein lay the clue. As soon as she labelled her thoughts and dropped them, she started to experience more Peace.

Chandra was overjoyed with the results. She committed to her practice and floated through life more happily. She was convinced that she was cured of her misery. However, six weeks later, she thought she'd "lost" it. Her Peace seemed to have vanished and she was back in the clutches of her old negative thinking patterns. No matter how much meditation she did after that, she was unable to re-find her Zen.

Chandra asked us why this had happened. We gently responded: *"Even after the revelations of the retreat, the stories you tell yourself about 'Chandra' still have power over you. Those limiting beliefs, like a familiar coat, feel comfortable, even though they constrict you."*

Chandra's treatment plan centred around her recognising that true liberation comes from living with her eyes open, while training the mind to do nothing at the same time. Specifically, she learned how to recognise herself as the Awareness that could hear her critical inner "self" repeating a story, while knowing that it was still just a story (see **Chapter 5**). This ignited her Peace.

Of course, she's encountered challenges since then. The ego-self does resurface, bringing up negative bullshit patterns and conditioning. But Chandra now knows what to do. She turns inwards and focuses on her own Love instead, empowering herself to navigate these moments with grace and resilience.

Overall, Chandra's life has become calmer. She still meditates but her approach is different. Meditation is not something she just practises on her own for an hour a day. She's realised that life, with all its ordinary moments, IS the meditation, and spends as much time as she can being present to it. The smells on her morning walk, and the sound of the water running as she showers – she savours it all.

Wake-up Call: Becoming More Aware Of Awareness

As you've begun to experience, becoming aware of Awareness itself is a potent method to transcend the bullshit story of the "self". It becomes even more effective when you combine it with conscious breathing and the *"Who Am I?"* self-enquiry process.

To start this exercise, focus on heart breathing for a few minutes. Follow the breath in through the nose and out through the heart. As you do, zoom in on the pause just before you breathe out, allowing yourself to enter the limitless space that's presented to you. Lean into it and become more intimate with it. Notice that the mind quickly becomes calmer.

Now, with your eyes open and fixed straight ahead, imagine that your Awareness is stepping back from the body, or drifting towards the ceiling, observing "you". The more you practise, the easier it will become. However, in the beginning, take a moment to notice the following simultaneously:

- Where you are.
- What you're sitting on.
- What colour the walls are if you're indoors.
- Whether there are any other items in the room or the environment around you.
- What you're wearing. And,
- What your hands and feet are doing.

Breathe deeply, let your senses embrace the world, and watch your Awareness widen like the sky at night. You might even feel a sense of detachment from your physical form. If this sensation makes you uneasy, take another breath and allow yourself to relax into the experience. Tell yourself that you're OK. Then, stretch your Awareness and FEEL it touching the earth and sky. Recognise that it's everywhere and contained by "Nothing". Point out to the mind that the True-Self "You" has no physical form – it never has and never will.

Now, try to recognise that as you look at the world through your own eyes, you're essentially viewing it from Vastness itself. Pause here and breathe until you truly grasp that there's no distinct entity known as "you". All that exists is the True Vast Eternal Nothing. As you continue to observe, connect with the truth that within this Vastness, there's no inner voice or sounds at all.

Spend a few more minutes breathing as this Awareness and grow more comfortable with the eternal Nothing that you ARE. This IS the gateway to creating every reality you could ever conceive of.

Say to the mind: *"I AM NOTHING. The True Self 'Me' is NOTHING."* Feel these words resonate deeply within you, touching the timeless truth at the core of your being.

Next, while remaining aware that you are Awareness (keep sensing your Awareness behind you), ask *"Who Am I?"*. Feel the expansion in the chest or body, and repeat these words: *"I'm aware that I AM Stillness, Silence, Peace, Love and Joy. I'm the True Vast Eternal Nothing. I don't start and I don't end. It may seem like this Vastness resides in my body but, actually, this body is a part of that never-ending Vastness."*

Observe the sensations in the body as you repeat this. You should be experiencing tangible expansion. If not, continue saying: *"Who Am I? I AM NOTHING"* until the mind-self actively recognises that the Vastness just became that bit vaster.

Now, get up and walk around whilst observing everything around you. Stay aware that your Awareness has stepped back from the body. Ask the question again, *"Who Am I?"*, snap the fingers, and say: *"I AM Stillness, Silence, Peace, Love and Joy. Even as I'm walking, I'm aware that Awareness is all around me, observing me silently! I am NOTHING."*

How are you feeling as you repeat this? Recognise that you're aware that "You" are everywhere. Repeat the process and acknowledge the spaciousness in the body again. Then point out to the mind that this is the True "You". As you stretch your Awareness, relax into the grounded Stillness that you ARE. There's Silence too, and a deep Peace that has nothing to do with controlling your thoughts or 3D environment. This is the Peace of BEING "You".

Take a minute to affirm this to the mind (doing so repeatedly really does help it to surrender and step back). Then, once again, acknowledge that you're experiencing yourself as the Awareness that's aware of the present moment and the four existential elements of the "Self". Breathe through the heart and FEEL the expansion within. This is *IshQ,* and the more you recognise it, the deeper the Great Unknown will reveal itself to you.

Now, sit down and close your eyes. Initially, take a few minutes to enjoy the intimacy of your breath. Then, still keeping your eyes shut, become aware of everything around you simultaneously. Notice that your Awareness of the True Self just deepened.

Allow the waves of Conscious Awareness to wash over you, then pick a moment and open your eyes. As you do, you'll observe that Awareness slips into the background BUT you're still aware of it.

It's STILL there. Point this out to the mind as you switch between experiencing the True Self with eyes open and eyes shut.

Say to the mind: *"Even though my Awareness of the True Self may be sharper when my eyes are shut, I'm still aware of Awareness when I open them. This Awareness never goes away. Even if it shifts into the background, I can still recognise myself as the Awareness that's aware that I'm reading these words, and that I am Stillness, Silence, Peace, Love and Joy as well. This is IshQ."*

As you repeat this mantra with your eyes open, notice how the mind and its noise melts into Conscious Awareness. Remember, the mind is not separate from the Stillness, but is an integral part of it. Only through Awareness can the distinction between the ego-mind and the observer be recognised. Realise the truth of this!

Continue alternating between repeating the *"Who Am I?"* with eyes open and then shut. Keep observing yourself as Awareness. BE the expansion. This IS the source of your power to manifest everything that you desire in life.

The next step in expanding your Awareness is to text while staying aware of what you're doing. The aim is to practise being the Awareness that's observing the small "self" writing.

Before you begin, take another moment to anchor yourself firmly back in the NOW. Close the eyes and take a few deep breaths, focusing on the rise and fall of the chest, and the sensations of the breath entering the nostrils. As you exhale, consciously direct the breath towards the heart, allowing it to expand and soften.

When you feel grounded in Awareness, start writing. As you type, maintain your connection to the silent observer that sits behind your thoughts and feelings. Notice the sensations in your fingers as you message, and the rhythm of your breathing. If you find your attention drifting towards the mind's bullshit, use the breath to guide it back within the body.

Keep breathing in through the nose and out through the heart, allowing the words to flow effortlessly. The goal is not to overthink or overanalyse; instead, trust your inner wisdom and let the text emerge naturally. As you continue to write, consciously expand your Awareness by taking in all your surroundings. This might be initially challenging, but with consistent practice, it will become easier.

This immersive experience holds transformative potential, offering a glimpse into how heightened Awareness can shape your thoughts and actions. Aim to repeat this practice at least once a day, gradually extending it into your everyday life. As you cultivate your Awareness, notice how your life expands with newfound clarity.

Take a moment to acknowledge the profound sense of Stillness and expansion you've experienced doing this exercise. Now, ask yourself one more question: *"Is there anyone inside this body known as 'me'?"* Keep asking until you're very clear that there isn't!

Do You Need A Daily Routine To Wake Up?

In the realms of Consciousness, there are no universal to-do lists to assist you in awakening. However, following a daily practice can support you to live more as the In-Lightened True Self. It's important to recognise, though, that practices, while valuable, are just tools. There's no point doing them if you just fall back into the bullshit as soon as you've finished them.

To truly In-Lighten, you must commit to being the change. We can't say this enough. You have to embody the person who IS waking up and vibrating at a faster frequency. You must BE the person who is dedicated to chipping away at the ego-self, knowing that one day Grace WILL step in, and the bullshit mind will "die" for good.

If you want to BE the person who lives more as the In-Lightened True Self revelling in *IshQ*, you MUST BE the person who's willing to change focus and live deeply within. You must choose to experience yourself repeatedly as Stillness, Silence, Peace, Love and Joy.

No one can do it for you. No one else can experience the Bliss of being uniquely "You".

To help you to establish a solid foundation, we've compiled a daily practice that you can devote as much time to as you desire. Remember, there are no rules. Embracing this practice will instil discipline, which is essential in training the mind to recognise that it's NOT the boss of "You". This daily ritual is also a good introduction to the 28-day *IshQ* Challenge that follows in the next chapter.

Your Basic In-Lightenment Blueprint

1. Give yourself a SLAP. Make the *"Who Am I?"* self-enquiry process your daily, eyes-open meditation. Repeat it as soon as you wake up and when you go to bed at night. You can also repeat it during the day, whether you're in the shower or preparing breakfast. The more you dive into the practice, the quicker the mind will learn to step back automatically.

Focus on heart breathing, ask yourself, *"Who Am I?"*, snap the fingers, and repeat the process until you sense that Vastness in the chest or body. Once you recognise the space, repeat: *"I am Stillness, Silence, Peace, Love and Joy."* Say each word slowly and FEEL it. As you talk to the spaciousness, your experience of *IshQ* will deepen.

Ask the question again, feel your heart, and as you receive that opening sensation, observe your Awareness expanding. Then ask: *"Can anyone give this Awareness to me? [Reply to yourself] NO. Can anyone take it from me? NO. Can I lose it? NO. Can I find it? NO. Does it start and does it end? NO. Was it there before I was born? YES. Is it a memory? NO. Is it happening in the NOW? YES. It's who I AM right NOW."*

Continue with: *"So, if no one can give it to me and no one can take it from me, this must mean that it comes from me. It IS me. It also means that I don't need anyone external to me to feel the True Love that I AM. I KNOW that no one else can ever give me the Love that fulfils me beyond all else. The only way I can get it is to recognise that I AM it."*

Remain present to the words and allow them to guide you deeper. Then say: *"You see, mind, no one can give me Stillness, Silence, Peace, Love and Joy, and no one can take them from me either. They are the inherent elements of the True Self. I am the source of these elements, and as I embody them, I radiate them outwards. They are not dependent on my external circumstances or the approval of others. They are my natural state of BEING."*

Become the words. Observe that they're pointing you to the delicious space that exists between, beyond, and around all words. This is the start of your SLAP. Recognise that as you SLAP yourself awake, you expand more into who you truly ARE. You're finally letting go of your indoctrinated bullshit and reclaiming your birth right of being the brilliant, radiant, and eternal "YOU"!

2. Journaling. Next, it's time to embark on an exercise that will take you beyond the bullshit, into the expansiveness of BEING. Grab a pen and paper, and let's go.

Use this prompt: *"Now that I'm starting to wake up and live more as the In-Lightened True Self, how do I show up differently?"*

Unlike other prompts that pacify the mind, repeating this one aloud, and writing down the answers that you sense in the body, is going to take you well beyond the mind. Write the prompt at the top of the page, read it aloud, and jot down the first answer that arises within you. Then voice the question again and note the next answer. Keep asking and keep writing. It doesn't matter if you get the same words. All you're aiming for is to recognise the expansion that occurs as you do this exercise.

Here's an example of what this journaling assignment could look like for you.

"Now that I'm starting to wake up and live more as the In-Lightened True Self, how do I show up differently?"

- I KNOW that I'm free.
- I turn inwards and experience myself as True Self-Love more often.
- I now rely on the True Self to fill up on Love and not on anyone external to me.
- I LOVE being the Awareness that recognises that I AM Stillness, Silence, Peace, Love and Joy all at once.
- I'm bold, courageous, and strong.
- I'm a lot less worried about my 3D world. In fact, I don't worry about it at all.
- I can't truly describe what *IshQ* feels like, but it's delicious.
- I show up as Love and Joy way more than the old bullshit story of "me".
- I'm not actually interested in the bullshit story of "me".
- I'm sick of defending my right to suffer. And,
- I KNOW that everything's working out for me, always has and always will.

Keep going until you've filled at least one page of your notebook. And don't worry, you can't get it wrong. Just make sure you repeat the prompt each time and FEEL the answers in the body – don't do this just with the mind. If you focus on answering with the body, you'll find that your Awareness expands quickly.

The more you do this exercise in "Mindlessness", the faster the mind will learn that it's NOT the boss of "You". It will then naturally start to step back. Trust the process; you might be amazed at how expansive and empowered you feel after practising this.

3. Receiving. Even though repeating the *"Who Am I?"* self-enquiry process, and recognising yourself as the True Self, will expand your vibrational frequency (SELF) naturally, we recommend that you nurture your ability to receive on a daily basis.

To start, tune into yourself, and ask: *"How open am I to receiving?"* Score it on a scale from 0 to 100, and note the result. Then ask yourself, *"In my life in general, Am I BEING expansion or am I BEING contraction?"* If it's the former, that's great! Continue with the *"Who Am I?"* self-enquiry and Q&A, and recognise yourself as the expansive True Self. But if it's the latter, you're unlikely to be feeling very receptive. You need to transmute your unease first.

See yourself stepping into the middle of your troubling emotions, flying through them, or diving into a pool full of them. You don't need to know why you're feeling contracted; instead, face it and acknowledge it. Allow yourself to experience your raw emotions without buying into them or wanting to change them.

Reconnect with the question, *"How open am I to receiving?"* Notice if your initial score has shifted. A climb? Wonderful! Continue with the *"Who Am I?"* exploration. But if the score remains stagnant or dips, it hints at resistance around receiving.

Trace its source. Recall moments of receiving – love, abundance, whatever resonates – and any accompanying awkwardness. Unpack that discomfort. What unease bubbles up? Focus on transmuting it, dismantling its grip until you envision yourself effortlessly embracing all you desire, free from emotional turbulence (or with significantly less resistance). Do NOT allow the ego-self to entertain any bullshit story that justifies a contracted inner state.

Catch yourself when the tension intensifies and your being shrinks against the day's demands. This contraction, this resistance, is the very seed of lack. Don't let it sprout, don't water it with wallowing thoughts. Instead, pivot inwards. Ask, *"Who is this 'I' who's fixated on this feeling of lack?"*

Feel the question dissolve the illusion of a separate, suffering "self". Your circumstances may point to limitations, but the ego-mind amplifies them. So ask again, and again, until the horizon widens, revealing the limitless expansion and gratitude within.

As you experience yourself as *IshQ* more often, you'll no longer feel separate from life. You'll become more present and your vibration will expand automatically. You'll start to see the world as it truly is – full of abundance and unlimited possibility.

4. Gratitude. Life, in all its rawness, is a mixture of blessings and bumps. Unlock the secret to inner alchemy, and even the roughest edges get polished into beautiful stones. That secret is gratitude. Not just a polite nod to sunshine and roses, but a gentle *"Yes"* and a heartfelt *"Thank you"* to everything – the laughter and tears, the triumphs and stumbles, the whispers of Joy and the roars of fear. For within each experience, even the seemingly bleak, there is a hidden opportunity for transformation. Nourish it with gratitude, and watch your existence expand into something beautiful.

Begin this practice by challenging yourself to feel grateful for your most difficult life experience. It might seem like scaling Everest in stilettos, but push through. However tough life has been, recognise that this ordeal has taught you something about you. Did it ignite a fire of determination or deepen your appreciation for life's fragility? Or did it, perhaps, spark cynicism and mistrust? This exercise is not about erasing your scars. It's about releasing the chains of emotional pain that bind you to them. Believe it, dear reader, you do hold the power to let them go.

Every *"Thank you"*, no matter how tiny, chips away at the bullshit story that you tell yourself about who "you" are. In fact, repeating *"Thank you for my life, exactly as it is,"* might be the closest thing you get to "True Prayer".

True Prayer isn't just about begging for fancy toys like bitcoins, dream jobs, or the perfect beach body. It's about declaring your radical trust in the Universe (or whatever you want to call it) and finding gratitude for everything, even the messy, uncomfortable parts. Because hey, even the bullshit serves a purpose, right? It pushes you, stretches you, and ultimately helps you to wake up to the True Self. So, thank the bullshit for being your ultimate teacher in disguise.

Try saying this affirmation to yourself every morning and see how expansive you feel: *"Thank you, Universe, for every experience that has graced my life [list them if you want to]. Although some of them have brought me to my knees, I honour the wisdom they have given me. I now choose to release my attachment to all lingering, painful emotions, and trust that everything's working out for me. It always has and always will. I KNOW that the Universe KNOWS exactly what I desire and is doing everything necessary to bring it to me."*

When you can meet life with an open heart, thanking it for every twist and turn, a magical transformation occurs. But, please, don't take our word for it – go within, take that leap, and experience it for yourself. You'll be so glad that you did.

Remember, gratitude isn't a one-time revelation; it's a daily practice, a gentle reshaping of your perspective. Embrace it, and watch your life unfold into a masterpiece of resilience, Joy, and boundless Love.

Dealing With Death

Ah, death... We all have to face it at some point in life. It's the one non-negotiable aspect of existence, following birth, and yet so many people seem to fear it. Both Noah and I have gazed into the harsh eyes of death.

Noah was forced to stare at it while navigating the challenges of advanced cancer. To survive, he had to confront his fear, transmute it, and pivot within to live beyond it.

As for me, my encounter with death began early in life. At the age of five, I witnessed people being shot dead on the streets of Beirut. By 15, I had mourned the loss of one of my beloved grandmothers. At 22, I had to grapple with the mass murder of my family. And most recently, I had to cope with the sudden death of my mother at the onset of the Covid pandemic.

There's no denying it – death can be really challenging to deal with, even for those committed to waking up to the True Self and living a more In-Lightened life. However, facing death can also be incredibly liberating. It's not the end; it's simply a transition from one state of being to another. Every day, we experience death on a cellular level as our cells die and are replaced by new ones. This is the natural order of things.

So, why do so many people fear death when it's an integral part of life? Instead of resisting it, it's time to embrace it. Recognise that there's no greater gift in life than death itself. In this realisation, we are ONE. Let's explore how to deal with death now.

Wake-Up Call: How To Find Peace In Death

If you've lost someone that you were close to, be particularly gentle with yourself at this time. Remind yourself that there's nothing you need to do spiritually right now, other than be present to the grief.

Even as you're waking up and living more as the expansive "Self", you still need to treat your "self" with kindness. There are five stages to grief (denial, anger, bargaining, depression, and acceptance) and moving through them is not linear.

Grief has the power to rip your heart open. Don't resist it. There's a cathartic purpose to it, even if it feels gut-wrenching. If it stirs up unresolved emotional pain, welcome it. Grief has a way of showing you that it's time to release the painful story of "you".

Allow yourself to do whatever you need to. Cry, scream, shout, or shake. Focus on experiencing fully the raw emotions that flow through you. Don't force yourself to say anything to appease the mind. After all, what can you say? The mind can't make sense of death. It's so final that no amount of talking can appease it. So, instead, say nothing and surrender to the pain within.

When you feel ready, remind yourself that the love and affection you have for the person will NEVER die. Death marks only the end of the physical body. The Conscious Awareness (the *IshQ*) that flows through the veins of every human lives on. Allow yourself to take warmth from this realisation, embracing both the Love and grief that coexist within you.

If the person who died was someone with whom you had a difficult relationship, their death is likely to affect you as well. Perhaps you're feeling guilty that you're not that upset, or maybe you're still feeling angry with them. However your sadness, anger, or fear presents itself, take the time to go within and transmute it by imagining yourself sitting in the middle of it, or flying through it (see **Chapter 4** on Letting Go). Do this for as long as you need to.

When you feel you're ready (which could be as soon as day one), you can incorporate the *"Who Am I?"* self-enquiry into your day. Repeat it as often as you can. In turning within and recognising the True Self, you WILL find it easier to cope with death.

As you explore the boundless space of the True Self, you'll come to understand inherently that the pool of Consciousness beyond the physical body is universal. In other words, the Conscious Awareness of Noah, myself, you, our Zen Masters, the great spiritual teachers, famous people (alive and dead), and all those "ordinary" people who have passed away, is IDENTICAL. It's the same Consciousness that permeates all of us, regardless of our race, religion, or social status. We're all one, interconnected by one invisible thread of eternal Awareness.

Repeating the *"Who Am I?"* self-enquiry, and investigating the True Vast Eternal Nothing, will cement this truth. The more you recognise yourself as the Vastness, the deeper your KNOWING that Consciousness continues after the body expires. It's like an unbroken line on an ECG heart-rate monitor. That heart will one day stop pumping, but that line of Consciousness will carry on eternally.

It's the Vastness you experience when you ask yourself the question *"Who Am I?"* that continues after the body dies. This is because the spaciousness within is not the impermanent body, but the eternal

Consciousness that animates it. Ask yourself *"Who Am I?"* with curiosity, and feel the edges of your identity soften. Recognise the opening sensation, and immerse yourself in its embrace – this IS your true nature, beckoning you closer.

When you can recognise that the True Self "You" is the same in life as it is in death, you'll KNOW that death holds nothing to fear.

This is the clarity that comes from recognising yourself as the In-Lightened True Self. So, allow yourself to surrender completely, letting go of the outer bullshit, and tasting the sweet nectar of unshakable Stillness and Peace that flourish within.

The In-Lightening Shift Begins

Living an In-Lightened life really is straightforward. All you have to do is commit to moving beyond the bullshit story of "you" consistently, and devote yourself to knowing the True Self. However, this doesn't mean you have to live a life of renunciation or solitude. It's not about controlling the narratives of the mind either. It's about relinquishing the need to engage with them and paying attention to the breath and True Self instead.

As you awaken, you'll progressively let go of your attachment to what you think your life should be. You'll KNOW unequivocally that it has the potential to be "Everything and Nothing". This realisation is what makes life so much fun, or so much hell, right?

To make life more "hellish" – you can stubbornly cling to your bullshit and continue buying into the sad narratives of "you". Yes, we understand that you've been through difficult and traumatic times, and acknowledge the psychological pain you've endured. We also recognise that you may feel "not good enough, unloved, bored with life, abandoned, inadequate, broken, too fat, too poor, too old, unwanted, homeless, and more."

We know that when you repeat your bullshit story of "you", it feels real. And when you look in the mirror, it looks real. However, the harsh truth is that you're the only author of this bullshit script! No one else is thinking about it – they're just reflecting your self-perception back at "you". Hence, the decision to keep playing the role of the victim, or to step into something infinitely vaster, really is up to you! Alternatively...

To make life more "fun" – you can choose to focus your will on stepping beyond the bullshit and shifting inwards to experience yourself as Stillness, Silence, Peace, Love and Joy. You can commit to living as the Awareness that's aware of it all. You can also repeat the *"Who Am I?"* self-enquiry process and Q&A, expanding your Awareness until the ego-self learns to step back automatically, and the Bliss of *IshQ* comes forth more and more.

So, what do you choose? If any doubt remains, ask yourself again: *"Who is this 'I' who's still clinging to the debilitating stories that I tell myself?"*

The answer is: *"There's no such 'I'. All these stories are just a fabrication of the mind, constructed by the ego-self known as 'me'. It's time to move beyond them and focus inside on the cathartic* Love *that I inherently AM!"*

For our part, we KNOW that you're ready to awaken and experience Joy. Every human inherently is. You're not unique in this regard. The Universe has NOT singled you out for a lifetime of misery – unless you enable it by continuing to buy into the bullshit that you've created around the story of "you".

To help you to master this, we've designed an intense 28-day programme in the following chapter that will guide you on how to SLAP yourself awake, ignite your inner revolution, and deepen your experience of true Love and In-Lightened living. It WILL truly liberate you.

The time has come, dear reader, for you to just BE the expansive True "You" that you already ARE. The more you move beyond the mind, and embrace the True Self, the faster you're going draw to you all of the magic in the Universe that's waiting to In-Lighten you.

CHAPTER 11

OPENING TO *ISHQ* – THE FINAL CHALLENGE

"Allow the next 28 days to take you on a transformative journey that will lead you beyond the bullshit mind, anchoring you deeper into Bliss than you ever thought possible."

28 Days To Boost Your Experience Of The "Self"

By now, you've probably realised that tapping into the In-Lightened True Self isn't about strenuous meditation practices. It's more like a mindful stroll – just a few deliberate breaths, a whisper of "*Who Am I?*", and voila, that opening in the chest! Even if it's just a glimmer, that's a giant step towards waking up. And yes, trust us, you'll experience it again, and again.

Remember, living as the True Self is simple. It's not a convoluted puzzle. It's a combination of surrender and application. If you want to bathe in Stillness, Silence, Peace, Love and Joy, then make dropping the bullshit your daily mission. Commit to turning within, and revelling in the real gold – your radiant, Loving "Self".

In essence, living an In-Lightened life must become your devotion – and it will. The more you experience yourself as the True Self, not much else will matter. All you'll want to do is deepen your recognition of it and train your attention to leave behind the dramas of your 3D reality – for good.

The path to In-Lightenment is whispering to you in every moment. Can you hear it? And are you willing to receive what it longs to offer you?

Ready To Go Beyond The Bullshit Towards Bliss?

The time has come to step fully into the vibrant expanse of the True Self. To help you, we've designed a 28-day challenge, a treasure chest incorporating the essential techniques and teachings that we've refined over three decades of awakening. This journey builds upon the wisdom you've already gained and delivers a daily SLAP of liberation, gently shaking you free from your persistent, self-limiting narratives.

The adventure unfolds in seven graceful steps, each designed to deepen your connection to the True Self and the four elements you eternally embody: Stillness, Silence, Peace, Love and Joy. You'll repeat these steps over four weeks, allowing them to guide your attention inwards and expand your recognition of your true nature.

Just as that puppy needs consistent training, learning to navigate your inner landscape requires unwavering dedication. Commit to this journey with us for 28 days, giving your mind ample time to adapt to this new way of being. With persistence, pivoting inwards will become a natural reflex, silencing the ego's incessant bullshit, and guiding you towards the profound depths of the True Self.

Therefore, we encourage you to embrace this programme wholeheartedly. Let it become your best friend, your guide to boundless freedom. Wait and see; your whole life will become an opportunity to move beyond the bullshit and come back to Bliss.

As you let go, and turn inside, you'll start to experience yourself as so much *IshQ*. It will feel like it's overflowing within you, expanding you, and radiating out to everyone you meet. It will illuminate your life, sparking an inner Joy that words can barely describe.

So, if you're ready to step into Peace and Joy, the last leg of your inner revolution is about to begin. Prepare to discover the dazzling potential that's waiting for you.

How To Get The Most From Your Challenge

1. **Choose a specific time each morning.** Commit to dedicating at least 10-15 minutes to do the steps for each day. Beyond that, set the intention to practise them during the day (it won't take long once you're familiar with the process). This will serve as a reminder to remain present and committed to the challenge, regardless of what's unfolding in your daily life.
2. **Sit upright or cross-legged in front of a mirror.** Don't lie down as you may fall asleep. As you progress through the weeks, you can visualise a mirror, but initially, it's best to sit in front of a real one. As you stare straight ahead, observe that your thinking subsides and you automatically become more aware of your breathing patterns.
3. **Get intimate with the breath.** Spend at least 5 minutes practising any breathing technique that resonates (we've made a few suggestions in the daily steps). Regardless of the method, recognise that even the slightest pause between breaths serves as a gateway to the In-Lightened True Self. As you hold the breath, enquire: *"What's in this pause?"* Explore the truth of what's there (hint: it's the True Vast Eternal Nothing).
4. **Listen to Theta beats.** You can find them on YouTube. This will support greater relaxation when following the day's steps (except for Day 1 of each week, which has a different focus). In a Theta state, your ability to access deeper states of Awareness is amplified, and practising breathwork enhances this effect. From the second week, experiment with and without the beats to see if your experience changes. (Disclaimer: Individual

responses to listening to Theta beats and breathwork can vary. If you have any concerns about your physical or mental health, or if you experience any discomfort during the exercises, pause and see a doctor. Remember, always seek medical advice when you need it.)

5. **Follow each day in sequence.** The steps have been structured in a specific order for a reason. Even if you've read the entire book, we advise you to focus solely on the instructions for the current day. This will ensure a more profound experience.
6. **Repeat the cycle four times.** Once you've finished the first week, return to Day One and repeat. By the second week, you're likely to find yourself simultaneously more aware of all aspects of the True Self – Stillness, Silence, Peace, Love and Joy. Embrace this. It signifies the expansion of your Awareness and heralds a new experience of being. It's the start of the spiritual mastery that you've been longing for.
7. **Familiarise yourself with the *"Who Am I?"* process.** The more you make this practice your own, the more effortlessly the words will pop into the mind. Your goal is for the *"Who Am I?"* self-enquiry to become your mantra for life.
8. **Do NOT engage in bullshit stories and feelings.** Ultimately, you don't want to care about how your ego-self is feeling during this process. All you want is freedom and to experience yourself as the abundant In-Lightened True Self that you already ARE. Remind yourself of this often! And,
9. **Revel in the Bliss.** Above all, savour these four weeks. You're giving yourself an amazing gift. You're going on an extended holiday from the mind and its madness. Allow the next 28 days to take you on a transformative journey that will lead you well beyond the bullshit, anchoring you deeper into Bliss than you ever thought possible.

Day 1: Time To Transmute (Use On Days 1, 8, 15 & 22)

Welcome to an important day of emotional alchemy! Today, you'll focus on transmuting your emotional reactions, both joyful and painful. Remember, transmutation takes patience and bravery. So, go step by step, and be gentle with yourself!

The Practice:

1. Spend 5 minutes breathing naturally, and tune into what's going on in the mind and body. Notice whether your mental state is calm and expansive, or noisy and contracted. Observe it all without getting caught up in any inner dialogue.
2. If you experience any uncomfortable sensations or emotions, address them directly. Release them through shouting, crying, or shaking, etc. Don't focus on the reasons for them; that will only keep you stuck. Keep moving until you sense that you're feeling emotionally lighter inside.
3. Next, transmute by observing any thoughts or feelings that are bothering you (or expanding you) and their corresponding sensations (usually in the stomach or chest). Imagine that you're sitting on a chair in the middle of them, or on a plane flying through them and just notice what's happening inside.
4. You can also visualise or sense these sensations expanding until they fill your body. Let them engulf you. Sit in the middle of them and let them wash through you and over you. Be present to your experience, while dropping all attachment to it.
5. Simply observe. Sit calmly and upright, fully present in the face of it. Keep your eyes fixed straight ahead. Don't let yourself think about it. Observe everything that's going on around you, using all your senses. Eventually, a shift WILL occur. The key is to remain centred and let go of any motive of wanting to change how you're feeling or what you're experiencing.

6. You can also visualise yourself in a library. Whatever you're experiencing (positive or negative), see it as a book of thoughts, feelings, and beliefs. Then drop the book and walk out of the library door into space. Keep dropping the book and leaving the library until you feel more detached from your current narratives. Recognise that by doing this, you're actually letting go.
7. Transmuting emotional reactions when your nervous system is triggered, and you're experiencing strong physical reactions (like heart palpitations), can be challenging. However, with practice, it IS possible to navigate intense moments. Allow yourself to become aware of all your physical sensations and recognise that they are the body's natural response to stress and fear. Observe them without judgment, whilst also reminding yourself that whatever is happening to you right now, it's NOT the same trauma as that which happened to you in the past. Repeat these words to yourself often, recognising the truth of them. Meanwhile, stay as present as you can and challenge your default dialogue about the situation. Throughout, keep in mind that transmuting strong emotional reactions takes patience and self-compassion. So, be compassionate to yourself and take warmth from the fact that the True Self is always there for the small "self". No matter what happens in your 3D reality, you CANNOT lose the Love of the True Self – remind yourself of this frequently! It WILL help you to release the emotions you're experiencing. And,
8. Finally, practise, practise, practise. The more you transmute the little stuff, the easier it will be to release the bigger stuff. This exercise will help you to realise, beyond any doubt, that you're not the ego-self version of "you" or its associated emotions.

Daytime Integration:

Spend the rest of today being as present as you can to the nature of the mind. Become a detective, observing that it's usually the mind-self that stirs up your internal bullshit, not external circumstances, or the actions of others. Similarly, when feeling good and inflated, notice your attachment to that state. Zoom in and witness the mind's limiting beliefs and judgments at play.

Specifically, pay attention to whether your internal dialogue tends to be predominantly positive or negative. If you're unsure, tune into the body and recognise whether you generally feel contracted or expansive in your everyday life.

If you find yourself in a mostly expansive state, your default thinking is likely to lean towards the positive. However, if you tend to feel more contracted, your default narrative is more likely to veer towards the negative. If that's the case, don't despair. As you recognise more often that you ARE the In-Lightened True Self, you'll come to KNOW that you can rein in that barking "puppy" and let the bullshit stories and feelings go.

One of the biggest hurdles people face is not having a proven set of tools to deal with their inner turmoil. We, therefore, suggest learning and practising the letting-go techniques outlined in **Chapter 4**. The more you practise them, the greater you'll be able to trust in your ability to handle the bullshit when it strikes.

Set the intention for the rest of today to transmute your reactions as soon as they arise. Regardless of how familiar the drama may be, KNOW that you can pivot your attention inwards, away from it. Allow this knowing to fuel your determination to let it go. As you push through it, you'll quickly recognise that Stillness, Silence, Peace, Love and Joy are lingering just behind to embrace and expand you.

Day 2: Tuning Into Sounds (Use On Days 2, 9, 16 & 23)

Today's journey takes you inward, focusing on all the sounds that surround and permeate your existence. Remember, this practice seeks to expand your Awareness, not shut down the mind. So, be kind to yourself and playful!

The Practice:

1. Begin by dedicating at least 5 minutes to the *Conscious Circular Breathing Technique* (see **Chapter 4**). With your eyes open, inhale deeply through your mouth (push your stomach out), imagining that it's your first breath of life. Hold the air in your lungs for a brief moment, then exhale through the mouth (pull your stomach in), as if it were your last breath. Do this for a few minutes and recognise that you're feeling more expansive as you do it.
2. Listen to Theta beats on YouTube while doing the breathing exercise and following the day's steps. Do not allow yourself to fall asleep.
3. Maintain eye contact with yourself in the mirror. Notice that this stops you rehashing the bullshit.
4. Focus on the sounds surrounding you. "Stretch" your ears and take in as many sounds as possible. Notice that when you cling to a single sound and start analysing it, the mind becomes more active. Don't allow it. By expanding your Awareness to encompass as many sounds as possible, bombarding the mind, you'll force the ego-self to step back and quieten. Observe the inner shifts that occur as you do this.
5. Apply the same process to any words that you hear in the mind. Instead of trying to decipher them, brand them all as "sounds". Try this and see what happens internally.
6. As you focus on all the sounds simultaneously, including any mental chatter, you'll notice that the mind surrenders and Awareness expands. It will become obvious that this Awareness is not confined by the physical body, but rather permeates everything. With this spaciousness, you'll no longer feel like you're listening from the ears of the ego-self known as "you" – you'll recognise that all sounds are actually happening within "You", not outside of "you". And,

7. Finally, ask yourself, *"Who Am I?"* and repeat slowly: *"I am NOTHING. I am the True Vast Eternal Nothing. I am NOT these sounds. I am not any sound. I'm the space that exists between, beyond, and around all sounds. I'm ALWAYS aware that I am the True Nothing from which everything in life flows."*

Daytime Integration:

Allow the truth of these words to resonate within you, guiding you deeper into the True Self. Spend the rest of today noticing as many sounds as you can (you don't need a mirror to do this). As you go through this process, observe how the mind searches for sounds and words, and attempts to label them. Recognise that the True Self never does that. It notices all sounds but identifies with none of them.

Challenge yourself to class all the words you utter to yourself and others today as "sounds". When you find yourself speaking, recognise that it's the mind saying the words while your Awareness witnesses them. Then, let go of any attachment to those words. Refuse to engage with them, and notice the calmness that arises as you create space between your Awareness and the cacophony of sounds within.

To highlight the impact of sound on your being, turn on the radio or TV loudly. Observe how the body reacts to the noise. Then, turn it off. How do you feel inside? Notice the inner shift as your being relaxes, allowing you to become more attuned to the natural flow of the body. The same effect occurs when you engage with the sound of thinking and then let it go.

Set the intention for the rest of today to see how long you can stay aware that you're way vaster than the sounds you hear around you.

Day 3: Journey Into Silence (Use On Days 3, 10, 17 & 24)

Today, you're going to dive deeper into the heart of existence, exploring the True Silence that whispers beneath every sound. Remember, this journey is about expanding Awareness, not escaping the world around you. So, stay present and curious!

The Practice:

1. Spend at least 5 minutes practising the following *Box Breathing Technique*. This is a form of Pranayama that entails visualising the lines of a box being drawn. Let's begin. Start with the left vertical line. As you imagine or sense this line being drawn, inhale (receive) through the nose for a count of 4, ensuring your stomach expands. Then hold the breath (integrate) for a count of 4, visualising the top horizontal line appearing. Third, exhale (release) through your mouth for a count of 4 as the right vertical line is drawn, pulling in your stomach. Finally, hold your lungs empty for a count of 4 (relax and rejuvenate) as you envision the bottom horizontal line. Take a moment to explore the pauses at lines 2 and 4, recognising that they really are the entry points to the True Self.
2. Listen to Theta beats on YouTube while doing the breathing exercise and following the day's steps. Do not allow yourself to fall asleep.
3. Stare into a mirror and maintain eye contact. Observe how this practice prevents the mind from rehashing the bullshit.
4. To discover True Silence, focus your attention on any sounds that you can hear in the present moment. Then, regardless of their volume or intensity, observe that Silence surrounds them all.
5. Stretch your ears to recognise the True Silence that's always there. This is the sound of the Universe and you can hear it if you focus your attention inside your ears. It has a frequency that sounds like a faint hum.
6. Notice how your Awareness expands as you tune into this Silence.

7. Keep focusing on this Silence and you'll sense it emanating from you. Become the Silence. Recognise that experiencing yourself as Silence deepens your recognition of the True Self, for they are essentially the same thing. And,
8. Finally, ask yourself, *"Who Am I?"* and repeat slowly: *"I am Nothing. I am the True Vast Eternal Nothing. I am NOT these sounds. I am Silence. I am the space that exists between, beyond, and around all sounds. I'm ALWAYS Silence. I'm ALWAYS aware that I am the True Nothing from which everything in life flows."*

Daytime Integration:

For the rest of today, pay attention to the Silence that exists around every sound. Practise this exercise both in front of a mirror, looking into your own eyes, and in other environments. Ultimately, your aim is to tune into this infinite Silence regardless of your surroundings.

Anytime you notice that the mind is attaching to one particular sound, focus intently on it, then stretch your Awareness until you can sense the Silence all around it. Imagine it's a dartboard and you're aiming for the red bullseye first, and then the green ring around it. Alternate between focusing on that sound (the bullseye) and the Silence (the green ring) that encircles it. As you continue this practice, recognise that Silence never changes, regardless of the intensity of any sound around you.

Deepen your connection to this Silence and you'll soon realise that you can recognise it even in the midst of a music festival. Remember, you don't need Silence around you to maintain your Awareness of it.

Set the intention for the rest of today to practise focusing on Silence. Notice that as you do this, your Awareness expands. This is the Bliss of surrendering to what IS. Enjoy it. See how many hours you can BE the True Silence that "You" always ARE.

Day 4: Unveiling Stillness (Use On Days 4, 11, 18 & 25)

Today, we're going to get intimate with the wellspring of Stillness within, diving into its depths. Remember, this journey is about uncovering your inner sanctuary, not external control. So, be the detective and embrace it all!

The Practice:

1. Spend at least 5 minutes practising any breathing technique that resonates with you.
2. Listen to Theta beats on YouTube while doing the breathing exercise and following the day's steps. Do not allow yourself to fall asleep.
3. Stand in front of a mirror and stare at your own reflection. Notice how this practice helps you to break free from the cycle of repetitive, bullshit thinking.
4. To tap into True Stillness, ideally focus your attention on a plant or tree. However, if this isn't feasible, select a small object and place it in front of you.
5. Observe the object and acknowledge its complete Stillness. You will feel a resonance in your body. Recognise that True Stillness permeates not only living beings but also inanimate objects. If you're using an object this time, focus on something living next time, such as a plant.
6. Once you sense the True Stillness of an object, see if you can recognise that it's the SAME Stillness as that of the True Self.
7. Now, while moving your head and body, observe the unwavering nature of Stillness. Notice how the body moves, yet Stillness doesn't. Take a deep breath and allow this truth to draw you deeper into the Stillness that's ALWAYS there.
8. Ask yourself, *"Who Am I?"* and repeat slowly: *"I am Nothing. I am the True Vast Eternal Nothing. I am* NOT *these sounds. I am* NOT *any sounds. I am Silence and I am Stillness. I'm the Stillness that*

never moves. I'm the space that exists between, beyond, and around all sounds. I'm ALWAYS Stillness. I'm ALWAYS aware that I am the True Nothing from which everything in life flows." And,

9. Finally, as you say these words, recognise the grounded Stillness in the body. Observe the slowed pace of breathing. Feel the Stillness. It's palpable.

Daytime Integration:

Spend the rest of today staying aware of the True Stillness within. Look at your reflection in the mirror and recognise the Stillness that you ARE. Experiment with moving the body whilst observing what happens to that Stillness. Try shaking your head or dancing, and notice how your inner Stillness remains undisturbed.

If you struggle to recognise Stillness, go outside and focus on a tree or another living object (an animal will also work). Observe it and see if you can tune into the Universal Life-Force Energy flowing through it and around it. This is True Stillness. This is Nature.

Next, acknowledge that the Stillness you sense around the tree is the same as that within you. Use the Stillness you recognise externally to help you to anchor into it internally. Really allow yourself to become your experience. Notice how grounded the body feels as you allow your observation to take you deeper into Stillness; however, your Awareness remains alert.

As you experience yourself as Stillness, you can experiment by focusing on the Stillness of another person. If you're drawn to Osho, Eckhart Tolle, Christ, or any other awakened being, you can tune into them and anchor yourself at their level of expansion. It doesn't matter if they're alive or dead, True Stillness (i.e., Consciousness) is the same and continues eternally.

To KNOW the eternal Consciousness within any individual, allow your Awareness to focus on them and energetically scan their being until you sense their Stillness. You'll intuitively know when you've found it, as you'll feel it resonating within you. Once you've connected with them, allow your own Stillness to align with theirs. You'll discover that by tuning into and sensing the vibration of a Master, even one who's deceased, you'll be drawn into a deeper state of Stillness, for they are mirroring to you that you are a Master too!

Set your intention for the rest of today to remain as still as you truly ARE. See how many hours you can maintain your connection to True Stillness.

Day 5: Cultivating Peace (Use On Days 5, 12, 19 & 26)

Today, you'll embark on a journey to expand into the True Peace that is your birth right. Remember, this practice is about tending to the garden of your inner serenity. It's not about imposing conditions in order to contrive Peace. So, keep going; it will be so worth it.

The Practice:

1. Spend at least 5 minutes practising any breathing technique that resonates with you.
2. Listen to Theta beats on YouTube while doing the breathing exercise and following the day's steps. Do not allow yourself to fall asleep.
3. Stand in front of a mirror and stare at your own reflection. Notice how this practice helps you to break free from the cycle of repetitive bullshit thinking.
4. To find True Peace, start by noticing the other elements first. Begin by stretching your hearing to take in any sounds around you. Then observe the True Silence around those sounds. Once you've found that, focus on an object and recognise that True Stillness is there too.
5. As you recognise all sounds, True Silence, and True Stillness simultaneously, you'll naturally meet True Peace.

6. Observe how your experience of True Peace deepens as you acknowledge it within. Allow this Peace to emanate from your being. You may even notice a sensation of warmth or tingling around the heart centre. And,
7. Finally, ask yourself, *"Who Am I?"* and repeat slowly: *"I am Nothing. I am the True Vast Eternal Nothing. I am Peace. I am NOT these sounds. I am NOT any sounds. I'm Silence. I'm Stillness. I'm the space that exists between, beyond, and around all sounds. I'm ALWAYS Peace. I'm ALWAYS Stillness. I'm ALWAYS Silence. I'm ALWAYS aware that I'm the True Nothing from which everything in life flows."*

Daytime Integration:

Spend the rest of today focusing on the Peace that you ARE. Practise observing all sounds, True Silence, and True Stillness all at once. Keep observing. As you fully embody your experience, you'll come to recognise that you're suddenly BEING True Peace as well.

During this process, you may observe that Peace is sometimes as readily available as Silence and Stillness. At other times, you may need to go through the steps and allow Peace to reveal itself later. Try repeating the entire process in front of a mirror, and then attempt it while walking. As you become more aware of Peace within your being, point it out to the mind.

Say: *"I am True Peace. This never changes. It doesn't matter how much sound there is in the mind, or emotional disturbance in the body, True Peace is always available to me. No one can give it to me and no one can take it from me. It's ALWAYS there. It's always 'ME'."*

Observe the sensations that occur in the body as you repeat these words. You're likely to experience an even deeper sense of Peace (if not, repeat the steps until you do).

Next, shift your attention externally and focus on a challenging situation that you've had to deal with. If you can't recall one, think of a disturbing event happening in the world. Notice the changes in the body as you concentrate on it. You're likely to feel contracted, right?

Now return to the steps for the day. Breathe in and out. Tune into the sounds around you. Direct your attention to True Stillness and True Silence simultaneously. Then observe how True Peace emerges. Recognise that this Peace didn't waver even when you were thinking about that troubling event. What did change though was the focus of your attention! You shifted from concentrating on the Peace within to focusing on your inner dialogue about something in your external world. This moved you from expansion to contraction, didn't it?

Remember this moment. It's OK to pay attention to what's happening in the world around you, but if you're intent on waking up, try not to engage with it emotionally (or at least transmute the reaction as soon as you become aware of it). Remind yourself that you don't need Peace in your external environment to maintain your internal experience of it. You also don't need the people around you to experience Peace in order for you to embody it. All you need to do is direct your focus inwards, away from the bullshit, and BE it.

Set the intention for the rest of today to remain connected to True Peace. If you do encounter emotional turbulence, face it gently and transmute it. Then pivot inwards and, once again, recognise yourself as the Peace that you always ARE. Challenge yourself to maintain your connection to True Peace throughout the day and see how many hours you can sustain it.

Day 6: Meta-Awareness (Use On Days 6, 13, 20 & 27)

Today, we embark on a profound exploration, tuning into the very essence of your being – pure Awareness. Remember, this enquiry isn't about intellectual understanding, but a direct experience of your boundless nature. So, stay focused and open to the wonders within!

The Practice:

1. Begin by dedicating at least 5 minutes to the *Box Breathing Technique* (see Day 3).
2. Listen to Theta beats on YouTube while doing the breathing exercise and following the day's steps. Do not allow yourself to fall asleep.
3. Face yourself in the mirror and lock your gaze. Observe how this simple act prevents you from dwelling on bullshit thoughts.
4. As you sit in front of the mirror, observe everything about you and around you. Where are you sitting? What are you wearing? What colour are the walls, the ceiling, and the floor? If there are others around you, become aware of them too.
5. Notice everything at the same time. As you do, become aware that Awareness has moved back from the body. Sense it behind you or above, looking down at you.
6. Acknowledge that you're consciously aware of this expansive Awareness. Understand that it isn't limited to a single location but permeates everything. It's a misconception to believe that Conscious Awareness is contained within the body. Remind yourself that the body and mind are inseparable parts of Awareness.
7. Notice how you begin to experience yourself as formless and expansive. Realise that as you gaze into the mirror, you're peering out from eternal Vastness. The eyes are merely portals through which Conscious Awareness observes itself. Allow yourself to become aware of who, or what, is actually looking back at you.
8. Next, ask yourself, *"Who Am I?"* and repeat slowly: *"I am Nothing. I am the Awareness that's aware that I am Nothing. I am the True Vast Eternal Nothing. I'm the Awareness that observes the words but never communicates in words. I'm the space that exists between, beyond, and around all sounds and all words. I'm Stillness. I'm Silence. I'm*

Peace. I'm aware that I AM 'Everything and Nothing'. I'm ALWAYS aware that I'm the True Nothing from which everything in life flows."

9. Recognise that you ARE the Awareness that's aware of every sound, True Silence, True Stillness, True Peace, and Awareness itself – all simultaneously. Notice what happens inside of you then. And,
10. Finally, observe your expanding self-realisation. You're beginning to experience yourself more fully as the True Self – the captivating Unknown.

Daytime Integration:

Spend the rest of today being aware of Awareness. How often do you actually observe what you're doing? This is not the same as observing yourself living life while giving yourself continuous bullshit feedback about it. Becoming aware of Awareness means that Silence has intervened. Pay attention to whether you still take the same actions as you become more aware that Awareness is observing "you".

When you feel comfortable shifting into BEING Awareness, start to experiment with how you "use" it. For example, during moments of physical intimacy, notice whether you can remain aware of the body even as you engage with another person. Keep part of your Awareness behind or above you, observing yourself as you entwine with your partner.

See if you can observe the body experiencing pleasure whilst acknowledging that it's not the True "You" who's enjoying the sensations. Whether you're kissing, touching, or gazing into someone's eyes, remain aware that Awareness is observing both of you. Remind yourself that you're way vaster than the body experiencing transient feelings of pleasure and comfort, but rather the Universal Life-Force Energy that connects us all.

Next, become aware of Awareness while talking to another person or during social interactions. The True "You" is the Awareness that's "floating" just behind your body, while the True Self of the other person is lingering just behind theirs. Use all your senses to recognise that communication is taking place between your mutual Awareness.

You don't "talk" to another person's Awareness in the same way that egos communicate with words. You talk through the mutual somatic recognition of this eternal Awareness. You're both Universal Life-Force Energy. Recognising this will create immediate resonance between you. See if you can observe this silent connection the next time you talk to someone.

As you move through the day doing this, notice how quiet the mind-self becomes. Observe that even though your Awareness is silent, you're still connected to everyone and everything.

Finally, as you end the day, revisit your mirror practice. Sit in front of the mirror, gaze into your eyes, repeat your breathing exercise (we like heart breathing), and sense your true nature. Ask yourself, *"Who Am I?"* and affirm, *"I am Awareness. I am the observer of this reflection. I am a formless, eternal presence. I hear words and thoughts popping into the mind, but I never talk. I'm aware that I AM the Awareness that's aware of it all. I'm aware of my connection to all things. I'm aware that I AM the Life-Force Energy that drives all of life. I'm aware that I AM Stillness, Silence, and Peace. This IS the truth of who I AM."*

Allow yourself to sit with this knowing for as long as you wish, basking in the Consciousness that you ARE. See how many hours of the day you can hold your connection to Awareness.

Day 7: Recognising *IshQ* (Use On Days 7, 14, 21 & 28)

Today, it's time to fan the flames of your true essence, *IshQ*. This practice isn't about seeking love outside; it's about uncovering the expansive Love that already burns within you.

The Practice:

1. Begin by dedicating at least 5 minutes to the *Conscious Heart Breathing Technique.* As before, inhale through the nose, imagining the breath moving internally over your head, down your spine, and up through the front of your legs until it reaches the heart centre. Then exhale through the mouth, visualising the breath exiting as a stream of air through the heart, filling the room that you're in. Repeat this cycle five times, paying attention to the sensation of Love within.
2. Enhance your practice by listening to Theta beats on YouTube while doing the breathing exercise and following the day's steps. Do not allow yourself to fall asleep.
3. Lock your gaze in the mirror, keeping your eyes fixed. Stare straight ahead and keep breathing through the heart.
4. To experience yourself as Self-Love (*IshQ*), it helps to experience the other three elements of Consciousness first. Begin by immersing yourself in all of the sounds surrounding you. As the mind quietens, tune into the Silence that cradles those sounds. Next, go further into Stillness by focusing on any object in front of you. Finally, expand your perception to encompass everything, embracing the True Peace that arises as you do this.
5. Now, take a crucial step – observe that you're aware of Awareness itself, the vast canvas that holds these elements together simultaneously: all sounds, Silence, Stillness, and Peace. As you focus on this Awareness, you'll eventually become aware of the presence of *IshQ* bubbling within "You". It may take a few attempts to do this, but KNOW that it IS there. It's always there.
6. To enhance your experience, spend a few moments focusing on your environment – the air, the light, smells, sensations, and the rhythm of the heart breathing. Embrace it ALL as a unified whole. Then ask yourself, *"Who Am I?"* and repeat slowly: *"I am Nothing. I am the True Vast Eternal Nothing. I'm Stillness. I'm*

Silence. I'm Peace. I'm Love and Joy. I'm IshQ. I am the space that exists between, beyond, and around all words and all sounds. I'm ALWAYS IshQ. I'm ALWAYS Awareness. I'm aware that I'm always the True Nothing from which everything in life flows." And,

7. Finally, allow yourself to lean into your experience of *IshQ*. Focus on the physical sensation as it spreads throughout the body. You'll start to experience yourself as so overflowing with *IshQ* that you'll want to stand on the rooftops and declare it to the world. You'll get to a point where you feel such gratitude for life that it moves you to tears. This is the power of *IshQ*. Allow this Love to radiate from you.

Daytime Integration:

Spend the rest of today experiencing yourself as *IshQ*. Set the intention to focus on it for the next 24 hours. If the flame of *IshQ* feels like it's waning, repeat the steps above. With practice, you'll find that just breathing through the heart while repeating the words *"Stillness, Silence, Peace, Love, Joy and IshQ"* will lead you deeper into it.

Observe how calm, but alert, the mind is when you're in this state of being. It's primed and ready to engage in practical tasks, but not emotional bullshit. This is how you live as the In-Lightened True Self. Observe what BEING this person FEELS like somatically. Point it out to the mind. Say: *"I AM Stillness, Silence, Peace, Love, Joy, and IshQ. My external circumstances may change but Bliss never does. It doesn't matter how much noise there is in the mind, I choose to focus only on the Bliss that's always available to me. No one can give it to me and no one can take it from me. Bliss IS ME – always."*

Notice how your experience of *IshQ* deepens as you recognise and embody this truth. As you relax into it, try the following as an experiment. Think of a challenging situation in your life that you still find hard to accept. Now, as the expansive *IshQ* that you ARE, pay attention to it and, with all the humility that you can muster, thank it for being a part of your life story.

As you do this, notice that the heart centre expands. You may even feel like you're bursting open with Joy and gratitude. This is *IshQ*. Experiencing yourself as this is the closest you'll ever get to knowing yourself as "God". Take a moment to acknowledge the truth of this statement. Then set the intention to continue experiencing yourself as *IshQ* for the rest of today, for as many hours as possible.

Moving Forward, Living as *IshQ*

Congratulations! You've just completed a remarkable journey – 28 days of expanding your Awareness of the Stillness, Silence, Peace, Love, Joy, and *IshQ* that you ARE. The steps to knowing the True Self and True Self-Love are now woven into your being. Remember, every human is wired to know their own Love, including YOU!

To deepen your experience, practise heart breathing and shift inwards every day to recognise yourself as Love. You may even choose to repeat the programme if you feel drawn to doing so. We KNOW that you can never get bored of moving your attention beyond the incessant bullshit to live as the In-Lightened True Self.

As *IshQ* flourishes within, you'll naturally want to share it. Breathe it out through your heart centre, extending it to everyone you meet. Offer your full attention, allowing rays of *IshQ* to envelop them in a silent embrace. Observe how your heart expands as you radiate Love, a subtle yet profound transformation. This is you, BEING Love.

With each breath of *IshQ*, you In-Lighten the world. Set a daily intention to see how much Love you can offer to the planet. Remember, your source of *IshQ* is infinite. The more you give out, the more it flows back to you. Living beyond the bullshit story of "you", as the True Self, is your only purpose. It's the ultimate outcome to this eternal Game of Life.

As you contemplate your In-Lightened existence, ask yourself one final question: *"What is the truth when it comes to knowing 'Who Am I?'"*

The answer is simple: *"I AM Nothing. G. I AM the True Vast Eternal Nothing from which all of life flows. I come from Nothing and I return to Nothing. As the curtain falls, living as IshQ is my only true calling in life."*

This is THE revolution – Beyond Bullshit to Bliss. This is truth This is Love. This is *IshQ*!

And with that, a new chapter begins. Share your experience of the True Love that you always ARE with us at www.samspiro.com, or on Facebook at www.facebook.com/sam.spiro/. On Instagram, you can find me at www.instagram.com/samspirozen, and Noah at www.instagram.com/premprashahd. The embrace of Bliss is never-ending. You have now entered the realms of *IshQ*.

Printed in Great Britain
by Amazon

62202228R10160